5/3 May 1813

T 11 L408 GL12ᴢ. L264 ∧g L.L. G8227 8.
W 12 7.2 1 G4L389 82 3. 622L4
T 13 X478 L8.12144 61884 .X^m 1595 87
F 14 X^m 159.7 G28 5X59. X478 615844L. L2
S 15 X478 ∧1ΓΓ. G3V4 GL4G2 69728. L12
G478 Mip 2.L 14884L. 2131637G 14
S 16 L537. 2574 6. 2224411 65 77. G1428..
M 17 X478 L144844LΓ@417.. 82. -5.. L2L4L4
T 18 X478 82 L1. L8 12154
W 19 X478 82 7G47425 615844. G8597 X26∧1
T 20 X478 7. L222. &c. L21. L2224G L264 82 17
F 21 L264 82 -2758157 L222.G
S 22 L264 1264. 4.G5779 157 G478 64 1488
S 23 X478 6408376
M 24 L208 GL1221. X478 1.5.
T 25 7.2 {6c1217 L264
W 26 7.2 {7465 7147 X^m 6c14271.5 81375
T 27 7.2 M.t (∧)
F 28 7.2 G15V.7.G.Γ.
S 29 X478 2V4L∧1.LL44L. ∧L38.G5779 82
..1595 157. Γ3G18. X478.. 41355 75V
S 30 L27410 -2795. L264 ∧g L313G22
M 31 L208 GL1221. X478 1.56

ϟ3Ə[4L

Cipher

Cipher

Jeremy B. Jones

— BLAIR —

Printed in the United States of America

Cover design by Laura Williams
Interior design by April Leidig

Blair is an imprint of Carolina Wren Press.

The mission of Blair/Carolina Wren Press is to seek out, nurture, and promote literary work by new and underrepresented writers.

We gratefully acknowledge the ongoing support of general operations by the Durham Arts Council's United Arts Fund and the North Carolina Arts Council.

ISBN: 978-1-95-888853-7, hardcover
ISBN: 978-1-95-888861-2, e-book

Library of Congress Control Number: 2024950739

To Abraham & Ezra—you beautiful, old souls

Also: 3 5ϭ 8˥4 ξ37ʃ2Γ ϭ5L32ξ5L8

hear them cry
the long dead
the long gone
speak to us
from beyond the grave
guide us
—bell hooks, *Appalachian Elegy*

We are the ancestors of our descendants.
They are the generations we have made.
—Tiya Miles, *All That She Carried*

To write a diary is to make a series of choices
about what to omit, what to forget.
—Sarah Manguso, *Ongoingness: The End of a Diary*

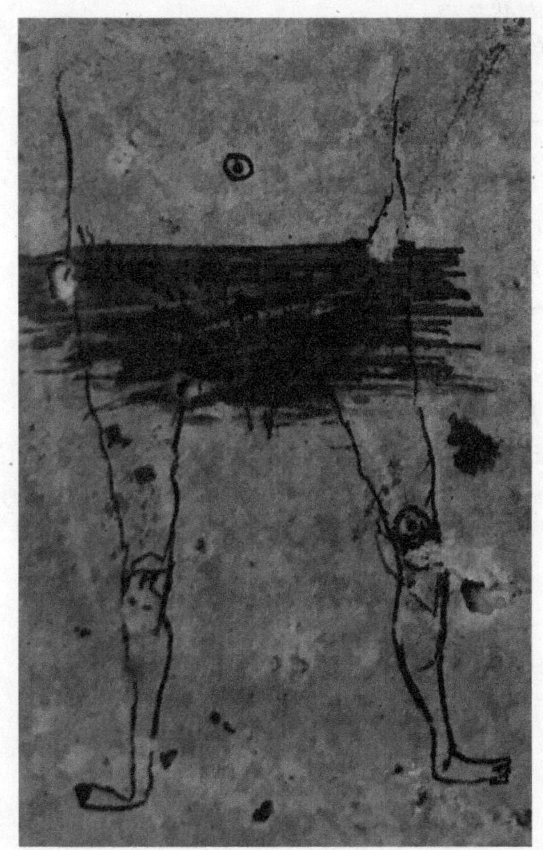

From the diaries of William Thomas Prestwood

Cipher (n) | 'sī-fər

1. A method of transforming text to conceal its meaning
2. One that has no weight, worth, or influence: a nonentity
3. A key to a code

Author's Note

I've tried, as best I could, to find whatever truth is out there in writing this book. Truth, however, is notoriously slippery, and so I'm sure it has, at times, fallen from my hands. In nearly a decade of research and writing, I consulted countless sources—some written texts, some lived lives—and from these, I've fashioned this narrative. I've endeavored to rely on facts where they existed. When facts were hard to come by, I built what I could from what I knew. Readers will notice this work of speculation throughout the text, framed in a world of *perhaps* and *maybe* and *could be*, but even in this imaginative work there are truths—about what I wish were true, what I fear could be true, and what we know deep down must be true. After all, as Herman Melville writes in *Billy Budd*, "truth, uncompromisingly told, will always have its ragged edges."

One truth I've attempted to challenge is the hidden racial biases historically woven into white Western literature. "For reasons that should not need explanation here," Toni Morrison writes in her 1992 book *Playing in the Dark: Whiteness and the Literary Imagination*, "until very recently, and regardless of the race of the author, readers of virtually all of American fiction have been positioned as white." One effect of this positioning has been the establishment of whiteness as the default in American literature: characters are assumed white unless otherwise indicated, and white authors have traditionally identified the races of only nonwhite characters, as if to denote deviation from the norm.

I am a white man writing a book that is, among other things, about race. I have struggled to know how exactly to contend with, and hopefully confront, this presumption of whiteness that Morrison notes. To my mind, I had two options: to name the race of everyone who appears in the text or to largely avoid naming the race of anyone. Ultimately, I took the second approach, with a handful of exceptions.

Naming the race of every character would have proven especially complicated in a book like mine. In many cases, I simply couldn't know the races of people from the nineteenth century. The primary source material of the diaries provided only passing details about characters inhabiting that world, so I could make sketchy guesses at best. What's more, even when details could point me to other documents—census data, for instance—I was then presented with the murkiness of racial identity in nineteenth-century America. I worried that relying on a document as fraught as an 1830 census could ignore the lives of Black people passing as white, for example, or indigenous people who'd been enslaved. And, at the risk of devolving into questions overly philosophical for this brief note, what is whiteness after all?

"America became white," James Baldwin writes in "On Being White . . . and Other Lies," "because of a necessity of denying the [B]lack presence, and justifying [B]lack subjugation." Whiteness, in Baldwin's estimation, is simply a way to exclude, having no real basis in biology or nationality. Moreover, these notions of whiteness in nineteenth-century America were much different than they are today. Whiteness has always been a moving target, which is how it maintains its power.

In the end, I worried that the speculation required to identify people's races, especially in the nineteenth century, would not sufficiently grapple with the presumption of whiteness or its shifting, imaginary definitions, and could, ultimately, fail to properly recognize the complex identities people inhabited.

That said, I have identified the races of some people within the book when I believed their racial identities mattered within context and when I could confirm, to some degree, these identities. For most other characters—white and nonwhite—I have chosen to avoid naming race. My hope is that the general absence of racial markers will unsettle any presumptions of whiteness readers might bring unconsciously to the page.

Finally, the book moves between the twenty-first and nineteenth centuries. In the nineteenth-century sections, the narrative voice sometimes slides toward the diarist's perspective in order to shrink the "psychic distance," a term coined by the writer John Gardner. In other words, while I'm telling this story from the twenty-first century, I often aim to let the diarist's voice seep into the narration. To that end, readers will encounter some language particular to the time of the narrative. Most notably, the word *Indian* appears a few times in these nineteenth-century sections because it is the word the diarist—and everyone around him—would have used. I have also relied on the diarist's spelling of names. For example, I've used Clonse even though it was likely Clontz (or might have been Klontz or Clonts). The same goes for McLeard (McLurd), O'Nail (O'Neill), Corpeny (Corpening), and so on. I intend for these biographical sections to push readers into that nineteenth-century world, in all of its terribleness and beauty.

More than anything, I hope I've gotten out of the way enough for the book take on a life of its own. Let's go see.

PART I

ſʒς̇ϟ2γ4Lʅ

Discovery

1

In 1859, a forgettable man died. He left behind bedclothes, a spyglass, cooking pots, and an umbrella. He left history books and algebra books and mineralogy books and Greek grammar books and astrology books. A compass, millstones, half chains, feather beds, dead sons, living daughters, and grandchildren soon to scatter. There were also debts. Debts that his land holdings and this scattershot of personal property—sold for a total of $11.94—couldn't pay off. He entered the ground penniless in late November.

Only, stashed somewhere in his wake was everything, his whole life recorded in tiny handmade notebooks. On those pages he logged his first love, his wedding, the births of his children, the death of his mother, the 1821 eclipse, the hanging of Frankie Silver, some tumblebugs fucking in July, O'Nail's child pissing on his handkerchief, and dreams about murdering children and fleeing to Georgia. All of this he scratched onto pages he never intended anyone to read. He concealed each entry in an invented cipher so that when he left this earth, his coded pages would be tossed away, forgotten, turned to ash.

But someone picked them up. Or someone neglected to throw them out with the unwanted grammar books. Somehow, either by accident or providence, the handsewn notebooks survived the Civil War, Reconstruction, the Depression, two world wars, rain, snow, sleet. Over a hundred years after the man himself faded away, his pages resurfaced in a sagging house more than a hundred miles from his body and debts and descendants. The house had been abandoned, but stacked up somewhere inside were fifty years' worth of symbols waiting to be cracked open.

In 1975 the city of Wadesboro, North Carolina, decided to level an empty house on South Rutherford Street. It had once been the home of a schoolteacher named Ethel Bennett, but Ms. Bennett had been dead for six years, and her house was falling to pieces on its downtown lot. Desperate people had found cracked windows and jimmied locks and taken up occasional residence in the small house, leaving bottles and needles and coffee cups where Ms. Bennett had once spread her cross-stitch. The city readied the wrecking crew.

There, just beside the local theater, Ethel Bennett's belongings were piled with the trash on the curb. She had no children; her husband had died in 1935, so she lived most of her life alone in that house. Now the knickknacks and picture frames and moth-eaten dresses from that life waited in trash bags on the street.

I like to imagine it was a sunny afternoon when Steven Scott Smith walked by these curbside piles. Perhaps the summer light caught something in the bags—a warped spoon lying on top or a forgotten earring sticking from a tear—and so the young man stopped to thumb through everything spread before him. Amid the photos and recipe books, he found a bundle of twenty-eight worn, rough notebooks, bound together by sewing thread. He picked them up, slid one free from the stack—it fit in the palm of his hand—and opened it there on the sidewalk.

Nothing inside the notebook made sense. Across the pages he found something akin to hieroglyphics: lines upon lines of scribbled shapes. He pulled another free, and there was more of the same. On some pages, he found charts and drawings and equations, on others doodled hearts appeared in the margins. A crude sketch of a naked man waited on the back of one notebook, black scribbles across his middle like an uneven censor bar.

Even if he didn't understand any of it, Steven knew by touch that the notebooks were old—small, handsewn artifacts. He knew enough to know that *old* might mean *valuable*, so he lifted them from their place, balanced the stack on his hip like a baby, and left before the house was scattered to bits.

....

I've never kept a diary. I'd like to say I'm not that interested in the minutiae of my day, but that lie is too thin to attempt. The truth is that I'm too lazy, too impatient. Diary-keeping is a practice, a ritual, and I've never put in the work.

When I was a kid, keeping a diary felt too gendered to approach. Girls kept diaries: frilly, padlocked affairs to be filled with hearts and stashed under mat-

A sketch from the back of one of the discovered notebooks

tresses. I was neither pushed nor lured into tracking my days or innermost thoughts in a notebook, so instead I went into the woods with my secrets. I learned to follow the old logging trail into the rhododendron caves below our house to be alone. I talked to trees or spied on my cousins. Anything I wanted saved, I took into those woods. Anything I wanted gone, I took there too.

I grew up in a place called Fruitland, surrounded by family and mountains. The one hundred acres of my people had been settled by a white farmer named Asbury Prestwood, my great-great grandfather, not long after the Civil War. His empty house stood on the hill above the creek, just through the woods from mine, and when my cousins and I absconded on summer days, we often ended up there, surveying the bottomland and barn and briar-covered banks from that old porch. Then, we landed in the creek, or sometimes in the trees, until Grandma walked to her parked car and blew the horn three times. Summoned back to her rock house, we scrambled out of our daydreams and up the hill.

Grandma surrounded that house in bird feeders. Seen from above, I imagine that plot of land was always awash in a blur of birds, cardinals and chickadees swarming her house from the orchard and hayfield and forest. And then leaving again. There were also the blurs of wild children who flew into her house, flocked to her table, and then scattered again, back out into that Prestwood land. With us fed and free, Grandma would finally sit by the picture window, talk to her birds, and write.

I never knew what she scribbled in her diary, never understood why she did it every afternoon, but I came to track time by her silhouette in that window, pen in hand.

It wasn't until college—when I was away from that land for the first time—that I came to understand what the page could do, what it might mean. Professors sent me to the blank page with unanswerable questions and tripped memories, and I found it accepted what I brought, just as the woods of my youth had always done. Before long, I gave the page everything: I confessed, I navel-gazed, I pontificated, I professed love.

Late in college, I decided I wanted to know where I'd come from. As a boy, all I really knew were the cows by the barn and the bees on the hill and Grandma's stern eyes on the porch and Granddaddy's baseball cap in the garden. I knew heavy dirt clods in a plowed field and flattened rocks by the creek. I knew the taste of blood and the smell of grapes. But I knew little of the people who'd come before me on this land. I'd gone off to a private school full of wealthy northeasterners and learned about Joyce and the subjunctive mood, but when I sat down to write, I wrote about home. Eventually I took my notebook and a tape recorder through the woods to Grandma's house. She sat in her easy chair by the window, framed by her bird feeders, and I pressed record.

From my notebook, I pulled up questions and then scratched down her answers, which came in the form of stories. I wrote about Grandma's daddy spoiling her, sharing milk they couldn't spare and letting her out of chores when her mama wasn't looking. Wrote about her grandfather Asbury bringing his family here to send his daughters to school, about his building the Methodist church up the road and farming anything that would grow on this land. I wrote of Grandma whacking her cousin in the back of the head with a frying pan at the kitchen sink, of her feeling a lightning strike while standing in a puddle outside Asbury's house one summer day. I wrote the edges of story after story about a people who'd abided in this very spot, living out quiet lives for generations. These, I was learning, were my people.

....

On his pages in 1810, the forgettable dead man wrote L45Ə4ʃ X[458. He received an arrest warrant later that year and wrote 822ξ 5ϐʅ ı|7ʃʅ 57ʃ ʃ5|ζ[84L ƏL3 274L. As the threat of a British invasion mounted in 1812, he scribbled ζ28 Λ5885ı327 2Lʃ4L.

Just before he died: ɥ2|L8.

....

To learn about DNA is to learn we are built of words, of letters lined up to spell us out. To make sense of it, I sometimes imagine my body on a gurney, beneath an x-ray machine: The screen fills with As and Cs and Gs and Ts—each sinew of muscle and stretch of bone woven of nothing more than these letters, bundles of two- and three-letter words making me who I am.

Then I imagine all of my people laid out there beside me, under the bright lights. Everyone who came before me—from my dad to Adam—pieced together by these same letters, words stacked into sequences, into sentences. I imagine each body is a different story with different words, but I quickly find repeating phrases, whole sentences laid down in body after body like a writer's tic. Pretty soon, it's easy to see that I lie there as only an accumulation of those same words and phrases and sentences—my whole story written in the bodies that surround me.

Until 1961, we were, each of us, locked-up diaries written by some unknown hand. There was no key to decode what lay beneath—and in—our skin. We carried on as a walking, indecipherable language.

Like most discoveries, cracking the code of our bodies was mostly an accident, surely improbable. And like all discoveries, it's too easy to pin it down as one mark on a timeline. The succinct narrative starts with Marshall Nirenberg, a young American scientist who had no business deciphering the genetic code: He had no formal training in molecular genetics and no staff. Meanwhile, across the world, scientists loaded down with degrees and teams of hungry postdocs were chasing after the key to translate our DNA, to read the letters, to understand where we come from. In his lab alone, Dr. Nirenberg petered around with *E. coli*.

Eventually, Nirenberg took on a German postdoctoral fellow named Heinrich Matthaei. At thirty-two, Matthaei was only two years younger than Nirenberg, and the two men worked without any fanfare in a lab in Maryland. It was 3:00 in the morning on May 27, 1961, when Matthaei added synthetic RNA consisting only of uracil units to a series of test tubes. He was throwing things together, like a chef with too many ingredients and not a single recipe, but Matthaei wondered if his man-made RNA—the word UUU—mixed with a couple of amino acids, would somehow copy the DNA sequence and translate it into something readable. He was spinning a decoder ring on a whim.

At first, it wasn't clear what happened, only that his cocktail had produced something radioactive. He'd coaxed the DNA into giving its code away to the RNA, and the result was a protein—a normal exchange in the body, what scientists would come to name as transcription and translation. But the produced protein was phenylalanine, and so Matthaei and Nirenberg soon worked out that the string of Us fed into the test tube coded for phenylalanine. They had the key. A way to read the Rosetta stone that is the body.

But no one cared. Nirenberg's application to attend the Cold Spring Harbor meeting in June was rejected, leaving him out of the conversations entirely. Later in the summer, he finally presented the findings from the experiment at an international biochemistry conference in Moscow, but he was a nobody in the world of molecular biology. Thirty-five people attended his talk. There was yawning.

But really another way to tell this story is to start a decade earlier. To follow James Watson and Francis Crick, the two scientists who created a double helix model to represent DNA in 1953. They were the men who first understood the shape of our genes.

But to tell that story, we have to know about Oswald Avery, who first proved that it was indeed DNA that carried inherited traits. This was ludicrous, of course. Four letters made up all of humanity? All of life?

But to know about Avery, we need to know about a nineteenth-century monk named Gregor Mendel, about his pea plants and the proof that we carry with us recessive and dominant traits from one generation to the next.

In its roots, the word *discovery* suggests an uncovering, an opening up. I sometimes imagine discovery as an unwrapping—a process that rarely comes all at once, but often in tears and tugs: "to lay open to view." Nirenberg grabbed a corner loosened by Mendel and Avery and Crick and Watson and tugged. It snagged at that conference in Moscow.

But while there, he met James Watson, the double-helix-model-maker from nearly a decade prior. He told Watson about the experiment, about the test tubes and the uracil and the transcription—the key! Watson was polite but didn't believe him. For eight years the brightest minds in molecular biology had been working at this problem nonstop, and Matthaei's mash-up of synthetic Us and radioactive acids made no sense. This was no way to come at the problem of the complex system of human life.

Still, Watson was curious enough to send a colleague to listen to Nirenberg's lecture anyway. After the thirty-five attendees filed out, the colleague reported back to Watson that what he heard checked out: Nirenberg might well have done it. Watson told his research partner, Francis Crick, and they quickly arranged for Nirenberg to present the findings again there in Moscow, this time to an auditorium full of scientists. After his last word, he received a standing ovation. The paper tore.

....

Steven Scott Smith carried his discovered notebooks to historical societies across North Carolina. He hauled them into libraries, where he flipped open the pages of gibberish to anyone who would look. Most people simply waved him away. Others studied the pages but then shook heads and apologized. No one knew what he'd found in the trash on South Rutherford Street.

So he drove to more libraries. Called archives. He copied pages and mailed them to the American Philosophical Society. They wrote back that they were not interested in whatever this was. For years, Smith pressed on. He was sure that he'd found something that mattered, so he opened up those tiny notebooks over and over for anybody he could corner.

In 1978, three years after the demolition of Ms. Ethel Bennett's house, Smith showed them to a state archivist in Raleigh. This archivist, a man named George Stevenson, had no idea what the scribbles meant either. But he knew a guy.

Years before, Stevenson had met a National Security Agency (NSA) cryptanalyst with a penchant for history. After a career of breaking codes for the government, this man had retired and moved into the North Carolina mountains to read and write, so Stevenson pulled an address, xeroxed a handful of pages from the first notebook, and attached a note: *I don't know whether the notebooks contain astronomical observations, a journal, or something entirely different.* Then he sent them off to an old codebreaker in the Smoky Mountains.

2

"The poor unfortunate sailors," Nathaniel Browder wrote in his diary. "They are lowering the boats for the abandon ship while I sit here in K ward smoking a chesterfield." It was the summer of 1926, and Browder was shirking his duties. This had become his way. For a month now, he'd refused to follow orders, to make his bed, to stand up straight. "He refused all regulations as to dress," his wife later wrote: "and, in fact, all rules." Instead, he put his feet up and smoked a cigarette while everyone else sweated into the Pacific Ocean.

Browder was done with this ship, done with this uniform life. He didn't start off this way. For two years, he'd yes-sir'd and no-sir'd and floated around at sea and swept decks and shined shoes. Then something shifted. "I must study the vital writers," he'd written in his diary just before making plans to get kicked out of the Navy.

Browder's parents had died five years prior—first his mother, then his father three months later—leaving him orphaned at age seventeen. After they'd gone, he couldn't find his footing, his whole world incurably shaky. He received a scholarship to Maryville College in Tennessee, but he dropped out quickly, packing his bags and moving back home before the summer. Only there was no home back home. He had no house, no family in Hickory, North Carolina. His parents had left him some money, but he couldn't access it until he was twenty-one, so he found himself adrift when he returned. It wasn't long before Browder—a bright, angsty eighteen-year-old—became hungry and bored. He joined the Navy.

But by 1926, he knew he wasn't built for menial tasks and blind faith. He wanted to read and think, to put his brain to work. And now he was twenty-two: His parents' inheritance waited for him on the other side of the world. All he needed was a signature, and he could start a new life.

He'd watched Walter pull this off a year earlier. His friend had transformed into such a pain that the Navy only wanted him excised, so they cut him loose.

"I suppose Walter will [be] getting out of bed about this time," he wrote while he painted cargo doors. Browder expected to be booted faster—it took more than a month of bad behavior before they dropped his rank and sent him to the kitchen—but he stayed the course, becoming the worst sailor he could be. As summer approached, a court-martial was finally ordered. "Nervously excited," he scribbled in his Navy-issue notebook before the trial.

Browder became free on July 1, 1926—given a Bad Conduct Discharge. "Report to Gen. office. Turn in my clothes." On his way out of the general's door, he mentioned a mathematical error he'd long ago noticed in the payroll, one that resulted in overpayment to his supervisor. "I believe they would have shot me if they could have gotten away with it," he wrote. Then he left—"bath, shave, and a new pair of shoes"—and set sail for Tacoma to see the world's tallest totem pole.

....

It was dark when I sat at the dining table at Grandma's looking through old pictures. I'd come through the woods, taking the trail we'd worn as kids from my house—"The Yellow Brick Road." In truth, it's hard to know if we'd worn that trail or if it predated us. In those woods who could ever know if we'd created a path or simply taken up a line already cut there by our fathers or grandfather or great-grandfather or great-great-grandfather. And, really, who's to say that the lay of the land didn't pull us all where we were always going to go anyway, if every path in our forest wasn't predestined by the plates never quite settling underfoot.

By then, I'd moved away from that land that raised me. But I was home visiting my parents, and I'd set off to Grandma's after supper, past the lilting tractor shed and abandoned beagle pens and rusted-out mill saw, to hunt through her boxes, searching for old family photographs.

I sat, and Grandma stood over my shoulder, leaning on her walker—*her husband*, she called it—and we worked through a box holding piles upon piles of photographs. I learned quickly there was no system for the stacks rubberbanded together or stacked in corners. Few of them carried dates or names. The whole box started to feel like a memory: flashes of images and emotional responses but hardly any method to the madness.

We settled into a routine quickly: I fished out a photo; she called out the names of faces I could never recognize. *Oh, that's your granddaddy's second cousin*. As I made notes and stacked the photos on the table, she reached in past me and lifted out a yellowed newspaper clipping buried beneath Christmas cards of matching families and Polaroid photos of camping trips. She scanned the page and then held it in front of me like a handkerchief: "Look here."

I took what turned out to be a 1979 article from the nearby *Asheville Citizen Times* titled "Secret Journals Yield Honest Picture of WNC." I set in, reading about the discovery of diaries written by a nineteenth-century man characterized as "an intellectual," "a naturalist," "a mathematician," and "a tireless lover."

He "kissed the girls all over Western North Carolina during the course of his lifetime," the article opened. "But he was true to the gentleman's code: he didn't tell." The story detailed the recorded life of a man who could read Greek and Latin and who "loved a good time and a willing woman."

I enjoyed a tattered and salacious local news story as much as anyone, but it did feel strange to read about century-old sex affairs with the grandma who once drove me to Vacation Bible School looking over my shoulder. I finished and handed it back to her with an eyebrow raised and a smile saying, *Well, that was something*. I readied to dig back into the photos.

"He was one of ours," she said before I could turn back to the box. "My great-great-granddaddy."

....

From Tacoma, Nathaniel Browder crossed the country, slowly. He took a stage to Olympia and relished in the fact that he wasn't scrubbing decks or painting cargo doors or worrying over scuffs on his shoes. He was on his way to a theater, where "a comely maid did make flirtation with me but I have not the heart to reciprocate."

He walked south for miles before hitching a ride to Los Angeles. He took a bath. "Boy I feel good. Free, and money in my pocket to go Home."

It took a week, but he arrived in Hickory, North Carolina, in mid-July: "the checker game is still going," he wrote. He found his friends. He went for a ride with his friend Gene, and they wrecked and nearly died near Lenoir.

The next day he visited Mr. Biggby, the executor of his parents' estate to see about his money. "I did not tell him how I got out of the Navy. I have told no one. Nor am I ashamed of the truth. It is my greatest achievement."

Then he wrote no more in his Navy notebook-turned-diary; he left that line as his last before taking his inheritance and setting out to make a life.

....

The forgettable man had lived and died not far from where Browder and Gene wrecked that car and nearly died in 1926. On that very same day, in fact, a hundred years before the wreck, the forgettable man had written, [2б4. ϟ[3|ſL47ς3ϟξ.

He'd been in a fight with his wife and skipped dinner the night before. And now the kids were sick, and he wasn't feeling great himself. The next day, he would puke at Setzer's house. Setzer would not like it, so the forgettable man would writeς48+4L Λ|2X'ſ|Ә in his tiny notebook.

This, I've decided, is how life works, the tangled-up mystery of the whole thing: a sailor kicked out of the Navy nearly dies not far from where a dead man once puked, and one day that not-yet-dead sailor will unearth the entire life—the puking and the sex in barn lofts and the hiding of runaway slaves—of the dead man.

Because after Browder claimed his inheritance in 1926, he gave college another college try, eventually earning a degree in education from the University of North Carolina at Chapel Hill. He married a woman named Blanche and taught high school for nearly a decade. They had kids. He took graduate courses in English (*I must study the vital writers*), started a job with the Federal Writers Project, interviewing tobacco farmers and writing their stories. He decided to learn drafting, moving to Raleigh to enroll in courses, and then found a job with the State Highway Department. He tried to patent his invention—a glass automotive valve—but didn't have the money. The U.S. entered World War II, and he was recruited to work for Signal Corps, moving to Washington, DC. He found a place poring over symbols and gibberish to find meaning. Somehow the work was like both drafting and reading—something akin to math in translation—and so he made a career of it, staying on at the NSA until he retired in 1965. Then he took Blanche back to her hometown in the mountains of North Carolina, where they made a home out of remnants of an abandoned church and Browder finally had time to think about history and write.

That's how he wound up opening a package in 1978 from a state archivist hours away. In the envelope, he found Stevenson's note and a few copied pages of symbols from 1808—mostly Greek and Latin characters lined up, some numbers. He fetched a magnifying glass and set to work.

I want to think this whole trajectory miraculous (Browder's meandering life finally resting in an old church so that he could receive some grainy copies of a 150-year-old cipher, *and* those grainy copies only existing because of years of saving or overlooking those pages so that they could end up in trash bags on the sidewalk beside a run-down theater for a passerby to notice and eventually deliver to the state archives). It seems remarkably inconceivable, but, really, I think that every single atom of this earthly life might be equally as miraculous, if not more. Up against the enormous genome of, say, a whisk fern, this story is as mundane as the dirt we're made of and will one day become.

Take a wound-up sequence of DNA that we call a gene. It could be a few pages long, thousands of matched up letters wound together: AT, CG. It has a meaning, albeit coded, tangled up, and tucked away. Our bodies transcribe that message into RNA and send it off. RNA translates the code it's been given into slightly longer words, strings of triplets: ANA, AAA. But between the transcription and the translation, some DNA is edited out—whole phrases cut away in the decoding, others foregrounded.

This editing and translation pulls words from the code now: CURE, maybe. Perhaps CARE or CAT or ART. The story is written down in complete, decoded form onto new paper. And all of this happens to simply create a protein. To keep us alive every millisecond of every day.

....

I didn't believe my grandmother. She was in her mid-eighties with a waning memory, and I'd been pestering her for stories and photographs and family names for years. She knew I'd be interested in an ancestor keeping a coded diary, and yet this clipping had languished in a box for forty years. If we'd descended from this man, I was sure I'd have heard about him before now.

I looked back at the page. Beside the article was a photo of an old white man with a tweed jacket and a pair of glasses threatening to swallow his face whole. He stared into a magnifying glass that stared into pages of cipher text. "Nathaniel C. Browder, a retired codebreaker," the caption read. The article told of the 1975 discovery of the diaries, of Stevenson's mailing copies off to Hayesville, and of Browder working to decipher them.

I imagined Grandma had read this article back in 1979, seen the diarist's surname, Prestwood, and clipped the page from the Sunday paper. Her maiden name is uncommon, so it stood out. I'd never met a Prestwood beyond our family, so I allowed there was at least some distant connection, but I doubted that this man laid out under a magnifying glass was her great-great-granddaddy.

And also, I realize now, much of my disbelief came from my entire sense of who I come from—maybe of who I am. What I knew of the Prestwood people who settled this land was that of a quiet, abstaining lot. They married young, worked the land, and went to bed. In fact, they lay quietly just across the creek in a small cemetery, beside their wives and children, as I reread the article at Grandma's table. I couldn't fit this philandering, educated man—William Thomas Prestwood—into the narrative I'd been given, the narrative I'd written for myself.

I went back home through the woods, letting my eyes adjust to the dark to find a path, and opened the family tree on my computer. Then I knew to believe grandmothers.

....

It took Browder thirty minutes. After a hundred and twenty years of the notebooks passing from hand to hand; after three years of Steven Smith carrying them to libraries and archives, Browder sat down with a handful of pages and his magnifying glass and broke the code in half an hour.

"Simple substitution," he wrote later, "similar to the cipher described by Edgar Allan Poe in the story 'The Gold Bug.'" In a matter of minutes, he gathered up enough clues to begin filling in a letter for each symbol on the pages. Like Matthaei and Nirenberg had done with their uracil and phenylalanine of DNA, once Browder understood how to translate one symbol, he quickly understood them all. From them, a man began to take shape.

In truth, the cipher didn't interest Browder much. For a career cryptanalyst, the code was tee ball. He might have tied a hand behind his back. Stood on his head. What caught Browder was the unvarnished, ground-level view of the previous century. He had spent a decade of retirement tunneling into the past, writing a history of the Cherokee people, a biography of Hernando de Soto and other Spanish explorers. Finding the laid-bare life of a nineteenth-century man in the mail made him lean in a little closer, stay up a little too late.

So he drove five hours across the state and bought the stack of notebooks from Steven Scott Smith for thirty-five dollars. Then he returned to his study and stacked the twenty-eight notebooks like a set of dirty dishes waiting only for him. He rolled up his sleeves and got to work.

For six years, Browder sat at his desk and worked over the symbols of William Thomas Prestwood, running his fingers along the indentations in the notebooks, leaning in to make out water-damaged days, translating a log of half a century's worth of gold panning, weather patterns, bird migrations, algorithms, and the menial tasks of a nineteenth-century yeoman's life: sowing turnips, building fences, hoeing corn, killing hogs, damming creeks.

He was the only man alive who knew that Prestwood had "reap'd wheat" in 1810, that he'd "taken Amy Lundy and daughter as prisoner" later that year. That he'd "got battalion order" in 1812 and written "court" just before he died in 1859.

ə|2|ζ[ʼſ ϟ28827ς85ʅʼſ ϟ|.ʼς [|ζʼſ ə4ζζʅ & Γ4|8 [4L ϟ|78, Prestwood had written for no one to ever see on May 30, 1811. But in 1978, he was long gone, buried somewhere along the Catawba River, and a Cold War analyst sat alone in the mountains, hammering on his typewriter the forgotten life of a forgettable man: "Plough'd cotton Stay'd Cl.'s Hug'd Peggy & felt her cunt."

"The reader is left," Browder wrote once he had completed the work, "with the lasting impression that here in these pathetic little books is the very essence of Everyman's life from the cradle to the grave."

PART II

Λ3LſϚ, Λ44Ϛ

Birds, Bees

♐♒ *Advice for My Sons* ♌♒

January 1, 1823

Above all things, my sons,
do not SEDUCE innocent girls.

3

We were on the coast when my son first asked about sex. He was seven and impossibly precocious. I was thirty-seven with my pants around my ankles, changing out of a wet swimsuit in a rented house in South Carolina. In truth, he wasn't asking about sex; he was asking about anatomy. In truth, he was pointing at my balls and saying, "Why are you bigger down there?"

Sarah, my wife and this boy's mother, was in the bathroom, watching this unfold in the mirror like one might watch a particularly clumsy cat scale a wall. Hoping for the best.

"Oh, here?" I asked, pointing, too. One of the cat's paws slipped.

Not long after having Abe, this seven-year-old looking at my crotch, Sarah and I'd agreed to use anatomical terms with our kids. No "wee wees" or "tee tees" here. We're a people of penises and vaginas. So when he nodded, I gave it to him. *Testicles.*

He liked the sound of that, tried it out a few times—the word like a roller coaster, hanging on that first syllable for a beat before rushing down. But then he regained focus: "What does it do?"

When Sarah was pregnant, I told her I didn't fear dirty diapers or runny noses. I feared teenage hormones. I feared messing up so much that my son climbed on a Harley at age thirteen, crossed out his *Dad* tattoo, and roared off for good. I'd like to think this is why I started backing into the corner while trying to pull up my pants. It wasn't that I was a coward but that I was aware of my power. Aware of all that could go wrong. I was being selfless, really. Humble.

I looked to Sarah, hoping to pass the baton just before I shrank into nothingness, but I knew everything I needed from the flash of her eyes in the mirror. *Your turn.*

Yesterday, after finding his aunt's pads in her room, Abe had laced Sarah with questions, starting with, "Why does she wear a diaper?" Then he'd learned it all: the bleeding, the shedding of the uterus's lining, the monthly wherewithal stashed in the bathroom. "Does Grandma still bleed?" he wanted to know. And then: "So she can't have babies?" This was the precise moment when we learned he is smarter than we are.

So, yes, it was my turn. I stood up straight and we set off: the sperm and the egg. The Great Mystery.

It wasn't so bad, really. He knew about the egg already. He'd witnessed his little brother change from a bump in Sarah to a little person singing "Pop Goes the Weasel" on the bed while we talked about conception. I was feeling better already as I rounded the homestretch: we make sperm, women make eggs. Two become one.

"But..." he said, and I sensed more than knew what was coming, like a bird before a storm. "But how does the doctor put the sperm with the egg?"

"Oh, a doctor doesn't do it." I pulled up my shorts. "We'll talk about that part later."

"Then how does it get in there?"

I buttoned my fly as fast as I could. "We can talk about it later." I was a heartbeat away from bribing him with candy.

"Does the boy, like... pee it in the girl's vagina?"

Then I gave up. I handed him the keys to the car and the account number to my 401K and poured a drink.

When I admitted, "Yeah, that's kind of right," he lifted off the ground, literally jumping in his excitement. I was taken aback by this. He was ecstatic. But then, suddenly, I saw it all as if for the first time, too, and it did feel worthy of leaping: the act, the result. How could any of this be real?

Later, because I'm a sadist, I brought it back up. I was compelled by his enthusiasm, by the newness with which I could see all of it by explaining it to the child who would, one day, put me in a retirement home:

"It's kind of weird but also cool to think that you used to be inside me but also inside Mom, right?"

He was in the back seat of the car. We were all there, our family of four that used to be two on our way to dinner. He nodded and said, "And that Mommy used to be in Grandma."

That night, the generational work of it all settled over him, and he wanted to know which parts of him were from my family and which were from Sarah's. He drew a line with his finger, bisecting his body: "Is this side yours, and that side Mom's?"

The great bundle of it suddenly felt too much for me to comprehend, much less to explain. I avoided DNA. I searched for some metaphor: A stew? A puzzle?

"You're you," I said finally, hoping I sounded like a wise monk stepping from a cave.

And then: "But you're also all the people who come before you."

I tried again: "You're you *because* of all these people who come before you."

But also: "There's no one like you."

Eventually, he was satisfied enough to go back to reading *The Boxcar Children*, and I was left standing alone in the kitchen, thinking about all the lives in our skin.

....

Browder was eighty years old once he'd finished transcribing Prestwood's life, one symbol at a time. He had moved in with his daughter in Raleigh by then, leaving the mountains behind after Blanche passed. It was a useful arrangement—his daughter camped out in archives and historical societies for him, looking for records and reporting back with her findings while he chiseled away at the code. In 1984, once he'd written an introduction and rounded out William's life with genealogical research, he printed and bound seventy-five copies of his work, sent them to regional libraries, and died.

I found a copy on Amazon not long after leaving Grandma's house in the dark and doing my own genealogical research—decades after Browder's death. Someone with the handle *pfortnash* advertised a used copy of *The Enciphered Diaries of William Thomas Prestwood* by Nathaniel C. Browder for $79.99 plus tax. I laid down my money and waited for my great-great-great-great-grandfather to show up in the mail.

When the package arrived on my stoop in Charleston, South Carolina, many weeks later, I didn't know Sarah was pregnant with Abe. She didn't know she was pregnant. We wouldn't know for another month, once she'd taken the bar exam and we'd packed our bags for a trip to Panama, that we'd created a tiny human bug, our first. A baby who would one day grow into a boy asking me about anatomy in a shared bedroom at the beach.

I entered into those diaries looking only for sex. From the newspaper article, I knew Prestwood had been promiscuous and thorough, so I skipped right past

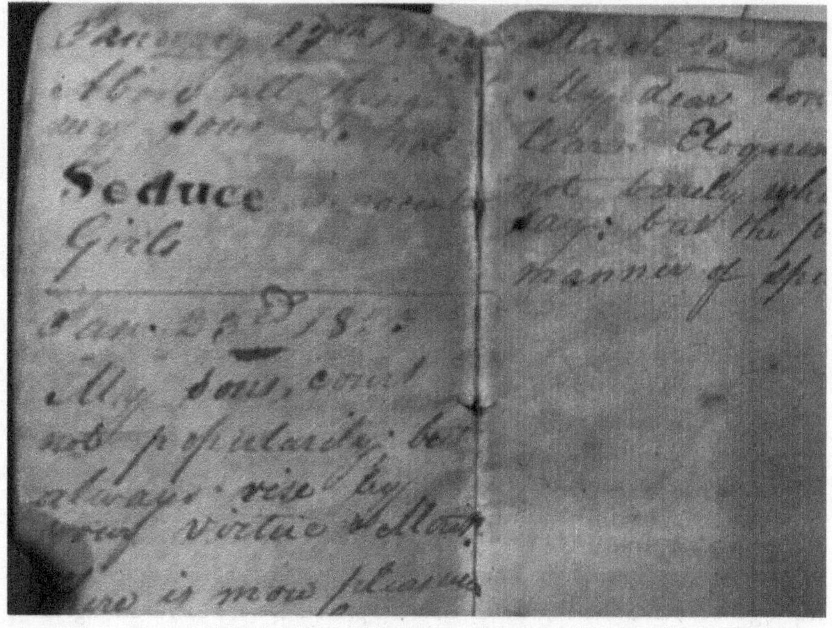

"Advice to My Sons," a plaintext section of Prestwood's diaries

mentions of mockingbird migrations and gold mining and state executions in search of lewd acts in closets and barn lofts. I'm not ashamed of this.

A few weeks later, I drove to North Carolina for July 4th. As I had done until I moved away from the mountains of home a decade before, I took a sleeping bag down to Clear Creek, just below the Prestwood homeplace and the Fruitland Cemetery, holding the Maxwells and Prestwoods who had come before me. My people, and other families from Fruitland, came out of the woodwork, throwing up dust from Townsend Road and filling the empty bottomland to set up tents and cover long wooden tables with potato salad and pound cake.

I hadn't been a regular attendee for years. We had been in the faraway place my people called *off*—Honduras, Ecuador, Iowa—but the drive from Charleston was easy enough on a summer weekend, so I'd come this year, William's diaries in hand, to sleep on the ground with a handful of families I'd known all of my life alongside a creek that had grounded my people for two hundred years.

Like a mischievous schoolboy, I showed my cousin Isaac the dirty words in the nineteenth-century diary at the edge of the trees above the creek, out of earshot of our parents and grandma and Sunday school teachers who prepared the food. Before long, our childhood friends Adam and Andrew noticed and wondered what we were looking at. We were a group of thirty-year-old men chuckling at the sex life of a man who'd been dead for 150 years. Real-life grown-ups. Eventually, my uncles caught wind; we opened up the circle. Then Grandma beckoned us over with a single word, the one she always called out like the sharp but perfect high lonesome sound of a Bluegrass singer: *Boys.*

We came.

In my boyhood, Grandma had been circling the table, sticking spoons in casseroles, cooking potatoes on the camping stove, wagging a finger at kids blurring too fast through the makeshift kitchen. Granddaddy would've already set up the horseshoe stakes and would be tossing with the other men, all of them in long pants and short-sleeved, button-up shirts, though they'd now have undone the top button or two in the July heat: the lot of them sporting wide baseball caps advertising plumbers or seed companies.

But now Granddaddy had been dead for fourteen years, and most of the men wore shorts and tennis shoes and threw cornhole instead of horseshoes. Grandma stayed planted in the folding chair while the other women fluttered about. Even sedentary and old, she called us all to immediate attention with the same word and voice she'd used all of our lives, every time we'd brought blood or broken a window or pulled blooms from her bushes. *Boys.* I carried the big green book over, left it on her lap like a time bomb, and we scattered.

My copy of the diaries stretches for 231 pages, the text filling two columns per page, and it's not as if William was playing the field every day, dropping *prick* and *bubbies* and *fuck* every line. To find the good stuff, you have to dig, to know just what you're looking for. I expected Grandma would get bored with the monotony of hauling logs and hoeing corn while I took up a cornhole game.

When I later retrieved the closed book from her lap, I suspected she'd found nothing racy and given up.

"Pretty interesting, isn't it?" I asked when I sat back down.

"Oh, it's about as I reckoned it would be," she said smirking at me. The glimmer in her eye told me everything I needed to know: She'd found William's private life.

....

Here it is: My great-great-great-great-grandfather dreamed of sucking on Rebecca Williamson's bubbys. He felt ZC's cunt and Celia's cunt and Peggy's cunt. He fuck'd Nancy and asked Betsy Gandy for a fuck and wanted to fuck Mary Norwood and tried to fuck CR, but a cow named Caroline interrupted. He had sex with another woman just before his wedding. He bragged about having two mistresses at once. He courted dozens of women. He disappeared with them into bedrooms and closets and forests and barn lofts. His last entry before he died recorded sex with a mistress. He might have loved them all. Or none of them. He wrote little of love, but he tracked every affair—fashioning a symbol for each mistress across fifty years of writing:

....

The Kamasutra lists sixty-four arts that an attractive woman should master. Fixing colored glass tiles on the floor. Tying turbans. Storing water in reservoirs. Mastering tongue twisters. Teaching parrots or starlings to talk. Knowledge of gambling.

Number 44 demands an understanding of code languages.

Vatsyayana, likely writing in the third century, offers women a system for using these code languages, a way to create a cipher by pairing and then substituting letters. Change, for example, all As into Qs.

Julius Caesar relied on a similar method when sending messages to Cicero during the Gallic Wars in the first century BCE. He simply replaced Roman letters with Greek letters and snuck the messages in plain view. Later, Caesar developed a system that shifted a cipher alphabet three places ahead of the plaintext, making an A a D, a B an E, and so on. The Caesar Shift, cryptanalysts later called it.

OLNH WKLV.

Without a key—without knowledge of the shift or the method behind the madness—these substitution ciphers locked up messages soundly in the ancient world. They were unbreakable.

William's diaries would have been similarly sealed tight. No one could have discovered that ς[ϟξ37ϸ 27 Λ[ΛΛ][ς meant "sucking on bubbys." He could have scattered his smattering of numbers, Greek characters, and shapes across Persian war zones and backstabbing Roman political circles and kept his life hidden.

But a scholar in ninth-century Baghdad could have known William's secrets. By then Islamic scientists had woven together enough mathematical, statistical, and linguistic knowledge to begin jimmying the lock of substitution ciphers.

In a ninth-century manuscript, a scholar named Abu Yusuf Ya'qub ibn as-Sabbah ibn 'omran ibn Ismail al-Kindi describes a method of breaking these ciphers, a method that later became known as frequency analysis—a method Browder surely used to crack William's code, that Nirenberg used to understand DNA.

In al-Kindi's description, a codebreaker takes a page of ciphered text and a roughly equal amount of plaintext. Then he counts the occurrences of letters in the plaintext—in Arabic, the letters A and L will naturally show up a lot (because of the article *al*), so it's easy to assume the letters occurring most frequently in the cipher text will match. Then the codebreaker performs the same task on the cipher text and begins making some assumptions, filling in the pieces as he can.

This is the invention of cryptanalysis: WDNH WKDW, FDHVDU.

By the time Nathaniel Browder received copies of William's symbols in 1978, wars had been won and lost, assassinations carried out and thwarted because of cryptanalysis.

Cryptology had become an industry in the eighteenth century—a hundred years before William's life. Countries across Europe created Black Chambers, staffed with cryptanalysts who worked to find and decipher information. By the time Browder received those xeroxed pages, Nazis had enciphered and shrunk messages onto microdots. The American marines had taken on Navajo words to encrypt communication. Sir Arthur Conan Doyle had fashioned Sherlock as a cryptography expert, Edgar Allan Poe had written "The Gold Bug," and Chaucer had encrypted passages in his *Treatise on the Astrolabe*. Babbage had cracked Vigenère, Turing had smashed Enigma. Handfuls of unbreakable codes had been created. And broken.

And, too, Samuel Pepys, the seventeenth-century English diarist and navyman, had written of sex under chairs and necking on bridges by hiding the saucy accounts in other languages. Eighteenth-century explorer William Byrd II had "rogered" women from London to Virginia in a shorthand code for his secret diaries.

In short, William Prestwood's simple substitution cipher isn't remarkable in the history of cryptology. His womanizing barely compares to Byrd's sexual appetite. William is himself a cipher: a nobody in the scheme of history.

This is what intrigues Browder, what sent him across the state and planted him at a typewriter for years: William's ground-floor view of all of the nineteenth-century happenings. His bystander status. It's clear in Browder's lines of research that he's interested in whose paths William crosses. He dives into genealogy and census data to find these connections: Thomas Wolfe's uncle buys the Prestwood family Bible, William befriends Daniel Boone's great-nephew, William's mother is connected to a Declaration of Independence signatory. For Browder, William is a narrator for a wider world, catching glimpses of the power players from the sidelines.

But for me, William is the protagonist. William is the history: a key to what's inside me, to where I'm from. My cipher.

....

We are equal parts our parents, as they were equal parts their parents. We're each packaged with full copies of two separate lives: everything that has fleshed out our parents' bodies is now our bodies. The obviousness of this makes it nearly unbelievable. But what it also means is that the same spun-up ladder of millions of DNA sequences that rests in a single cell of their bodies also makes the whole us.

This is too much for me. That the information that gave me a sizable nose and thinning hair is written on a single skin cell on my dad's arm or a stray hair from my mom's head. Our whole genomes wait in a cell we might slough off without ever knowing, all of our secrets trailing us as dust.

I think of those microdots from World War II, when Germans stashed messages within a single period of communication, sneaking coordinates and plans past Allied forces by shrinking them down into punctuation: everything tucked away in plain sight. They might have carried on that way forever, but someone eventually noticed. A microscope in the bag of a captured German spy made an Irish codebreaker suspicious, and soon he'd unraveled all the tiny, hidden messages waiting there: thirty pages of instructions and names vanished into throw-away dots.

For centuries our earlobes and curled tongues and eye colors made scientists and philosophers scratch their heads; they dug for answers about what—who—we're made of, but they couldn't see what lay hidden out in the open, right on our skin. Like that Irish codebreaker, Crick and Watson noticed something awry. They spotted a double helix on a blown-up image of a cell and knew the shape of human life—two wound-up strands. Now scientists sit in labs working away at the DNA in our skin, decrypting messages to know just who we are. Unspooling us. We'll all be found out sooner or later.

I do the math. I am 1.56 percent William Thomas Prestwood. Or he is 1/64 of me. That's nothing, negligible. His DNA has been whittled away by Fabius and Elizabeth and Asbury and Clementine and Albert and Azalee and Ray and Betty and David and Joy—and many more branches that never touched William's.

I may owe him for the pop my right elbow makes when I straighten it in the morning, but not much more. He's long gone, barely a part of me. I contain multitudes.

And still, I want to know. I want to know where exactly he lies in my skin, what he's given me. I imagine myself divided, like my son had wanted, not in half but in sixty-fourths. What slice of me is he? I ought to hire a codebreaker to find him hiding out in there.

But, of course, it's not math. A life—this long line of begets—is not a mere matter of DNA, of genetics. The way William laid his hand on young Fabius's head might have carried through the fingers of Asbury and Albert and Betty, learned without any work at all. My daddy's hand on my head might have been William—a gesture passed on without a gene. He could be anywhere right now. An unknowable haunting guiding my hand even now as I rest it on my boy's wild hair just before bed.

....

I read the decoded diaries as our baby grew inside Sarah—our genes stretching out to give shape to a new life, copies of us coding someone who is not us. I carried the transcript in my bag to and from the small college where I taught, pulling it out during empty office hours or after dinner to open to a random page and search for any curiosity there. I flipped through the diaries like one might a magazine in a waiting room.

But in the winter, satisfied I'd found all the dirty words I could, I started reading the diaries in earnest, chronologically. I first found William at age twenty, lovestruck and confused, and followed him to his grave at seventy-one. During those fifty-one years, he wrote everything and nothing: every day of his life he whittled down to a line or two. "Went to meeting" earned as much space as "Mother died."

He offered no reflection or introspection, little context or defense. He simply logged his life—or what he thought important about his life—in short form. Across those pages, I saw flashes of the history I'd learned in high school blurring by in the background: The War of 1812 looms, then passes. Cherokee families are hauled into camps in 1838. He attends Frankie Silver's execution. But what was foregrounded across the two hundred pages was a man tending land and searching for life.

Then it happened. Sometime in the winter, the diaries were no longer simply a distraction or an oddity—no longer a Where's Waldo of bedroom words. Amid the white space and unspoken motives, a man took shape, a man from whom I'd descended. When I read the pages, I saw him. When I left the pages, he came with me. He took up residence in my brain as I took up residence in his passed-on life. He was real.

4

William Thomas Prestwood spends much of the vernal equinox of 1808 pulling a cow from a bog. He is twenty and has decided it time to make something of his life. All across Darlington County, South Carolina, seeds are finding purchase, the air heavy and wet, and perhaps William has been imagining those fields turning green in a matter of weeks, thinking about his grandfather's ever-dividing land, about his own drunk father, about the thinness of human life. Thinking about nothing changing. Or everything changing.

The truth is, some of this life-change decision has to do with his sister forever nagging him to take hold of something, to quit floating and reading and thinking. To become a man. The truth is also that some of this life-change decision has to do with love—with the tight-chested version of himself he becomes around Mary Norwood.

Today, in the mud, pushing on a cow, it has been a week since he last saw Mary Norwood. And that exchange had not gone well. It was Sunday, and he rode with her brother Alex to the church meeting. When they set out for home, Alex walked with Mary, rather than mounting his horse. William tried to keep pace with them on horseback, but it was difficult. Finally, he asked Mary to climb on, to ride behind him so they could all carry on their way. This was only logical; why should she and Alex amble along beside a perfectly capable horse? But William may've also been thinking of how he'd look with Mary Norwood—a *woman*, six years his elder—gripping his waist, hair trailing them both as they made their way home in the Sunday sun.

She'd rather walk, she said.

And so began William's recorded life. Later that day, in his first entry, he recounted the rest of the ride home:

> **March 13:** I kept up conversation when I could.... After a while I said as I can't be of no service to you I will go. Repented for my aukward conduct.

The next day, he plotted out the possible trajectories for his life:

> **March 14:** Rise. Reflected on yesterday's conduct. I swore I would alter my station of life. (Provoked to it by my sister.) Determined one plan of three to be executed; viz., either marry MN, or keep Bachelor's Hall, or travel.

Three possible futures scribbled in ink: teach, travel, or take the hand of Mary Norwood—pull her up onto his horse and rush through the fields, the world turning green in their wake as they charge toward the coast, his parents arm in arm, looking happy for once, waving goodbye.

Of course, he chooses Mary. Mary will become his life. He's set it in ink. And so he is knee-deep in a bog on a Tuesday with a mud-stuck cow belonging to her father. He is putting in work.

The next day, William hauls this curried favor to Mr. Norwood's shop to find Mary, to start his life:

> **March 15:** Thought to spark Miss MN but my Uncle CC was there. Did not do it.

No matter the finality of his plans on paper, what becomes clear in the living world is that it is easier for William to push a cow from a bog than it is to carry on a conversation with the woman he loves. Oozing with *aukward* conduct, William avoids Mary for weeks, eventually deciding to court her where he is comfortable, alone and writing:

> **March 27:** Burnt a letter. Started to meeting. Did not talk with MN. She looked crossed-eyed. Come home to sleep.
>
> **March 28:** Skinned Mr. Norwood's cow. Put out the fire at night.
>
> **March 29:** In the morning halled rails. Mother started to Grandfather's. I went to writing a letter to MN. Alarmed by fire. Subdued it. Went to writing. Fire alarm. Subdued it. Wrote a while. Went around the fire. Finished writing. Slept.
>
> **March 30:** Sent the letter to Miss MN (night by Byner).

The whole of William's life now hangs on a letter written in fits over two days. Then he waits. He works on the road. He visits his grandfather. He buys a gun.

April 3: Slept late. Heard that MN had received my letter on Thursday. It not returned. Had toothache.

....

I found the tiny notebooks Steven Scott Smith lifted from a now-demolished house in the archives at North Carolina State University. I drove hours to sit and wait for them in the special collections wing, which felt like the private library of a rich statesman from a century before: dark wood, forest greens, cloth covers behind glass. Soon, before me stood a row of nondescript boxes, chronologically arranged.

I felt like I should be in an all-white tunnel, dressed in a hazmat suit with gloves as soft as butterfly wings. Instead, I took a box from the counter, sat down at a table, and yanked the first notebook out. I paused for some rise of orchestral music but heard only the faint clacking of a keyboard before I turned to the first page of the notebook sewn by my ancestor.

The first entry in the first notebook was a plaintext account of a resurrection, of a young girl brought back to life in Brown Creek in 1783. William recorded what the nine-year-old girl saw when she was dead: two men in a house, one small man chained to the floor joists, the other a pretty man flying in the air. She soared away from the house with the pretty man, to a garden where children played. He invited her to stay but warned her she wouldn't be able to return home if she did. She missed her sister, she said. The pretty man told her to go back and to warn the people of their wicked ways. She was to tell her mother not to "jangle with her children," not to "threaten them with a whip." She was to warn her sister that she was stubborn and "had evil ways." She was to tell Joseph Ingram not to begrudge the poor when he helped them, to warn Rebecca Laughter she was spoiling her pretty child, and to warn everyone that if they did any bad thing, they should be sorry for it. If she was good, he said, he would come back for her. If she was bad, she would go to a bad place, "between the boards" of the house. When she returned to the house, back to the chained-up man, she saw there her own body, which she "remembered perfectly well," and so she sank back in and awoke.

It took strained eyes and time to make out this account in William's looping longhand, but I managed it. Beyond these opening pages, however, I was lost. The shapes meant nothing to me. But I could feel them. I ran my hands along the indentations of the symbols and imagined the weight of the fountain pen in William's hand, the force it required to leave this mark: the pages like reverse braille, grooves where my forefather had been.

As I touched the pages, I thought of the trails back home, about the worn paths through the woods first cut by my great-great-grandfather, about the ways that we stuck to them and held those lines long after Asbury Prestwood had passed on.

But the etched lines on the thin paper didn't meander like our footpaths in the forest; they ran arrow-straight across the page so that immediately I was taken aback by the precision of the entries—every day neatly marked, a measured line separating the symbols from the date—and the microscopic control required to carry the small symbols across each page without sagging or drooping.

In my decoded transcription, it was easy to imagine William throwing down a few quick words between plowing and dinner, a rush of the pen. But when I saw the notebooks before me, I realized how slowly he must have moved, at least at first. How much repetitive care went into this logging of a whole bunch of nothing and a little bit of something for fifty years.

Then I thought I could see him, by candlelight, pondering MN's latest silence and his hazy future, picking out a handful of stars from a break in the clouds above the long fields outside, and then putting pen to paper, the scratch slow and deliberate above the pops in the fireplace. I imagined him there writing to me, to tell me about the feel of the early fall air, how it has been suddenly emptied of water and made to stretch his lungs wider. How he wished he'd known in his younger days to sometimes leave the log rolling for later, to simply sit and watch a clutch of leaves scatter from the faintest of breezes, as if birds flying briefly before diving into earth. But he wasn't putting any of this on paper; he was writing that he "saw folks" and that he started "to plant corn" and that "JP not dead, got wet." He was not writing for me, not for anyone. He was recording. He was prioritizing what mattered—what he thought would matter.

April 4, 1810: Skinned my shin.

In the first box, I also found Browder's *Elementary Military Cryptography*, published by the War Department in 1945. Even though I had no white gloves or string music in the special collections, the warning on the handbook added some gravitas to my document digging:

> **RESTRICTED:** No person is entitled solely by virtue of his grade or position to knowledge or possession of classified matter. Such matter is entrusted only to those individuals whose official duties require such knowledge or possession.

I had begun wondering if I should be doing any of this: unearthing the purposefully buried life of a man. He'd blanketed his shin-skinning and corn-planting and woman-laying in code for a reason, and what right did I have to come along two hundred years later and run my fingers along the edges of his life in a library in the middle of the state? Was I shrinking his life by bringing it out into the open, making him smaller than he ever was, less of a man?

The easy out, of course, was that someone else has already done it: Browder had broken the code and printed the transcription and sent copies out to libraries. *He started it.* If these materials were classified in the nineteenth century, Browder declassified them forty years ago. I was merely the writer who received the tip-off.

But Browder came to these diaries with historical interest, at an arm's length, looking for a historical figure. I came with something more complicated, more personal. I wanted to find the flesh and blood of a man who'd made me spread out across these pages. I was looking for resurrection.

In the margins of some entries, I found sketches of hearts—the briefest emotional admission within the recording of passing details ("read *Sorrows of Werther*, thought of MN"). Some hearts were upside down. Some were colored in, others mere outlines. I set out to skim all the diaries for these emotional marginalia, for recognizable shapes amid the made-up cipher. It didn't take long before the pages became a kind of Rorschach test. In water-damaged sections or ink drips, I was sure I could see something—a heart? a cloud? a face?

I returned, instead, to the tactile. I felt the thinness of the pages, the crinkled texture where water had been. I held each notebook in my palm like a flower. None of them was the same size: some long and skinny, others nearly square. They were like off-brand Moleskines, crude and brown and practical. As I traced the edges of the covers with a finger, I realized a few of the notebooks were built from recycled legislative documents. On the inside of one were snippets sounding like the book of Revelation: *in the year one thousand eight hundred... and who shall appear... a bag or powder horn... armed with a sword.*

As I held them, I imagined each tiny timeworn notebook like one of those expanding pills from my childhood. Water dropped on it and suddenly it was larger than my hand, stretching wider, filling up the table, and then, from one of the ink blobs in the margins appeared the face of a man. Hair sprang up, ears rounded, a chin dropped. Then, a body. And soon, William Thomas Prestwood lay on the table of the special collections, naked and prepped for autopsy. I leaned in. I reached for him. But before I could crack open a rib, he twitched, blinked an eye. He stopped my hand before fixing me with his gaze.

....

In April, the birds return. First the mockingbirds, then the martins. Before long, woodpeckers fill the air. Mary, however, has not returned William's letter.

One Saturday, William wakes up and burns a collection of paper and hair. Then he rides into town to pay his taxes. Thousands of other events shape his day—perhaps he brews coffee while the hair burns, maybe discusses the weather with his mother before setting off to town. He writes none of this down. He doesn't fit any other memories into cipher except for these: burning hair, paying taxes, and seeing a poor boy playing a banjo on the road to town. He also writes that while in town he receives his orders for general muster and he learns that Mary Norwood will not return his letter.

William is tired. Yesterday he and Binah rolled logs until nightfall. He should have gone straight to bed, but he and his sister stayed up late, gabbing like teenagers.

Who do you like better, he asked her, *P. Wright or C. Jones?*

Why? Martha asked.

Fun, he said.

When she turned the tables and hinted that she thought Binah was his mistress, he didn't deny it. He grew boastful, telling Martha—promising her—he would have two mistresses before the year was out.

So perhaps William rose this Saturday morning ready for the world—ready to burn anything and settle his debts. But then he learns that Mary has no intention to write to him, and so he and his sister make plans: *I and sister had plotted to get MN to my house.*

The next day, William rides a piece with his mother as she travels to Chesterfield, South Carolina. On his way home, he spies Mary Norwood with her mother along the road. He pushes his horse to reach them, to be seen.

As he passes, Mary's father calls out to him. William stops. He follows her father onto the property, and in that moment, William might look like a man for marrying, a man who could swing a woman onto a horse for the rest of his life. Or he might look like a desperate kid who can't take a hint. Alone with her father, William says he's in mourning, only he has no crepe to wear to show it. That night, he dreams of Mary. The next day, the martins come.

....

I've started writing letters to William. It makes no sense; I know this. I tell him about my days, about life two hundred years later. I work out questions about his life two hundred years ago.

Yes, I've merely tricked myself into keeping a diary, substituting "Dear Diary." for "Dear William." But it's different, more complicated than that. I imagine him reading them. Actually reading them. Not like a ghost over my shoulder or through some kind of neon time travel, but I imagine his resurrected body opening my letters with resurrected fingers and finding traces of my life there. I imagine him getting to know me.

I know it's crazy, and I do it anyway.

I feel that I owe him something, like I ought to give some part of myself away, in some kind of trade. Or penance. He's given me everything on his pages—or perhaps I've taken it as I return over and over to these transcriptions that he never expected anyone to read. I learn about William's life, about his pain and desire. His secrets. I need some skin in the game. So I write to him, this dead man I'm getting to know, and expect him to somehow read my words.

True to form, I'm impatient and undisciplined in this work—I write to him one day and then don't return for weeks. But I do eventually return. I keep this up, and before long, it feels like a conversation. A conversation with a man long gone from this world who is somehow a part of me.

Dear William:

I found you. As you walk to the mill and find turkey eggs and dream of stolen horses, I carry you in my bag, those worn-out diary pages reconstituting you two hundred years after you tucked your secrets away there. You're with me at oil changes and on airplanes. You're with me here in the near dark, as I lay this day to bed.

I want to tell you about how you will move on from MN, about all that will follow you—a long line of lives stretching to my hand as I write this to you on a chilly night in February. I want to tell you of my father, of his mother. About how she tracks birds like you, how she loves to talk to them when they appear beyond her window, how she scratches her day down into notebooks.

I want to tell you that I'm learning your code so that it'll be our shared, timeless language. 3 5ϐ ꞁ2|L ς27

A friend in West Virginia sent me a fiddle last week. I thought of you. I wondered what you might teach me if I could lay it in your arms and step back. Sometimes when I play the banjo, people will ask if music runs in the family. "No," I'd always said. My parents don't play instruments, none of my grandparents played. But now I wonder about you and your fiddle playing, about what might have floated generation to generation to me. Maybe the music is settled somewhere in my skin because of you.

We could play. That's a miraculous thing, isn't it? Another shared language. I know nothing of stolen horses and turkey eggs, and you know nothing of oil changes and airplanes, but the songs I hammer out on my banjo are the same tunes you played, trying to draw Mary to you. "Fly Around My Pretty Little Miss" is a good place to start. It has so many names, has changed in little ways from one mountain ridge to another, but "Western Country" or "Susannah Gal" or "Fare Thee Well, My Blue-Eyed Gal" or "Little Betty Ann" or whatever you might've called it two hundred miles and two hundred years from here would connect us. The first stair-stepping run down would light a little flash of recognition in your eye, and soon enough we'd be in it, a man and his dead ancestor making music for no one to hear.

The music, your codes, the birds—everything carries on, William. A whole world waits, pages upon pages of awful beauty reaching out before us, beckoning us on. There's nothing to do but go.

5

William was born along the Great Pee Dee River in South Carolina, a place European explorers had once named the River of St. John the Baptist. The name didn't stick. No camel-hair-covered, locust-eating man had ever set food into these cold waters, but the Pee Dee people had been living and dying on that land for seven centuries, so later settlers simply called the valley the Pee Dee. Then they killed the Pee Dee people.

In 1756, when William's great-granddaddy moved south from Virginia and bought two hundred acres along the river, the Pee Dee tribe had been decimated. Some survivors of the never-ending battles with white settlers and the Cherokee people lived among the Catawba tribe; some lived among the Europeans. According to anthropologist John Swanton, when William begins his diary, "the Pedee and Cape Fear tribes were represented by one half-breed woman."

In 1808, the Upper Pee Dee valley is a place of plantations, of wide fields and trafficked bodies. William has come into this place carrying white wealth, born into the planter class. His family is not aristocratic, doesn't rule over any hundred-acre plantations, but they have plenty of land and money. His grandfather and namesake had amassed nearly three thousand acres when he died in 1806, but because he died intestate, much of his estate was siphoned off by mismanagement. William's mama's people, the Cokers, have even more land and growing power. At twenty years old, William is a burgeoning man—the only son of Thomas and Nancy—with options, with land awaiting him and family with means surrounding him in this brand-new country. The unsurprising trajectory of his life should be one of inheriting all that he can see and taking up residence in a house overlooking it.

In mid-April, William's father's bees swarm. Having laid her eggs, the queen uproots and takes with her a handful of workers. They start over. William, too, has begun wondering about moving on, letting go of Mary Who Would Be His Life, Mary who will not respond to his letter. He runs into Bill Mayhorn, and

Bill mentions a sister. A sister who will be at the next church meeting. A sister who might take a liking to a man like William. William makes a note. He's growing impatient. He is, after all, a grown man who dreams of "hugging Rebecca Williamson and sucking on bubbys," who's bragging to his sister of multiple mistresses by year's end. There is a wide world beyond Mary.

And yet by Sunday, he is sending messages to Mary again, always from a distance and by proxy:

> **April 17:** Easter. I told June that if MN was for jumping off I did care how soon she let me know it.

And on Tuesday, he's writing again. He's fretting again, burning bits and starting over:

> **April 19:** Gmother come. Burn piece of a letter (MN). Mother communicated that for me to put my property in some person's hands and keep school.

And so, at his mother's urging, William comes again to three paths: teach, travel, or marry. How long does one wait for a woman who won't return a letter, a woman who won't even climb on a horse to ease her travel?

And why won't Mother trust that he can care for his land? Why must she picture him indoors, a book in his lap? He could be a man like his granddaddy, like his uncles, like those Calhouns and Pinckneys farther south: men who stand on porches and make calculations about the Black bodies and white cotton spreading before them. Men who would clear those fields with the swing of a scythe if the numbers don't add up.

> **April 20:** Done nothing.

On Friday, it is abnormally cold, and June comes in the night to say that "MN did not want to jump off." This should be it: one possible future closed. On Sunday Drucilla Mayhorn will be at the meeting. She will be expecting him. He can sell his land and start teaching any day now, turning his obsessions with math and Latin on young minds. His life is only now beginning. Drucilla is waiting.

But on Saturday the woodpeckers return and William finds his missing horse up at Seedtick, and he knows in his bones that Mary Norwood is his destiny. On his way back through the woods, he sees the eerie green glow of ignis fatuus. Perhaps it is the luck of this—of spotting green lights rising up from the marshy nowhere, appearing there as if only for him—that further emboldens William, commits him to pursuing Mary no matter how far. He has his horse, the weather is warming, and the world is performing miracles all around him.

But William should know better. He knows his Latin, knows that ignis fatuus is a *foolish fire*. He knows that the mystery of the haze lures travelers from their paths, deceives them into inescapable waters.

And yet, he stays home on Sunday. He ignores the meeting and the promise of a woman named Drucilla Mayhorn. He only halfway listens when his sister returns and tells him of the many compliments Drucilla paid him. Instead, he spots June talking to his father in the field and rushes over to seek out news of Mary.

> **April 24:** In conversation with June, he told me that MN wanted longer time to consider (I am determined to be a neuter!!)

....

I was taken aback to feel sympathy and annoyance when reading the flat transcription of a dead man's notebooks that winter. Despite the occasional poetic syncopation in his recordings *(Went to M Brown's, to a frolic, to fiddle.)*, he didn't work with bright colors, wasn't packing an emotional punch on those tiny pages. He logged everydayness. He made lists out of his life. And yet I found myself shaking my head at his hypocrisy when he claimed he'd never write to MN but then took up the pen a few days later. I felt sorry for his awkwardness, for his inability to take hold of this woman he loved or find his place in the world.

I had a decade on the twenty-year-old William when Browder's transcription showed up in the mail. I was his elder, a married man about to have a son, and he was a heartsick kid doodling in a handmade notebook. He might have been one of my college students, wrapped up in drama and longing, and I felt for him like I might one of them. *Kids these days.*

But not long after our son was born, it struck me that every choice William made, every attempt that failed, threaded through time to reach me. I'd not be here—or at least not as I am—if Mary Norwood had finally given her hand to him. What if she'd climbed on his horse after church, given in to his pestering? What if June hadn't delivered the news of her indecision and he'd remained more steadfast? What if he'd fallen in love with Drucilla Mayhorn and made a new life that spring? What if he'd not paid his taxes or burnt hair or eaten beans on a Thursday?

Suddenly every choice he made on his pages was mine—or, somehow, me.

Then, in a rush, this realization pitched forward. While I sat in the dead of the night holding a sleepless redheaded baby, I felt the extra weight of fatherhood: my decisions were no longer only my own. I thought not only of the jaundiced baby wrapped up in a glowing light-therapy blanket and my genes, but also of his children—and so on. The word arrived like a neon sign through the haze of my sleep-deprived mind: *legacy*.

My sense of family already dug deep. Growing up, we had no boundaries on our land—we walked through unlocked doors and cut through yards without warning. My mother's people, the Maxwells and Gilliams, owned most of the land across the creek, so I could be let loose with a bag full of daylight and never get far from family. On holidays, we crammed into Grandma's house, pushing furniture into corners to make way for a table long enough to hold generations. I knew my parents hadn't raised me alone—my uncles and aunts and grandparents fed me and jumped my car battery and cheered at my basketball games and listened when I had little to say.

I knew in my bones that family mattered and that family stretched as wide as you allowed. But until that point in my life, I had seen this transaction as one-directional. I could see the ways that my family had shaped me, but I had never worried over what my life might mean for them—or for the family that would grow from my DNA.

Presented with the possibility—the promise—that my daily choices could leak into the lives of my grandchildren, of their grandchildren, I grew nervous. I wasn't having an existential crisis, but I had a sudden and double-sided awareness of both my smallness and my influence. I was a nobody, and yet lives branching off from mine would be altered by the way I cradled this baby at 2:00 a.m. As we rocked and he refused to settle in his crib, I knew that the thunderstorm of his brain was already sparking, fusing connections that would make him who he is. My touch—or my absence—thundered around in there as those synapses fired, and that wiring would light him up for the rest of his life. But not only him: he might someday be a father, fathering with the brain sparked by a 2:00 a.m. rocking by his father. His hand resting on some young boy's head.

I wasn't in my right mind. I was hardly sleeping, and the world was both brighter and blurrier than I had ever known. In saner moments, I saw that these late-night realizations were obvious notions—the basic tension in any time-travel movie—but I felt more than I understood them. In my skin, I carried a sense of the generational weight of every single life. When I cracked open those notebooks and found William riding his horse around Darlington County in 1808, I couldn't help but also think about all the life that would follow me.

What this mostly meant was that I thought about my childhood. And the childhood I'd be able to offer this boy. I remembered those never-ending days roaming the woods and rushing onto Grandma's back porch as she set the corn on the table, and I knew that my sense of the world—one cultivated in long stretches of forest and family—would not be what Abe awoke to here. We lay him to sleep in a small house on a quiet street in Charleston, South Carolina, a few blocks from a train station and a shipyard, hundreds of miles from his cousins and aunts and uncles and grandparents and great-grandparents holed up in the mountains. He would never get lost in our small backyard or rush into an aunt's house with a bloody nose. Of course, I knew his life would be different—should be different—than mine, but in the snatches of sleep I found, I dreamed often of the field above the barn and the brambles along the creek. I wanted to give them to him. To have them back myself.

. . . .

At the end of April William's father's bees swarm again. They multiply. Then, strangely, they swarm again the next week, but this time they "run away" and don't return.

William spends the beginning of May hunting his ever-vanishing horse, plowing his father's fields, drinking rum at his grandfather's house, and watching his cousin Caleb cut the head off a snake. He enters into conversations about selling his land. He plows, he hunts deer, he dreams of seeing a man hanged. At the end of the month, June appears again in the night:

> **May 28:** June come night. Said MN would have me if she could get [unreadable].

What Mary needs cannot be recovered two centuries later. The entry is water damaged, and so Mary's one demand is redacted, vanished into history. But it is fitting, this indecipherable request. From here, watching William's life play out in staccato bursts of farmwork and letter writing and rum drinking, I know

Mary is unreachable, unattainable, a foolish fire. Move on, William. Swing round to see Drucilla next week. Set out to find the world. Start your life.

> **May 29:** Funned. Heard that Wm. Gun seen three full moons. Last night dreamed seeing a man hung.
>
> **June 2:** Hunted my horse half the day. Slept.
>
> **June 4:** Stuck a stick in a snake's head.
>
> **June 5:** Pentacost day.
>
> **June 6:** Read a letter from James Coker. The snake at my plough. Binah communicated to me destruction.
>
> **June 9:** Wrote a letter to MN (no. 5).
>
> **June 11:** Went over Black Creek. Alex Norwood come.
>
> **June 12:** Trinity. Saw Uncle William.
>
> **June 13:** Sent MN the letter.
>
> **June 14:** Drank rum.
>
> **June 15:** Simon Williams told me that Jackson told him that I was to be married to MN.

Then again, I've always been too impatient. Perhaps I've never stood still long enough to rightly see the beauty shrouded in the ignis fatuus. As summer approaches, William finds his footing upon this rumor of marriage and stands up straight. He will marry MN. He makes a decision about the rest of his life.

> **June 16:** Went TC Jr. Offered him my land.

....

One summer, I drove the back roads through the part of the world that raised William. What I knew of Darlington County, South Carolina, I knew from the interstate: It was a crossroad sending vanloads of people another hundred miles toward the airbrushed strip of Myrtle Beach or onto I-95, to run to Florida or out of the South. And, of course, there was racing. I'd never watched a

NASCAR race start to finish, but I'd sat through enough screenings of *Days of Thunder* in high school shop classes for *Darlington* to mean *Raceway*. I knew Darlington as a place for speed, a place to rush past.

But beyond the interstate and NASCAR lights and forever-spreading fast-food stops, I found miles of irrigation machinery and cotton and corn. The land opened. And it kept going. The wide fields seemed to slow everything down, and I took my time alone on the straight road under the afternoon light. It was beautiful—I recognized this immediately—but it bore little in common with the place I come from: my South was one of tangled-up roads and trailers hanging on the sides of mountains and tiny fields cut out of any flat scratch of land. The South on a road in Darlington County was a place of land rolled out for miles. If not for the forest backing and sometimes interrupting everything, it might've resembled any piece of agrarian Midwest.

Then again, the trailers and shells of cars on cinder blocks appearing along the road looked more like home than anything I'd encountered in the Midwest, where farming is carried out at industrial-scale with GPS-controlled machinery.

Every few miles, a big, old house appeared out of nowhere, dwarfing the mobile homes and conjuring *Gone with the Wind*. Each one tempted me to pull over and peek in windows, but I didn't. Most were occupied but timeworn: the wraparound porches sagged, the paint chipped, the gabled chimneys crumbled. I have a thing for old houses, sparked by the centering presence of Asbury and Clementine Prestwood's empty house on the land of my childhood, but it didn't take long for the eeriness of each beautiful run-down structure to settle over me like a storm.

Each house loomed, ominous amid the rolling land, and I could think of only the bodies in the ground. I knew the houses were beautiful only because of stolen lives. I saw each place in a time-looped image, men on those porches two-hundred years ago forcing enslaved bodies to work that soil to death.

Is there any escaping that haunting? I imagined what it would be like to inherit, to live in one of these grand houses on this postcard-pretty land today—coming down the staircase every morning to sunlight caught up in those tall windows but knowing with every step that the boards holding me up are cut by bone and blood. The worst kind of evil is always beautiful.

As I drove, I thought of William and this world offered up to him at age twenty. I didn't know why he sold his land in 1808, why he let loose of the power and money planted in the ground, why his mother encouraged him to do so. I knew what I want the truth to be. I wanted the truth to be that he wanted nothing to do with the evils of slavery, that he wanted to make an honest living. I wanted the truth to be that I was descended of a man strong enough to build a simple life when the whole dirty kingdom awaited him.

But maybe he simply had no business sense. Maybe he was too flighty to handle the responsibility. Maybe he only wanted a quick payday to convince Mary to make a life with him. Maybe he had allergies. His pages wouldn't tell me, but as a man forever shaped by the land of my people, I was grateful William let his go. That June 16 sale changed William's life. And mine.

6

I knew that what I wanted to give my baby was a fiction. My childhood was summer. An eternal, romantic, unbelievable summer. I had no diary to search to piece those years together, so they floated in my head as a single, never-ending day, an amalgam of images. If I searched long enough for individual moments or memories in other seasons, I could find them up there—playing Nintendo on snow days or crashing my bike into leaf piles—but to conjure *childhood* was to conjure summer and Granddaddy in the garden and Grandma on the porch and me in the trees. Our parents are at work, so my cousins and I take over everything within reach while Grandma and Granddaddy carry on with the growing and making of food. Childhood lives forever there, a soft loop of blue sky and hayfields.

Our life in Charleston was sleep-deprived but sweet. We walked our baby through streets draped in Spanish moss. A park waited two blocks away, restaurants not far beyond. It was easy to imagine the rest of our lives stretching out on our short street.

I knew the childhood I carried with me and wanted to pass on to my son wasn't real, not truly. Those images happened and happened often, but I also fought with my cousins and fell off the oil tank and watched *Matlock* on the living room floor while eating frozen pizza. My head had recast the first decade of my life as forever roaming the land beside the apple orchard and below the beehives, and it was an illusion. I knew this. Still, I dreamed of that endless summer. I imagined Baby Abe as a loose-limbed boy skipping rocks in the creek below the barn.

This was partly because I knew that even accounting for the rosy coloring of memory, my childhood was bizarrely normal. I wanted for nothing; I feared little. My world was sturdy: mostly free of drama or divorce or death. If I could piece together anything like it for my son—even if it was an interpretation of a smoothed-over memory—I would. And the ingredients I needed were family and land.

But of course there were secrets on those one hundred acres in Fruitland, North Carolina. Most of them lay buried, each layer of soil its own code to work through. Above Grandma's house, we uncovered green and blue glass medicine bottles left there by somebody generations before. By the barn, Uncle Tim opened a hole from time to time and dropped busted machinery and worn-down tires into the earth. Then he spun around to the backhoe and covered it back over. Now the debris creeps back to the surface like weeds.

We booby-trapped everything as children: strung trip wires, covered deep holes with a layer of sticks and leaves, stuffed trees with plastic tinker toys, ready to fall on anyone passing through. We prepared for invasion.

By whom, we couldn't rightly say. Soviets maybe. Or else, the family living in a trailer out by the highway. We only knew we wouldn't abide anyone setting foot in our woods, so we'd summoned MacGyver and the A-Team and prepared the ground underfoot for battle. We wore trails to nowhere into the dirt, trying to lure these Russians/neighbors into broken ankles or bloody faces. We were sweet kids.

Deeper in the woods, my cousin and I buried a *Playboy* one summer. We absconded with a gallon freezer bag from Grandma's and tucked it tightly inside to keep it reasonably dry. Then we buried it in twigs and leaves and measured the number of steps from the felled tree to the X (and X and X).

Back then, I knew nothing of my grandparents' strange courtship on that land; it lay buried somewhere between their house and the creek. I only learned because I sat on that floral couch in college, my notebook in hand, and asked question after question. I dug. Slowly, from the bits I could unearth, I pieced together a story.

Grandma grew up as an only child in a small house above Clear Creek. Farther up the hill lived her grandparents, Asbury and Clementine Prestwood. On the backside of the hill lived her uncles and aunts. Cousins abounded. Her daddy, Albert Prestwood, tended the fields along and above the creek, same as he did as a boy: seemingly never-ending rows of corn and beans and potatoes. He took on a field full of dairy cows as a man, and once a week he rolled barrels full of milk a mile down Townsend Road, where they'd be scooped up by the dairy truck.

The road leading to Asbury Prestwood's house, on the land where the author was raised

When Grandma turned eight, her mom and dad took in a boy whose mother had died. By then, Grandma expected to be an only child forever: she'd long since stopped asking about a little sister. But suddenly, a teenage boy had moved into their small house, and her father had set him to work out in those fields. He was long and lean and quiet, and the house grew crowded but not uncomfortable.

And so it went: the Prestwoods above Clear Creek were now a family of four. Grandma read her books and sometimes talked back. The boy hoed corn and milked the cows until 1941, when he joined the Army and set sail for England.

I gathered this story like a bird makes a nest: weaving together details until they held. Grandma delivered these bits as if they were the most natural, most obvious details one could unearth: The boy knocked out his teeth working on airplanes across the sea; she went to prom where a one-armed librarian played piano. She graduated high school. He sent money from across the sea for a gift—a Bulova watch purchased on Main Street.

This long-gone boy was, I must assume, a brother when he left for war. He'd been someone to tease her, to be in her way when she needed the bathroom, to drink the last of the milk at night. But from the fragments of story I collected sitting on Grandma's couch, from the look in her eye when I coaxed it from her, I knew something rippled in this moment when she was eighteen, with this Bulova watch given from across the ocean as a graduation gift.

Then the war ended. The boy came home. But he was no longer a boy—he was in his late twenties. Grandma had finished high school. They set back to their life as a family of four on Prestwood land, but the air changed somehow. The sound of the creek down the hill no longer static but suddenly a call, a temptation.

From here, most details became inaccessible, nearly redacted. I couldn't pull them out of her, but I know that after the war, the now-adult boy and now-adult girl sat longer on the porch. They walked the edges of the field at dusk. They stood closer than they once had. And, eventually, they climbed into a car with Albert and Azalee, their usual family of four, and drove to the Methodist church to be married.

I didn't know any of this as a boy—didn't know that my grandparents in the rock house through the woods had been adoptive siblings, that my great-grandmother in the house above Clear Creek had been a mother to both of my grandparents. I didn't know that Albert Prestwood had set his hand on each of their heads.

Maybe none of this was hidden away from me. I don't know when such details would have naturally emerged. In my feral state roaming the woods I didn't often stop to ask about my grandparents' love life, about the possibility that they had shared a house as both teenagers and husband and wife. Even in my adolescent years, I mostly talked to Grandma about the birds. I talked to Granddaddy about baseball, about the Cardinals. Grandma and I sat in our chairs in the living room and watched the flashes of feathers outside, and Granddaddy and I sat in his parked car and listened to the broadcast of the St. Louis game through the fuzz of AM radio.

Finding that newspaper article in Grandma's house about William's enciphered diaries felt a lot like learning about my grandparents' affair on this Prestwood land—*this was here all along?* Maybe Grandma had buried them. Or maybe I'd never known enough to ask, couldn't read the land well enough to know where to stick the shovel.

Now when I sink into the blurred-edged summer day of my childhood, I fold in this knowledge of my grandparents: that they had been adoptive siblings before lovers. At first it wrinkled the picture—an Appalachian stereotype if there'd ever been one—but now the story somehow makes the skies bluer and the hay fuller. This land wrapped them up, their love a field of wildflowers never planted but shooting up all the same.

....

For William, the summer solstice of 1808 is a roller coaster; it brings rumors and dreams and broken promises and rum:

> **June 19:** Went to Mr. N. Swore I wou'd not send MN any more letters before she sent me one or I talked with her.
>
> **June 29:** Ploughed for TP. J Jackson interrogated on marriage, negative.
>
> **July 4:** 32 years of independence. Byner communicated that MN wanted to know some things from me. MN said she refused a proposal of matrimony on my account. I swore that she should be the last to lay it to my charge!!!!!!!
>
> **July 9:** Went to muster. T Coker is to buy my land. Quarreled with John. Come by to see MN. Did not court her. Had a frolic. TP got mad.
>
> **July 10:** Got 9 turkey eggs. Shall land and marry MN.
>
> **July 13:** MN wished we was married and bedded.
>
> **July 14:** June come. Misses MN sent to me for pears.
>
> **July 15:** Binah told me MN wished we was married.
>
> **July 17:** Eat watermelon.
>
> **July 18:** Went to Esq. Fort's and proved a deed for CC. Work'd with JS. Drank rum.

July 20: Holp CC thresh wheat. Dreampt fuck MN.

July 21: Threshed my wheat.

July 22: Cleaned my wheat.

July 23: Saw Rhonda Ganey's thighs.

July 24: Arose. Holp NS drive cattle. Saw KS and Aunt married. Attempted talk with MN. MN's chair harness broke. Give her strings. Sent her pears.

Mary still hasn't returned any of William's five letters. He still hasn't spoken to her about their lives together, about just where he wants to place the chest of drawers, about where he'd imagine she'd sit once the supper dishes had been cleared away. But something has changed. William has a buyer for his land and Mary has his pears. *Shall land and marry MN*; *MN wishes we was married and bedded.*

But, of course, doubts, like fingertips of green smoke, sneak in:

July 25: Dreampt that June told a carpenter fucked MN. Byner communicated that MN wanted June to fuck her. Byner told that Mr. N. was mad with MN for it. Went carousing. Thought I wou'd never drink any more liquor.

I imagine William, trying to shake this dream from his head all day—Mary opening her gown for a passing carpenter. He knows it's a dream, of course, but then this news of her desire for June. He can't let go of this sense of Mary's insatiability, of her uncontrollable want wrapping up any passing man. And yet she won't return a simple letter; she refuses the most courteous of rides. He goes carousing.

7

My cousins and I often forgot where we'd set traps, which trails led to hunks of plastic falling from the trees and which ones led home, so in the longest stretch of rhododendron below Grandma's—the inner sanctum—we installed a map. From the tractor shed, we took plywood, painted it white, and then charted the whole of our territory in permanent marker: some forty acres from here to the road, hayfields and apple orchards and forests. We marked our houses, the beehives, the creek. We also invented symbols to indicate all the traps lying in wait. Each one a delicious sign of danger.

If I found myself at Grandma's alone—my cousins off somewhere—I concocted new traps: perhaps a branch pulled tight with rope, ready to thwack someone in the face. Then, I dutifully sketched a triangle onto the map to alert everyone to this danger.

Naturally, the highest concentration of traps surrounded that rhododendron, protecting this absolute knowledge. A normal summer afternoon meant four boys, and sometimes three girls, huddled around a makeshift map on the ground in the middle of the woods, camouflage paint on their faces, preparing for war.

In Charleston, I bought a topographic map of home: Terrys Gap and Mills Gap and every other gap of Fruitland, North Carolina. I sometimes spread it out on our dining table and walked around it in the evening, staring at the rings, knowing each line would send me up, push me through trees, until I could see everything from Sugarloaf Mountain or Bearwallow Mountain. Translating the off-kilter circles into visceral memories satisfied and surprised me. How could a two-dimensional wash of green and rings prickle my skin and fill my head with the smell of mossy woods?

I'd begun to see codes everywhere around me since sinking into William's diaries, so it didn't shock me to recognize this map before me as another set of symbols to crack open. But the desire beneath the code set me back. I understood I was injecting my own—my longing for those mountain dirt roads while living in a city on the coast—but tracing the lines in that tiny corner of America laid out on my table, I came to understand the ways that human desire shaped the land: roads and fields cut into the topography to give us what we wanted, to take us where we pleased.

I thought of those Darlington County fields I'd rolled through recently and about what the open fields and giant houses might tell about what we want, about what we're willing to take to get what we want. About what we're willing to hide under the soil to feel better about what we want. "All forms of landscapes are autobiographical," Charles Wright writes.

The summer of the *Playboy*, I wore new trails into the soil to open it up. I knew life was changing when I went into the woods not to camouflage into the trees and watch the ants but to dig up a damp magazine and stare at a woman stretching across two pages, staring back at me. I'd started seeing something new in Vanna White on TV in the evenings; I felt some pulsing in me, each turn of the letter on the screen was tying a tighter knot in me.

Unearthing a woman from a freezer bag felt thrilling and wrong—like a trap I wanted to spring. At any point, the Russians or my parents or a younger cousin might sneak up as I flipped the pages, pointing a finger at my young sex-addled brain. So I disappeared into hidden spaces, patches of rhododendron surrounded by trip wires, and traced the shapes of female bodies on those pages. I marveled at the strangeness of hair cropping up from nowhere, something of protection and vulnerability in that intimate space I knew I shouldn't have seen.

One of my cousins heard that in Vietnam, during the war, naked women approached soldiers, wearing the same faces of longing on display in our *Playboy*. But these women were wired to blow. Explosives hidden—where exactly?—so that when a soldier went to one, they both flashed into eternity. As we fought off the unseen enemies in our forest around Grandma's—Russians, Vietnamese, neighbors—I wondered what I'd do with an explosive, naked body coming toward me from thin air. I would have gone to it. I knew that without a doubt. I would have reached out for her, knowing it might be my last breath.

The mysticism, the clamminess of puberty, I gave it all to the forest, and as it did with everything else, it took it in: the new girl in the red plaid, the climbing skirts of the high school cheerleaders, Vanna White, Ms. September 1992. I stashed it there, but seen from above, my paths laid out on a map across our land would have revealed everything I'd hidden: desire lines into secret wars and opening bodies.

....

William has begun thinking of Nancy Powell more and more, thinking perhaps of the curve of her beneath her dress. Of the curls that land between her shoulder blades. He asks Caleb who he'd prefer between the two—Nancy Powell or Mary Norwood? Caleb tells William he'd take NP any day.

The next day, Binah tells William that "MN would scold and not suit me." *Move on, William.*

> **August 1:** Llamas Day. June told me MN's sham. Studied a letter from MN.
>
> **August 2:** Dead pines.
>
> **August 3:** Wrote a letter to MN. Dated Monday.

In plain text William writes *Ultimatum.*

Then he waits.

It takes only two days. June comes with news: Mary thinks William is mad. Is it working? This cold shoulder, this line drawn in the sand?

He can't help himself. He writes to Mary.

> **August 8:** Holp JN. Had a race with his mare. Binah. Night sent MN letter.
>
> **August 9:** Holp J Coker. CC told saw phantom. Mother dreampt I married MN.
>
> **August 10:** Went to hunt a school. Small success. MN looked either mad or sorry.

Is the small success locating an appropriate school or Mary's looking mad or sorry? Has he played hard to get, turned the tables on MN and now she's sending messages his way? He carries on with his new aloofness, emerging easily from within his usual awkward conduct. He ignores her on the way to the mill. When Binah sees Mary coming, he sets to working on the road, his back to her. When he sees June a few days later, noting that he seems melancholy, he learns Mary has noticed "that I not talk with her in public."

William rides his horse Guinea and borrows a copy of *Gil Blas.* He dreams.

August 16: Dreampt that I had cloth coats and Mr. Norwood consented for me to marry MN. He didn't want June to have her. Worked on schoolhouse.

August 17: Went to mill. Borrowed corn. Byner communicated that JN [Mary's father] said I told him that June and Mary slept together. A dam'd lie. Rode Guinea.

August 19: Raised schoolhouse.

August 20: Worked on the floor. Went to Grandfather. Cut my leg. Fainted.

August 21: Went to Mr. N. No success.

Perhaps Mr. Norwood is the holdout, the person keeping MN from throwing in with William? Does he refuse to let William—William who pulls his cows from bogs and drives his cattle for him—marry his twenty-six-year-old daughter?

William dreams he kills two snakes, "not huge and not invulnerable." The next day, June comes with news: Mary will wait until winter. This is working, this forced distance, and yet Mary still upsets him in dreams: "Dreampt that MN wanted Dog cooked for me and I contemned."

He buys a hat. Binah comes with news: "AN said MN respected me." He forges a pass for June and comes to a decision to take hold of his life: "Determined to hold no longer an irregular intercourse with MN."

....

In the summer of my childhood, Granddaddy robs his bees. My cousins and I come crashing from another world to find him climbing down the ladder from the attic, suited in white and carrying his beekeeper veil. He says hello, makes a joke, and he's off, trudging up the hill toward those buzzing white boxes.

Back then his donning the helmet and protective clothing meant danger; it meant we'd have to avoid that patch of field for a day or two for fear of angry bees. But I realize now how much I loved the ritual of it, despite the threat of stings. When I work my way back into those memories of him, looking like a bomb technician lost alongside a cornfield, other memories emerge—foreign memories. I see the epic processionals during Holy Week in Guatemala when I lived in Central America: the robed priests swinging incense and releasing swells of smoke throughout the streets. Underfoot, the intricate alfombras of flower petals are trampled and dispersed, leaving behind only hints of the image that only moments before stretched across the cobblestone streets. Then I see my grandfather again on the hill, pumping smoke into the air, vanishing within it.

Everything that happened in that smoke was a mystery. From farther down the hill I'd catch flashes of moving arms, but mostly the afternoon seemed to consist of him stepping into an otherworldly outfit, disappearing into the haze, and emerging with sweet honey. My writer's impulse pushes me to research the minutia of bee robbing, but I resist. I want that mystery. Veils, smoke, and honey.

Now when I think of the birds and bees, I think not of eggs and fertilization but of honey, of mysterious sweetness appearing from smoke. I think of the stair-stepping call of the oriole in the woods beyond Grandma's house, of the lull of a cardinal's purr that rings out to me anywhere, sending me into the woods. I think of the current in a bee's body as it spins in a hive, rubbing against another so that the electricity triggers sound. I think of unexpected pitches, of honeycomb, of the sound of electricity.

I don't remember ever being settled or forced onto a couch for *the* talk. I took sex ed in middle school and high school: gym teachers mumbling through textbook sketches of urethras and wombs. More than any other place, I learned about sex at church, in rooms always underground—basements outfitted with posters of Christian rock bands and tattered, sagging couches. In those subterranean spaces of our rural Southern Baptist church, the youth leaders said the word *sex* freely and without blushing. We looked away.

In my mind then, our leaders—David and Linda—were old, on par with my parents. Looking back now, I realize they were in their late twenties, early thirties, not all that far removed from our high school worries. We talked about Moses and Jesus and baptism and resurrection, but we spent a good bit of time talking about love and sex. They knew the room, it's safe to say. As much as we groaned when we heard the word *sex* in those rooms beneath the church, as much as we let loose our ***not again*** calls, we were bags of itchy hormones.

Here's the message as I remember it: Sex is good, but wait. Sex isn't physical; it is spiritual. It is a connection beyond flesh, a merging not easily undone. *Don't ruin sex*, our leaders seemed to say. Let it be good and big and all-consuming. Something more than a carnal act.

This stuck for me. Admittedly, I was a rule follower anyway, but I wanted sex to mean something more than release. I wanted to give my body over to someone who would keep it.

My parents started dating in eighth grade. My maternal grandparents married just after high school. My paternal grandparents' courtship started before they could name it, before they knew what it was. I met my wife when we were eighteen. I played no fields. Made no bar pickups. Created zero online dating profiles. In the world I knew growing up, relationships started early and lasted.

I was twenty-five, just married, when I stripped down in a small house above Clear Creek. I didn't think about my grandparents walking hand in hand along that water, about my father proposing to Mom on the bridge. I thought of the two bodies buzzing in our new home and felt them move together.

8

By the end of September, the world has grown edgy. An enslaved man named Cato has run away. William may have let him go. It doesn't matter if he did or didn't; what matters is that P believes William helped Cato escape. And P is coming for blood.

P is a mystery. He appears in the diaries sporadically in 1808, always causing a ruckus. In March, William stops P from beating Binah. In June, William notes that it has been two weeks since "P encountered with Mother." Had they had an argument? Are they having an affair? William gives no hint. A few weeks before Cato runs away, William hears that P intends to whip the enslaved man.

When William sees Cato after he escapes, he says nothing to P.

All month William has been writing poetry and experimenting: observing dew on fodder, collecting data on rainfall, inverting maps to determine sailing lines, working out the distance of the planets based on the rotation of wagon wheels. He's also been fighting with his father.

In his diaries, William's mother is *Mother* (δ28[4L). His father, however, is always *TP* (8ə), Thomas Prestwood. It's hard, at first, not to read this as a young man's rebellion. I imagine William calling his father *Thomas* to his face, watching the twist of anger or hurt in the man's eyes every time he refuses to say *Father*. But hardly a month passes without a "quarrel" or a "fuss" or a "florry" between William and TP. Whatever lies between them, it is rocky and wide.

All year William has done as he's told—plowing TP's fields, threshing TP's wheat, hoeing TP's corn—but when his father burst into his bedroom at midnight in April, looking for his gin, William had had enough. "I tell'd him one roof wou'd not hold both of us if he done as he did."

The next day, he finalized his cipher and rewrote his previous entries in it, tucking his recorded life safely out of view. *M* becomes δ. *Y* becomes γ. *Life* is now I3Γ4.

δγ I3Γ4.

And now it is September and William has his own house and Cato has run off and Binah catches TP fucking Ruth.

William records this affair, the same as he records P's encounter with Mother, but he doesn't lay out any reaction to it. Perhaps he knows good and well about his father's adultery already. Perhaps this is only one more disappointment to attach to his father. Perhaps it means nothing because faithfulness isn't expected of a well-heeled man in 1808. Or perhaps William is enraged, ready to break open the earth and throw his father in. None of it shows. Instead, he follows up this news with a note about an early frost and his forcing A Ganey to stand on the dunce box at school.

The next day, Rhonda Ganey sees Cato, and before long, William is experimenting with water and magnification and hiding Cato at his house.

Perhaps, as he walks to Mr. Wood's house to return the dictionary he borrowed, William reflects on the movement of his life during this past year, returns to his possible futures as he saw them in March. It is October, and he has raised a schoolhouse, landed a job. He whips children, sends them to the dunce box, brings them new language. He finally has time to experiment, to read *Gil Blas* or whatever he pleases. No longer does the shadow of his promised land loom: He's sold it, pocketed the money, and pays no mind to planting schedules and trades in enslaved workers. That his mother knew he wasn't meant to live his life as a Lowcountry planter might have drilled a hole through him earlier in the year, but now he feels free to have let the notion go. She had seen him more clearly than he'd seen himself, perhaps.

Still, when he hears that Reverend Campbell preached laziness on Sunday, he is offended. The work of the mind is not laziness, William knows. He spends the day drinking rum with his grandfather and theorizing that the earth is heated by subterraneous fires in the winter and by reflection in the summer. He vows to experiment with two fires to better understand atmospheric change. Meanwhile, Cato continues to lie low in his house, out of sight of P and anyone else.

Binah comes with news of Mary. Mary believes that he "only intended fun" with her, Binah says. Mary Can't-Return-a-Letter Norwood believes William is only in this for a fling, only pursuing her for seven months for a one-off fuck. William sows his turnips. He comes to understand permutation. He wrestles with Colonel Reynolds. He sends no word back to Mary.

Then it rains and men come around looking for Cato. William stays inside, trying to ignore them. He watches the window and waits. Eventually, they go.

Perhaps he considers writing to Mary, of telling her about the chaos of his life: his decision to sell his land, his father's adultery, his stashing an escaped enslaved person in his new house, his leg wound slowly healing, his understanding of evaporation. His never-ending love for her. Instead, he goes to bed.

The next day—a day when J Ganey has to stand on the dunce box—Cato sleeps in Binah's house to be safe, and William learns from Jonathan Sellers that JP wants to find Cato, "play hell with his back and sell him."

In 1808 there are nearly as many enslaved people as free in South Carolina. They're in rice fields and cotton fields and kitchens and chains. One is hiding in William's house. Since the seventeenth century, half the enslaved people to have come to North America passed through South Carolina, nearly two hundred thousand lives sold in Charleston's port. Because of enslaved labor, the Lowcountry of South Carolina is one of the richest regions in the world. It's not only the rice and indigo and cotton, but also the trafficking itself that has pooled such wealth into one place. Slave traders such as Henry Laurens and Gabriel Manigault are among the richest men in the colonies.

The year before William begins his diaries, congress votes to end the transatlantic slave trade. They intended to do it in 1787, when framing the edges of this new country, but South Carolina's delegates said they'd just as soon form their own country than allow any infringement on the "right to import slaves," as John Rutledge put it then. Now that two-decade allowance has ended, and South Carolina is a place populated by bondage.

William writes nothing of his decision to hide Cato, nothing of his feelings about slavery. Perhaps he's read widely, carries in his soul an enlightened abolitionism, a desire to undo this evil system keeping his region afloat. Or perhaps he simply knows Cato and doesn't want to see him beat. Whatever leads him to open his door to the runaway man, his doing so is dangerous, upending the world he lives in.

At night, more men come:

> **October 6:** Three persons and Watkins watched my house. I suppose after Cato. I run them.
>
> **October 7:** Dreampt that I was accused of stealing Cato. Jonathan Sellers communicated a sale to Bramlette of Cato.

Then Harry, a man enslaved by Mr. Norwood, runs away, too. William observes that "the pole of the moon is elevated above my horizon in rising." Before long,

June comes with news. I imagine William when June approaches, a mixture of fear and longing. Will Mary finally consent to marry? Will Mary tell him to stop writing? How long will he be strung along?

> **October 9:** June come. Communicated that MN said she had never told that she wou'd not have me. Windward meteors. She be glad of me.

9

Here's the story I'd started writing: young William Thomas Prestwood sells his dirty land and holds himself chaste for the love of his life, Mary Norwood. He stops everything for her. He suffers (*I am determined to be a neuter!!*) and writes love letters. He hides men escaping slavery, a small but personal and dangerous fight against evil. Here is an upstanding, awkward young man who only wants love and a simple life. A man to be proud of.

But then I learn about Binah. She appears more often than anyone on William's pages in 1808. More often than Mary Norwood and Mother and TP. He notes when she leaves, what news she brings, when they roll logs. In March, William's sister suspects he's sleeping with Binah. He doesn't deny it. Even while he worries over letters to Mary, he goes to Binah, scribbling down her symbol (ה) after he reaches for her body.

I want to say that they are lovers, but they are not. Binah is a woman who was enslaved before conception. Her grandmother had been enslaved by William's grandfather, and for the past two years, Binah has been enslaved by William, a "gift" given to him. They are likely the same age.

He sometimes writes her name as Biner. Other times as Byner.

They are not lovers.

William fucks Binah. Binah is property. Biner is property. Byner is property.

But is it more than that? More complicated? He stops P from beating her in March. He shares with her his secrets. He seeks her counsel. He worries when she's gone. In Hebrew, Binah means *understanding*.

Binah is property. Biner is property. Byner is property.

June, who comes like Gabriel in the night with news of Mary and whom Mary wants to fuck, is an enslaved man, held by the Norwoods. How easy to imagine the three of them—William and Binah and June—unpacking rumors like teenagers (*she likes you, she doesn't like you, you'll be married, she's not your type*). They sip tea and conspire.

Binah is property. June is property.

How tempting to conjure up a messy crosshatching of relationships: William likes Mary; William fucks Binah; Mary wants to fuck June; June wants William to have Mary; Binah doesn't think Mary would suit William.

Property. To be used. To be put to work.

....

I am a white man born in the South, from white families settled in the South for hundreds of years. Finding slavery in one's family tree is like finding salt in the ocean. And still, I thought the mountain poverty of my people might have spared us.

After asking those birds-and-bees questions about where I come from on my grandmother's couch in college, I kept digging—learning about the place I was raised, the people who came there and stayed for centuries. I spent hours at the historical society; I read local histories; I floated around cemeteries.

I found that most of my branches—Joneses, Maxwells, Gilliams, Harrells, Whitakers—crashed into the mountains in the late eighteenth century, taking up land as soon as the Cherokee people and other tribes had been forced or tricked farther west. My people left the British Isles, mostly as Scots resettled in Ireland, to find something they could make their own. Like the majority of the Scots-Irish, they settled in Appalachia, taking to highlands that might have felt something like home. They farmed what they had, which wasn't much, but they made a way and abided.

I found no records of slavery in those families. In fact, many of my ancestors fought for the Union army. They were subsistence farmers who hadn't enough land or money to enslave another human being. This didn't necessarily mean they wouldn't have, but the fact that they couldn't rely on slavery meant something to me as I searched through archives in my twenties. I felt cleaner.

The Prestwood branch was a late arrival to Appalachia. That family didn't come down the Great Wagon Road or the Cumberland Gap like the Scots-Irish in my genealogy. Instead, they worked down the coast, settling in those South Carolina lowlands in the seventeenth century. And they bought human lives. I found this as soon as I found William's diaries. His father, his grandfathers, his great-grandfathers—these were men building a small empire on the backs of men, women, and children stolen from their homes and treated as livestock. Compared with other families and the town-sized plantations in Darlington County, they enslaved small numbers—William's grandfather held six enslaved people in 1800—but they owned and profited from these stolen lives nonetheless.

William's breaking away from this life at age twenty, his willingness to hide Cato despite threats, buoyed me. Somehow it mattered less that the Prestwoods and Cokers had amassed wealth by way of slavery because I could point to William Thomas Prestwood as a conscience to break the chain. A man who died in debt, seemingly by choice. Sure, I came from those slaveholders, but I also came from William. And I knew William. He wasn't a name in a family Bible but a man whose life was spread out before me. It had been buried and hidden, but pulled up and dusted off; he'd laid himself bare. And he tried to do right.

Then I found Binah and knew William to be just as broken and weak as the world he lived in.

....

In the middle of October, William dreams that the earth's roundness attracts thunder, causing lightning to strike for weeks—covering the globe in explosions. Rumors have spread that he has hidden Cato. His aunt tells him that Mary Norwood and June told her Cato had been at William's house. And so P has come around, making strange threats, threats of stealing a child. William decides to sleep at his grandfather's until everything settles down.

Since the windward meteors, he has been thinking nonstop of Mary Norwood again, seeking out news of her. He learns little, other than her cat killed J. Seller's cat and she has been telling people William is hiding a runaway slave. When Joe comes around telling William he has the power to divine, William hears him out. After all, he learned from Clark a month back that PC was "a witch and lively." He'd seen the ignis fatuus. The world might soon be covered in explosions. Anything seemed possible.

He asks Joe about Mary. And Joe uses his powers to tell William that Mary is nearby. She is close. What could it mean? Emotionally? Spiritually? Sexually? William works on his chimney and gets a toothache.

Cato left William's house weeks before, just after the windward meteor, but P returns, threatening to kill William "for he believed I had his negro." All of Darlington County seems rattled, the ground shaky. Other slaves have run; just that day William learns of another. The air is growing cold. Birds are scattering. William dreams of fire.

He keeps his head down. He gets a wool hat and continues work on his house, readying himself for whatever comes next. A waiting schoolhouse. A fight with P. A life with Mary Norwood. A life alone with his books and wool hat and new house.

He helps Mr. Norwood drive his cattle, steering clear of bogs and wondering if he might spot Mary on the way. He doesn't. That night, he has sex with Binah. She shares with him news of MN, news that she has moved on:

> **October 27:** Binah communicated MN wanted Isham Linton. Pulled corn.
>
> **October 28:** Snow. Birds come. Halled in my corn. Shucked corn.
>
> **October 29:** Housed my corn.
>
> **October 30:** Heard that Cato was in Chesterfield jail.

His corn put away, Cato caught, and Mary Norwood in someone else's arms, William hunkers down for winter.

10

In an ad on TV, a young husband and wife stand in front of a camera. "I thought I married an Italian," she says. He's smiling in a way that is also a grimace, his hands hanging aimlessly by his sides.

"It turns out he was 34 percent..."—a pie chart appears beside her head, and she pauses a beat as if she's about to say *Martian* or *the spawn of Satan*—"Eastern European!"

There's a flood of commercials in this vein. Some from Ancestry.com, like this one. Others from 23andMe. In the thirty-second spot, viewers are drawn to the suspense, to the identity-shattering reveal of a strange past, some unknown forefather in some remote patch of the world.

I'm drawn to these revelations, too: The grandfather who wears a kilt but isn't, it turns out, Scottish at all. The woman who always answered "Hispanic" when asked but then learns she's from all over the world, a stew of nationalities and ethnicities. The Canadian man who finds his lineage in Ireland and then forms a bond with his new Irish neighbor in the dead of winter.

I like the emotional rise and fall of the commercials, the connection to history. But I also wonder why any of it matters.

What does this knowledge do, exactly? How has the grimacing guy's life changed from one day to the next now that he understands he's barely Italian, and that one-third of his DNA hails from Eastern Europe? Does he suddenly take his coffee black? Will he buy an ushanka this winter? Maybe he'll swear off pasta forever?

I think of that line we learned in high school about DNA: *the basic building blocks of life.* It makes sense to feel rattled to learn that your blocks were made in China, not France, but they're still the same blocks you've had your whole life. They've not changed shape or color. They're your blocks.

Now Kelly Ripa is yelling slow, emphatic Italian at a baker. She's 74 percent Italian, Ancestry.com has let her know. "And," she's still yelling, "I found out that I'm from the big toe of that sexy Italian boot."

Kelly's DNA is drawing her home. Because she's learned she's built of blocks once located in Italy, she's learning Italian. She's becoming Italian? She was already Italian, even if she didn't know it? (Or her results were confused with someone else's and she's actually Eastern European and learning Italian for kicks?)

It's this chicken-and-egg game that confounds me—Kelly working into an identity not because she felt it or grew in it, but because she knows there is some genetic, some internal-organ connection to a place or culture or language or people.

Ancestry.com's commercials boast its genealogical database, the opportunity to take DNA results and then comb through a family tree. To find real people.

Sometimes, I watch these commercials and think, wouldn't it be amazing to find someone who looks like me, my doppelgänger forefather, just as the grimacing Italian-cum-Eastern-European guy did. I should swab my cheek and follow the crowd-sourced trail online.

And then my brain catches up to this desire, and I realize I have this man already. On this very day two hundred years ago, that man "got mumps." It rained.

I do not have the mumps. It's sunny. I'm eating sunflower seeds. And somewhere within me are building blocks made of building blocks that once had the mumps on a rainy day. But what does it matter? Why does it matter that William hid Cato and raped Binah? How does that change this sunny day and these sunflower seeds? What should this revelation change about how I live today—or tomorrow?

I have no idea what William looked like, if I would resemble him in the slightest. Above my desk, I've taped several old photos—most pulled from that same box at Grandma's where I found the newspaper article leading me to William. One of them is of my grandparents; they're young, probably just married. Granddaddy wears a tie and shiny white-and-black shoes. He's sitting on a rock beside a girl, my grandma, whose hair is a ruffled version of Princess Leia's and whose dress stops just below the knee. He has a pipe, she's leaned in close to him, her shoulder vanished by his arm, and they smile. I like to inhabit the photograph, to know them then, so taken with this love they've grown that they've built a house up the hill at the edge of the woods and laid out a future wherein they'll fill a home with food and children and music.

Another photo is of my great-great grandparents, Asbury and Clementine Prestwood, and their brood of children above the creek. It's probably 1906 or 1907. The children are barefoot, and Asbury wears a wild beard and round hat.

Asbury Prestwood (left), William Prestwood's grandson, with family in front of his new house, circa 1900

He's dressed up for this; his hat is clean, and the vest over his white shirt is smooth. But the tan of his hand and the cut of his arms reveal a man who spends his days working a field. It's hard to find much of his face for the beard, but his eyes are deep-set and serious.

In my head, I've taken this image and created William. I've trimmed his beard and cleaned him up, softened him about the face and body. I've taken the outline of Asbury and filled in a young man who reads Latin and has money in his pocket. Then I put him on a horse, lovestruck and ambling.

I don't look much like this man. In fact, even accounting for the two-hundred-year age difference, I have little in common with him. Finding his diaries on the internet didn't change my DNA overnight; my country of origin hasn't relocated because of learning of William's day-to-day life.

And yet I'll sometimes see something and wonder to myself, *What would William make of that*? Just last week, as I did the dishes one night, I thought about William sowing oats for geese. What did this mean, to sow oats for geese? Was he luring them in for eggs? For meat? For company? Then, I heard geese calling, flying overhead in the dark. Night geese. I'd never considered those big birds migrating in pitch black, looking down on lit-up, boxed-in lives. It was revelatory to me, alone in my kitchen, a rag over my shoulder. But then I wondered if I would have noticed them at all had I not been thinking about William's oat-sowing as I scrubbed a pot.

I don't know what to do with the bald fact of William's life, of his action and inaction, but I do know that he's in my head on his horse, settling into my gray matter, his life wrapping around mine like a strange double helix. One hundred and fifty years dead, this flawed, broken man is shaping me. Whether I like it or not.

....

William believes the earth is growing larger. Water will not stay level; his plumb varies. He is uneasy. If only he could see inside the earth or float above it. Then he could know.

MN wanted Isham Linton.

He dreams that his father hangs Malcolm M'Quage, but Malcom comes to life again.

MN wanted Isham Linton.

William reads and keeps school. He helps Caleb shuck corn and they get drunk. "Catched two squirrels in one tree," he writes later.

Then Binah brings news from MN, her fickleness comes calling again:

> **November 3:** Binah communicated that MN blamed me for not coming to see her.

MN wanted Isham Linton.

And later:

> **November 21:** Binah communicated that MN believed that I wanted to marry.

But William doesn't. Not anymore. He can't. The earth is expanding. He is a grown man with a house and a chimney and needs. He can't teach forever, he doesn't want to travel, he could never keep Mary Norwood happy. *Told her I would have 2 mistresses in 12 months.* The thought of writing letters and fretting over the future of MN for another year, for all of 1809, covers him up.

In his fussing over the unbalanced earth, someone suggests to William that he ought to learn surveying, to make a career out of his curiosity. He suddenly considers that there may be possibilities beyond the three paths he laid out in symbols nearly a year ago. He has sold his land, held himself for Mary, but as the year draws to a close, he gives up on all of that, gives up on Mary, gives up marriage:

> **December 6:** Fucked E. Jordan. Did not promise to marry her.
>
> **December 11:** Went to Jonathan Aichin to learn surveying.

Then, William is alive:

> **August 30, 1809:** Fucked N. M'Lemore. Heard she was married.
>
> **August 2, 1810:** Holp thresh wheat. Lay with P. Sellers.
>
> **August 6, 1810:** Put leather away. Felt ZC cunt.
>
> **January 19, 1811:** Borrowed two books. Went to our hill. Fucking Mrs. Powell. Forged a letter for HM.
>
> **January 20, 1811:** Court'd M. Windon. Come home. Asked Betsy Gandy for a fuck.
>
> **May 30, 1811:** Plough'd cotton. Stay'd Cl.'s. Hug'd Peggy and felt her cunt.
>
> **October 7, 1811:** Riding. Coming from a meeting. Fucking.
>
> **August 11, 1811:** Funned with P. Kelly.
>
> **June 21, 1812:** Went TC Jr.'s meeting. Saw MS's cunt at piss. Stay'd all night.

Dear William:

You're better off without her. We're better off without her because, without her, I'm here—two hundred years later. There will be more women. So many women. A shameful number of women. One of them is a hundred miles away and still a girl but one day you'll make her your wife and grow her a garden, and this is how I'll find a way into this world to read your words and watch as you sow oats for geese.

I married a good woman, William. A woman who can't lie or abide injustice, a woman who makes me better. And this is how a red-headed boy found his way into the world on the first day of spring.

We named him Abraham, and I'm sorry for that. It is a name that will soon cause you pain, a name that will take Mary Norwood from you forever when Abraham Sellers makes her his wife, but you should know that our baby Abraham is a tiny ball of empathy. He's been this way since he arrived. As an infant, when he heard another baby crying across the grocery store, he would set in himself, wailing in solidarity with a stranger. It's unnerving, and it's our fault. Sarah and I both cry during movies and worry over other people's pain more than seems natural. I worry over yours. And now we've sewn ourselves together to make tiny Abe.

You're sewn into him, too, of course. And Betty and Grace and Hiram and Asbury and on and on. All of you stitched together so that he'll shed tears for anyone who needs them. But then, in the whiplash of time, he's sewn into you, too. I'm in your skin even now as you fashion symbols for Betsy Gandy and E. Jordan, waiting to be pieced together in the North Carolina mountains centuries later.

That's too much to hold. For now, sow your oats, William. A war you can't escape is closing in, and our son is waking from a nap, and life is waiting impatiently in the soil of Darlington County.

PART III

37ʃ4Ə47ʃ47ɥ4

Independence

♐♒ *Advice for My Sons* ♌♒

November 6, 1822

The desire of my soul is that my son should be a man and not a child all his life.

II

Abe lay in bed. It had been a week since he had learned about conception at the beach, since we'd started marveling about the nesting-doll way we all come to be, each of us from a womb that was once in a womb. The light was already off, the book put away. I was a few steps from the door when he asked, "Do you have sperm as soon as you're born?"

His *r*'s were still taking shape, so at first I heard "you burn" instead of "you're born" in his question, and I considered jumping out his second-story window and fleeing into the woods instead of having to answer questions about burning loins. But when he asked again, I heard *born* and tried for an answer: "No."

"But I think I have sperm now," he said. "I feel something in there."

We got anatomical again, and I explained what was in there, but then he wanted to know when, exactly, the sperm would arrive. On his ceiling we'd stuck the solar system, each glowing planet orbiting his ceiling fan, handfuls of stars spreading out across the room. I thought suddenly of God's promise to Abraham as he looked up into the sky, that his descendants would be as many as the stars. Then I remembered the King James: "so shall thy seed be."

"It's just something that happens when you're a man," I said and knew immediately it was a bad answer. I just wanted the kid to go to sleep. For a beat, the answer felt vague enough and also right enough to click on the white noise and walk away. But I was a slow learner.

"So Alana is a woman?" he asked immediately.

Alana, his thirteen-year-old cousin, had recently had her first period. I didn't know how he knew that. But that was the mantra with Abe: *I don't know how he knows that.* I stood by his bed, unable to get out the door, and ended the way I mostly ended these end-of-day inquisitions: muttering.

"Well... not, sort—I mean, it'll happen when you're close to that age."

"And then I'll be a man?"

. . . .

Resurrecting an ancestor brings with it a reckoning. As soon as William lifted off those bound pages, he was a houseguest I couldn't banish. No matter his messy habits or the baggage by the front door, he was mine. And he wasn't going anywhere.

This was both a grace and a burden. How many people will know even the slightest details about a great-great-great-great-grandfather, about a life that led to their own? Will any ever know this ancestor's innermost secrets, his sins?

William, my cipher, became a kind of code through which I'd begun to read my life. I held him up like a decoder ring to everything around me. How was my life an extension of his? How was my life an effect of his? How was my life a reaction to his?

Through him I read our family land, with its long summer days enveloping my childhood, as a result of both William's debts and his family's history of slaveholding. When a beautiful woman walked by and I felt that instinctual prickling in my skin, I calculated my own desires by using the equation of his. When I considered my baby becoming a man and worried over the power this world would give him, I conjured up all the men before me, William now sitting at that table, looking sheepish and alive. In this nineteenth-century man, I had both a guide and a foil for becoming a man, for raising up a boy to become one in my wake.

. . . .

Almost immediately after having Abe, I understood my parents better—or more fully. I stepped into a kind of empathy I hadn't had access to before. When I didn't sleep or couldn't console Abe, who spent most of his infancy crying, I thought of my parents walking a dark house with me. I remembered those stories to which I'd given little weight years before: Mom taking me to the swing outside in the dark of the night; Dad driving at midnight to usher me back into sleep; Mom lying by the sliding glass door with me at naptime and playing Todd Rundgren records because the moving of the trees and the '70s pop calmed me down.

I cringed remembering my teenage tantrums, my manufactured aloofness, my annoyance with their questions about school and girls. I heard, like an echo, my mom saying all those years before, *Just wait until you have kids, buddy.*

And now I did. I had a baby who seemed to hurt, who wouldn't sleep. We fed him with a syringe when he wouldn't nurse. We wrapped his tiny, jaundiced body in a stiff, glowing blanket to leech the bilirubin from his system. I drove around until he fell asleep and then leaned my seat back in parking lots to snatch a few minutes for myself at 4:00 in the morning. Then I drove to my university in a haze somewhere between the land of the living and the dead to teach, trying my best to keep it between the lines.

When I was seventeen, I drove off the road late one night. I had been at a friend's house playing video games, and when I left, it was 1:00 a.m. and thick with fog. I rolled along the familiar stretch from Mills Gap Road to pass Fruitland Baptist Church and then descend the long hill on Gilliam Road, crossing Clear Creek. I drove those roads most days, rounded their corners by instinct, but that night, when I came down the short hill to the highway, I must have drifted off or been lulled by the fog because I thought, for a moment too long, that I was somewhere else. Before I could recover, there was a stop sign and brakes were slamming and tires were screaming.

Had a truck been coming, barreling down Highway 64 from Chimney Rock, I'd have been smashed to bits. Had I realized a moment later, I would have flown off the ten-foot drop along the road, nose-diving into the cornfield below. But I simply blurred through the quiet highway and came to a stop with half of the car in the grass and half the car hanging in midair. I tried to back up, but the front tires spun freely in the dark. I jumped out, afraid the car would tip into the field at any moment, and stood along the empty road.

Then I called Dad. We had no cell phones, but my parents had put a bag phone in my car when I turned sixteen—a hulking thing that plugged into the cigarette lighter and that I wasn't allowed to use except in emergencies. I'd used it once or twice when lost, and I'd pretended to use it a handful of times in sight of girls on Main Street. Without that phone, I might have considered walking the mile up the dark highway to our family land or trudging back up Gilliam Road to a friend's house, risking someone's dad greeting me at the door with a shotgun. Instead, I called, woke Dad, and he said he was on his way.

A few cars passed. No one stopped. At some point, a sheriff's car flew by but continued on its way toward Bat Cave without pausing. I don't know what kept it moving, how the deputy missed seeing me on the edge of the road, my car hanging there, but I was grateful not to walk away with a ticket on top of my embarrassment. Then Dad showed up with a chain, and after a few minutes, he had heaved my little car from its perch and onto the road. I drove it home, and we went to bed.

Over a decade later, when I realized I had a live child who depended on me, I also realized my parents had always had lives beyond me—lives before me, even. This fact wasn't always easy to see as a kid. I knew they had jobs and bills and friends, but I also understood that I could trump any of those if I called. Their willingness to let anything go, to drop whatever they held to help me, struck me as an impossible mark for a parent now that I'd become one. I worried I couldn't match their givingness in the same breath that I wanted to call them, to ask them to drive the hours from the mountains to the coast where we lived to make this live wire of a baby sleep. I was stuck in a space of wanting both to become them and to need them.

I remembered my unexpected knee surgery when Sarah and I lived in Iowa. I woke from anesthesia to learn that I'd be unable to bend my knee for two months, that I wouldn't be able to run for a year, that I'd be stuck on the couch downstairs and unable to get myself to the bathroom for some time. Sarah was a few weeks away from the all-consuming exam season of law school, I was teaching and taking classes, and we lived twenty miles from the university in a tiny town of immigrants and corn. Dad dropped everything to fly out and chauffer me around for two weeks while Sarah sat in lecture halls and I downed pain pills in order to sit in in front of twenty-year-olds and talk about writing. I was a twenty-six-year-old man with a wife and a house and two huge dogs roaming the yard, and I needed my dad to fly across the country to drive me to school, my lunch bag in my hand. I felt ashamed.

He told me once he arrived that he worked his job as a school administrator—a job he loved, a job full of meetings and decision-making that he'd left behind—so that he could make time for family. I remembered that he and Mom had come to every basketball game, every soccer match in high school, no matter the two-hour winding roads into small mountain towns, to watch us play for ninety minutes on what might have recently been a cow pasture. Maybe it was selfishness that kept me from seeing their sacrifices as a teenager, and even though I spotted them and understood them intellectually in my twenties, I felt them in a visceral way once Abe came into the world. I felt the promise and the weight of everything they'd given in my ragged, sleep-deprived body.

And so Sarah and I held Abe's tiny screaming form and breathed deep, and I realized there was nothing I wouldn't do to ease his pain.

12

On the first day of classes, I often asked my students to write down all of the assumptions they'd made about me when I walked through the door. They didn't have to share this list; I simply wanted to start them thinking about statements we make every day, even in small ways, like in the form of clothes or posture. We'd soon be talking about argument and audience, and so I wanted to introduce this back-and-forth immediately: how we make statements but also how we read the world—and the people—around us.

Despite my teacherly intent, I was also curious about how I presented to a room of eighteen-year-olds. None of them had met me before, so what did they decide about me when I crossed the room and set my bag on the desk? I was a youngish white guy. Average height. Relatively in shape but not rippling with muscles. Close-cropped hair and a face that wouldn't make babies cry but wouldn't land on a magazine cover either.

Really, what I was asking my students to do was decode me, to take all of my shapes—my barrel chest, the chicken pox scar on my nose, my chukkas and khakis—and transcribe them. Sometimes the bravest students volunteered their cryptanalysis. When I'd let my hair grow shaggy and walked in without a tie, someone wrote *hippie*. Without a jacket, I sometimes received *laid-back*. *New*, a student called out, reading my age as inexperience.

I wondered what the women I taught with would receive on this kind of first-day decoding. I already knew how their course evaluations read different than mine: Students commented on their voices, their dress, their hair, their formality or informality. I skirted all of this with two prominent genetic markers: I was white, and I was a man.

The latitude these features afforded me was impossible to fully comprehend or quantify. I could untuck my shirt, let students call me *Jeremy*, and these choices decoded as access, as friendliness in my classroom. My female colleagues would have been roasted at the end of the year had they made similar choices.

When I took off my jacket, sat on the table, and told students to call me by my first name, they understood these moves as a kind of relinquishing of power—a power I didn't earn but was given me by a broken world. Encoded in every step I took across the room on that first day was power, not because of anything I'd said or done but because of the skin and anatomy that I carried.

Stepping outside of myself and imagining my body walking into a room, I realized even my averageness earned me a kind of respect. I wasn't short or tall; I wasn't ugly or handsome. I wasn't big enough to be threatening or small enough to invite disdain; not strange or beautiful enough to stare. I performed a kind of average American masculinity. I tucked in my shirt, wore boots, maintained a short beard. Even my boringness gave me power.

But I wondered about the different reads between my white and Black students. North Charleston, South Carolina, where the university sat and where I lived, was evenly divided: around 46 percent Black, 46 percent white. My first-year classrooms mostly mirrored this ratio. What did my young white frame mean for a young Black man in his first college class? I suspect it carried a different kind of power, one always tinged with danger.

The paleness of my skin and the lingering traces of the Southern voice I'd once tried to lose created a bridge for white students. But for Black students that bridge might've been blocked by baton-wielding troopers. My voice and race might have decoded as the sights and sounds of the son of a slaveholder. The history I carried into the room was one of terror, and I could never know how that rippled up in my shoes and voice and crossed arms. I could never know how those students might have felt that menace in their skin while never thinking it with their brains, like an evolutionary twitch to survive.

William's coded life had provided me a new kind of lens to read myself not only in terms of what I did or said, but also in terms of where I come from, who I come from. I could see the historical legacy of my body in a way I hadn't grasped before, and I, too, understood both its power and fragility when I entered a room and took my place.

....

In March 1810, William sees ignis fatuus again. This new country, only a few years older than he, is rattling amid treaties and threats and embargos. William feels only the edges of this, hears of captured sailors and armed Indians when the militia musters and he's sent on patrol. What William can be sure of is that he has a toothache and he has seen the foolish fire again. But this time he's not the boy who saw in that flame MN. He's twenty-two, has swapped for new boots, had his watch repaired, and bought a jacket pattern. He's a new man.

1809 is gone, the book holding most of it lost into the hole of history, and so, too, the year slides from memory. What's recorded of the year survives on a few pages: snippets of dreams, mythology, and poetry. A sketch of a compass. In these flashes, William is a man about town, courting and fooling around with women not named Mary Norwood.

By March 1810, William has finished *Gulliver's Travels*, and now he's on to *Life of Abbott*. He's courting Miss D. Bagit and hugging S. M'Nail and dreaming of marrying Martha. He finds a buzzard's nest and comes upon cube roots by logarithm. He studies Greek and philosophy and algebra.

He does not think about Mary Norwood. He will not think about how she is no longer Mary Norwood but now Mary Sellers, about how quickly she married once he moved on. About what she might be whispering in Abraham Sellers's ear right now, about the heat of her breath just there, on the neck. He will not consider the sound of her name as Mary Prestwood or what she might think of the buzzard's nest or if she would agree with Hegel's understanding of consciousness or if she misses the thrill of longing, of waiting for word, for a letter, for some sign of distant desire. Instead, he dreams June Goodson kisses him, and he "presumes longitude from the light on the moon." He takes his horse to the road, as he's ordered to do, and scans the trees and fields for any threats, for the ghosts of redcoats.

James Madison is in the White House. Somewhere beyond the Cheraw District of William's world, out beyond the flat forever of the ocean, ships are circling. Farther beyond them, Napoleon stuffs a hand in his shirt and considers his place in the world. He decides, as he always does, that the world is his place—the whole of it. But it's growing harder to keep up with which country he is fighting, which corner of Europe has come out to oppose him this year. He pushes forward, into the everywhere, but his trade routes are blocked, and his country is desperate for the cotton wrapping around young William for miles in South Carolina.

But Napoleon is, if nothing else, an optimist. He's offered a reward to any man who invents a better flax-spinning machine. He has already made his brother a king—just like that, voilà, Joseph, *vous êtes* king of Spain. Anything in the whole wide world feels just beyond his window, out in that water.

He ponders the strange, huge experiment of the United States, with its captured sailors floating in the British blockade. A mess of identities, of loyalties. The hands and backs lifting the boxes and manning the mortars claim to be American but were born British and have now been repatriated by force upon those ships, been told to forget living and fighting and growing families across the ocean: citizenship is birthright; it is the ground beneath your newborn feet, the king on the throne above your mama and daddy and governor.

Napoleon knows a little about shifting identities, having come to France as an immigrant and now standing here as France in flesh. "I am the Revolution," he likes to say. But these Americans have invented themselves from thin air. They've not been overtaken by an invading army or slipped into another country. They've left their homes, found a bit of land, stitched together a flag, and chosen a name. A nation of rebellious, runaway teenagers. It's charming if not foolish.

William Prestwood doesn't doubt his Americanness as he rides the roads of Darlington County on patrol in his new hat. He came along five years after the Revolutionary War ended; his father and uncle fought for independence. He knows his place: these fields and these roads are the only fields and roads he knows. But lately, he's thinking of other places. Of other fields. Other roads. He wonders about a life beyond his father. Hardly a month passes without a fuss or quarrel between the two men. It is men, isn't it? William's no longer a boy living under his father's roof. He is a militiaman and a constable, carting Amy Lundy and her daughter to prison just last month; he appears in court the same as he courts a new woman every month. He is a grown man who understands the movement of the sun and moon. And yet he carries on with his father's business, plowing and grubbing his father's fields as if they're chores to do before school. He is flustered by his father, TP—indebted to him and infuriated by him all in the same breath.

May 28, 1810: Hell quarrel TP. Bee hive.

May 29, 1810: Plough'd for TP.

May 31, 1810: Work'd for myself.

....

Albert Asbury Prestwood, great-grandson of William Thomas Prestwood, on the land where the author was raised

In high school, I became aware of the inevitability of our land. My sense of the world was one of abiding, of staying put on the land that made you, of a great recycling of a people and place. My cousin was preparing to farm his daddy's land, which had been his daddy's land, which had been his daddy's land. The crops had changed—corn to cattle to sod—but, at eighteen, my cousin intended to settle in as we'd been doing for centuries. My teachers expected I'd be a teacher. My dad was a teacher; my grandmother was a teacher. (William Thomas Prestwood was a teacher.) The school counselors directed me to scholarships for soon-to-be teachers. They recommended schools with good teaching programs. It all seemed predestined: We'd become our fathers and find a patch of forest along Clear Creek to raise up a family.

I resisted. I knew the world had to be bigger than one hundred acres in Fruitland, North Carolina. From Asbury Prestwood's empty house, I could see clear across the creek to where all my people lay in the ground. The smallness of that terrified me—to live this life and the next on one parcel of land. I applied to colleges where I knew no one. I steered clear of any classes with "education" in the title. I lost my accent. I left the country.

I couldn't have foreseen that having a baby would make me dream of home, of that hill and those tombstones. The eighteen-year-old me would have wanted to slap some sense into the thirty-year-old father I'd become, pining for that small town I'd fled. The eighteen-year-old me would've been embarrassed by this desire to return; he would have seen it as an inability to break free, to find life on my own, beyond the one mapped out on that Prestwood land. But suddenly that mapped-out smallness was all I wanted.

After all, despite my best efforts, I'd become a teacher. My hair was letting loose, and I was looking more and more like my father every day. I sometimes conjured him up in tense meetings or moments when my sleeplessness and a crying baby lit my shortening fuse. I tried on his clearheaded calmness, his tightrope walk of kindness and honesty. Turning into him and raising up a family across the creek from where I'd be buried took on a sweetness I could have never seen coming.

13

There is today, according to some—namely the contributors and creators of the magazine *The Art of Manliness*—a crisis of manhood. "At the heart of the modern crisis of manhood," the magazine's creators write, "is the extension of adolescence, a boyhood which is stretching on for a longer and longer period of time."

Some of us, the claim goes, remain boys into our twenties and thirties—and "in some especially sad cases," even forties. I'm in my thirties, a father, and I feel this sometimes, feel that I might still be a boy who needs direction, a fatherly hand on a shoulder. Someone to help me balance my checkbook and split wood. I'm suspicious of claims that this feeling is unique to my generation or that it represents a "crisis of manhood," but I am curious about the invisible line—or, perhaps it is visible: sewn of rawhide and hair—between boyhood and manhood. At what point and by what act do we cross over?

I can't find a clear line in my own life, a day when I went from feeling boy to being man. The usual points on the timeline don't serve: growing facial hair, turning eighteen, leaving home, getting married. Today, with a mortgage and a wife and kids, I call my dad when I find a leak in the house, when my car sounds funny, when I have a weighty decision to make.

A cursory glance at rites of passage across the world seems to reveal that most of them boil down to violence and sex—sometimes both. A closer look suggests some of the acts are meant to control these urges not to amp them up, but the underlying idea is that we become men by doing violence and taking women. No, this is too simple. Before espresso machines and factories, men survived by killing and procreating. These rites put food on the table, kept humanity alive. It's easy, at my computer in an air-conditioned room, to name it all as brutish, but I see in these rituals—in the slicing open of animals and the punching of a friend in the face—even from this comfortable chair, the training to persist. To stand up on one's own.

I don't come from a place or a people with clearly defined rites of passage, but lots of the boys I grew up with had moments that set them a step closer to manhood: their first dirt bike, their first gun. Some of them growing up on farms were expected to butcher a hog or lop off the head of a chicken at a certain age. It's this passing down of adult things, the sharing of responsibility, that opens the door.

So much of the perceived crossing into manhood—whether by circumcision or marriage—seems to be about independence, about self-sufficiency. Alexis de Tocqueville described the relationships between American fathers and sons as "more intimate and gentle; there is less of rule and authority, often more of confidence and affection." But when a boy becomes a man, he is meant to become a "master of his thoughts" and a "master of his conduct."

As some of my friends watch their parents fade away in hospital beds, attacked by every kind of cancer, I can't shake off occasional flashes of life without my dad. I wouldn't default on my mortgage or get lost in a mall or stop bathing, but my life would immediately become harder. I'd stagger into minor crises, listening for his voice in my head and leaning on my own instincts (shaped by him, no doubt), but I'd be unsure. He cuts my grass when I'm away; he picks up my son from school; he asks, "How's it going, son?" so often that I have to tell the truth. How does one measure what independence means in the context of family?

As a father, this question sends me in both directions: How can I live without my dad, and how do I train up my boy to live without me? Is the central task of parenthood fashioning your children so that they'll never need you? And if so, is this process of parenting one of shrinking yourself until you're gone?

....

By the summer, William is reading *Aesop's Fables* and courting Nancy Powell—the same Nancy Powell Caleb told him he'd prefer over Mary Norwood a couple years back. He teaches and plants corn and has sex with Peggy Gandy. But this thing with Nancy Powell might be growing serious. They've been courting for a month now, and if he lets himself, he might sometimes imagine her as a mother to his children, as the face he'll see before darkness every night.

One Friday in August, he sees Mary Sellers née Norwood at the mill, but never mind that. Never mind how she looks both the same and somehow fuller. He buys a new shirt.

Then he learns that he's not alone in his courtship of Nancy Powell, the Husband boy has been coming around, too, and suddenly there's a familiar feeling in

William's stomach and the world might be spinning so fast that everything is off balance. But it's not. Everything—his constable badge, his stack of books—is as it was, so William puts on his new shirt, and he and ZC sneak off and draw close until their hands are inside clothes: *felt ZC cunt*.

Throughout August, William has become a regular Paul Revere, though no international threats take shape.

> **August 8:** Warned people on the road.
>
> **August 11:** Caleb Coker got drunk.
>
> **August 15:** Warned people on the road.
>
> **August 16:** Made a stool. Got sick.
>
> **August 18:** Went sundry places. Had fun with Mother.
>
> **August 22:** Eat watermelon on a plate. Enter'd to Singing School.

He keeps on courting Nancy, but before long it seems every man of a mind to marry has come courting Nancy—first J. Kervin and then A. M'Intire. William shouldn't care. He's not exactly been faithful himself, sneaking off and slipping his hands into dresses of other women, but he's been courting Nancy in public for over a month. He writes her letters. She writes back.

> **September 7:** Went school. Saw Jupiter at prayers. Wrote N. Powell a letter.
>
> **September 8:** Muster. Courted NP.
>
> **September 9:** Went singing. J. Kervin courted NP. Frost.
>
> **September 11:** Holp CC take up fodder. Felt Cl's cunt.
>
> **September 23:** Went meeting. Had a pull of whip with T Brown. Dispute A. M'Intire about N. Powell.

And then, William hears tell of Nancy getting married:

> **September 24:** Open N. Powell letter and Mother talk'd with N. Powell. Heard wedding (I & do).

Beneath the words "I & do" he writes "nut." It's all crazy—to marry so soon, to marry at all.

The next week, he learns about physiognomy. He takes to studying the practice, wondering if he might see something hidden in every person—in the cheekbones or earlobes. That something in the shape of the fingers might reveal the secret heart of a person. The thing someone might hide until it's too late to know it, until they're married, and he's still building a chimney for a life that may never come. He wonders if he might learn to nudge people, ever so softly, where he wants them—closer to him, perhaps.

When the wedding comes in October, he stays home.

> **October 3:** Did not go to N. Powell wedding. Pull'd down school house.
>
> **October 4:** Kill'd bull.

Instead, he gets a new book, *Persian Tales*, and reminds himself about the largeness of the world. There are ships on the sea that he cannot see, ships controlling empires and sending him down the road to shout warnings at no one.

William brings Pruny Kelly home and courts S. Joiner and has sex with Binah. He hugs C. Grigg and finds a knife at the mill and O'Nail's kid pisses on his handkerchief, but when Jonathan Pruitt tells him he saw a rainbow at night, William cannot wrap his head around it. He pulls his corn and imagines everything he cannot see.

> **October 22:** Sold my pocketbook.
>
> **October 31:** Housed corn. Got lost.

14

On the night that I was offered a job back in the North Carolina mountains, Sarah and I drove to Krispy Kreme. Abe—almost two years old then—was sleeping at my parents' house, where we'd been staying for my interview. Patches of snow and ice still covered the woods, but the ten-minute drive from Prestwood land toward the strip of fast-food restaurants was mostly clear.

Though my head was swirling with the prospects of moving back to the mountains, leaving our home in Charleston, likely settling back in our hometown for the rest of our lives, I couldn't help but think of us fifteen years before: eighteen-year-olds who hadn't seen much beyond this mountain town, puttering back and forth between our houses in my ugly car. I was desperate to leave then. Sarah may've not been as antsy at first, but once we left, we kept moving—to Peru, to Costa Rica, to Honduras. Back then, we'd first met at a mutual friend's house and been attracted to one another by ideas. Her curiosity about the world had matched mine in a way that led our conversation afield from everyone else's. It led us outward over and over.

On this night, we sat in the corner of the mostly empty Krispy Kreme amid a strip of seven fast-food restaurants and wondered, beneath the fluorescent lights, if we could come back home.

In Charleston, more restaurants and coffee shops than we could count surrounded us, and it didn't escape us amid the whiffs of fried dough that having a date back here might mean this very spot of tile floor and sugar glaze on a Saturday night. At the same time, we hadn't been to any of the countless swanky restaurants or hipster coffee shops in Charleston after 5:00 p.m. because of the sleeping two-year-old back at my parents' place. Moving back here would mean family nearby: cousins and aunts and uncles and grandmas and grandpas and great-grandparents. In other words, babysitters.

"Asheville is only twenty minutes away," I offered.

"Houses would be cheaper," Sarah said.

We were convincing ourselves.

The truth of it is that we weren't exactly moving to Podunk Appalachia. Our hometown had changed since we left. It now boasted a couple of coffee shops and a handful of bars and a few good restaurants on Main Street. People were moving here from all over the country for the land and the cultivated small-town charm. It wasn't Charleston, which Condé Nast had just named the top city in the world, but this wasn't the boonies either. Of course, our attempts at convincing weren't really about amenities. We were sorting out if we could settle down in a place where our high school classmates might handle our car insurance or money at the gas station. Might be our dentist or sheriff. We were feeling around for the line between intimacy and claustrophobia.

As we spoke, I thought about Mile Marker 16 on Interstate 26. On the drive from Charleston, Mile Marker 16 was the spot when the mountains rose up on the horizon, as if from nowhere, ushering us inward. I waited for that moment on every 240-mile drive back to our hometown because at the shifting of the horizon I felt wrapped up, swaddled like Abe had been when I held his tiny body and imagined him calf deep and growing taller in the creeks of my boyhood. By the time we had left the doughnuts and driven back into the woods, we had decided to uproot and reroot in the soil of home.

....

On Christmas Day, William drinks and studies Greek and goes for a ride through the woods. He's been taking off on horseback more and more often this year. Not only to patrol or shout warnings or haul people to prison, but simply to ride alone on empty roads "for pleasure." He sometimes gets lost but always finds his way back. Out there, he might think about navigation or the small of Pruny Kelly's back or the sound of his voice thrown in with everyone else's at singing school. He might consider the hypocrisy of arresting someone for forgery while he forges passes for enslaved men and women to move about. Or how happy Martha McEun and William Johnson looked when they married last month. He will not think about Mary Norwood Sellers. About the sharpness of her eyes when he finally caught them, when they saw him. Instead he will think of how quickly light must move from sun to moon to earth. About the possibility of a rainbow at night.

Two days later, out of nowhere, Mary wants to see him. Binah brings this request. It is cold, but he has repaired the chimney and can take some time to sit and think, to consider the man he is now, with his new boots and hat. He hasn't seen Mary for months, since the summer at the mill. Since then, he's courted four women and crept into dark places with five more. Still, he mounts his horse, his mind made up, and sets out into the December chill, riding to Sellers land, pulled toward her as he has always been.

But, once there, he doesn't stop. He thunders past Mary's house, his breath thin clouds in his wake, and rides instead to P. Sellers's porch, where he waits, hat in hand, for Mary's sister-in-law to come to the door after he knocks. Once she does, he lights up his warmest smile and asks to come in.

> **December 27:** Court'd P. Sellers.

And so he ends yet another year by closing the door on Mary Norwood, by breaking free of things of the past just as the new year comes.

> **December 31:** Rain'd, hail'd, snow'd. June got drunk. Mother come back.
>
> **January 2:** Kept school. June communicated P. Sellers wanted me to come see her.

....

Not long after we had moved back, Sarah and I took Abe to Grandma's. We brought dinner and sat at the same table where I had first learned of William Thomas Prestwood's diaries. Abe, a two-year-old wild man, ran around the living room, crashing onto the floor and picking up the ceramic birds from the windowsill. In the strange whiplash of time that parenthood provides, I saw myself spinning in circles in that living room. Abe was me, and in the same moment that I was telling him to be careful and not touch that, I felt whisked backwards in time, sent into his flesh every time he turned.

As we ate, and I foresaw all the things Abe might break, I remembered Dad cracking the living room window one summer. We'd been in the field by the apple orchard, him hitting me pop flies. I went for a short one but couldn't decide if I should dive for it or pull back and take the ball on a bounce. I went halfway, which is about the worst way to do anything. In a half dive, I saw the flash of the ball as it hit a rock in front of me and smacked into my mouth. When I came up, my front tooth was mostly gone.

One of the reliable truths of my childhood was the unlocked back door of Grandma's house, and yet on this day, when we needed the phone inside, we found the house locked and empty. Rather than head back into the forest to trail blood all the way home, I stood on the porch while Dad took a rock and gently cracked the small window through which we watched the birds, tapping it like an egg until it cracked. Then he removed enough glass to get us in.

We called Mom first, who called the dentist she worked for. Then she fetched us, and we went to town. It was a Saturday, but the dentist came into the office to take a look at my shattered tooth. He made a temporary fix and eventually constructed a new tooth out of whatever it is we use to fashion teeth from thin air.

Life carried on and Dad had the window repaired, and now my boy peered out that same window into the dark, seeing his reflection while I saw in him my reflection. And if this wrinkled-up time wasn't enough, fatherhood had inserted within me the power to consider, too, my father: to wonder if he ever saw himself in me, half diving for pop flies and bleeding in the reflection of the window to the house where he was raised.

We were all there, in the kinetic body of Abe—my dad, me, my dad in me.

"And you know they won't let me drive," Grandma said.

I knew. I heard every time I visited. The smattering of dents in the car and the doctor's orders had done nothing to convince her, so my dad and his brothers took her keys. Those vanished keys were, in part, why we'd come.

I imagined her stuck in this house, surrounded by her family and the birds but unable to leave on a whim, tethered to my uncles and aunts anytime she wanted to buy birdseed at the store or a biscuit at the Hardee's. On the one hand, I knew how lucky she was to be an eighty-five-year-old woman living just down the hill or through the woods from all her sons, to be able to call on someone a few hundred yards away when she needed something. On the other hand, she was alone in a house where she'd lived for nearly sixty years. What if she simply wanted to go somewhere?

I thought of the moment when her husband, my granddaddy, died. I was sixteen, and it was 9:00 or 10:00 at night when we returned from the hospital. I took my keys and left. I could tell my parents didn't think I should go—I had only had my license for a few months—but they only said *be careful* and turned on the outside lights. I rolled along empty country roads and ultimately into town thinking some about my grandfather but mostly about the headlights and the next turn. The steering wheel allowed me a clearheadedness that I couldn't have found inside a house, closed in by walls. Out here, I knew I could mash the brake or hit the gas and the world would follow suit. I felt in control.

When I lived in the mountains of Honduras, hoofing it everywhere and relying on sporadic, rattling buses to leave town, I longed for a steering wheel, for the ability to aim myself in a direction and then chase it with velocity, without permission. I was hemmed in without the wherewithal to grab my keys and go, so I felt that I could understand some of Grandma's stuckness, of her longing for those keys no matter the risk. But then again, she knew she'd never drive again. Her car was gone forever. She would need the rest of us for the rest of her life.

....

During the second week of 1811, William dissects a rabbit's head. School is back in session, so most days he's at the schoolhouse, whipping the pupils into shape, sometimes literally. But in his free time, he cuts into a rabbit to see what he might find. He starts the work on Tuesday, and then on Wednesday, he wakes, has sex with Binah/Biner/Byner, and sets back to it, cutting free another eye.

It's hard to say what he's learning in all this dissection. What is true, however, is that William will turn twenty-three next week, and he enjoys passing the time by finding out what's just under the skin, by opening up the world to see how it works. He observes dew and lights fires and considers physiognomy when he catches the eye of a woman.

In a notebook, William writes notes about history and mythology—scribbles about Euripides and Sophocles. He connects Jesus's charge in Mark—"But whoever causes one of these little ones who believe in me to stumble, it would be better for him if a millstone were hung around his neck, and he were thrown into the sea"—to a story from 2 Kings about a woman boiling and eating her child during a time of famine. Amid these plain-text searches for meaning, he develops a new cipher, and in it, he records his dreams.

William believes in dreams. He believes that something is hidden there, something to be uncovered. In notebooks now lost, he recorded other dreams—surely about MN and lost horses and glowing, green fires. But in this notebook, he writes first of dreaming that he returned to the "place of the dissection of the rabbit" and there he saw HM reading a letter.

In truth, the dreams William will record in 1811 might better be called *Ruminations on HM*. Many of the entries are daydreams, mentions of William lost in thought on horseback, and every one of the entries in the notebook reveals the life of HM in William's restless mind.

HM or H. Moore or Mr. M appears on William's pages over and over during the first two weeks of January. William writes about how HM's opinion is that light is fire, about how HM said that Lun's wife kissed him, about HM bringing William fodder on his birthday. On January 19, William forges a letter for HM. Then, letter in hand, HM leaves Darlington County:

> **January 20:** H Moore started off. We cried. Courted M Whindon. Come home. Asked Betsy Gandy for a fuck.

And here, three days after his twenty-third birthday, is the only mention of William crying in the whole of his recorded life. HM, a brief albeit intense flame, leaves, but he remains in William's dreams and daydreams for the next twelve months:

> **January 30:** Drempt that HM came back. Said he obliged to on acct of that forged letter.
>
> **February 4:** Dreampt H Moore sent me a letter with several in it. The handsomest writing ever I saw and money in them.
>
> **July 28:** At home. Rode out on Guinea. Thought Mr. M was studying about coming back.
>
> **August 25:** Forgot HM.
>
> **September 22:** Walking about home. Thought on Mr. HM.
>
> **October 27:** Riding. Coming from meeting. Thought on HM. Fucking.
>
> **November 24:** At fence. Thought HM was thinking on me and philosophy.

I don't know what to make of this relationship—a meeting of the minds? a father figure? a lover? I can't properly account for HM's persistence in William's stray thoughts, for the stickiness of the forgery in his gray matter, despite HM's brief appearance in his waking life. What is clear is that he mattered enough for William to record him over and over—and to hide him in a special cipher, built only for dreams.

Back in the waking world, he learns of across-the-ocean rumblings:

> **January 22:** Went and got my books. Stay'd CC. He was drunk.
>
> **January 23:** Grubbed for TP.
>
> **January 28:** Kept school. TP went mill. Heard the embargo.

Napoleon, in a flare of opportunism, has revoked the French blockade of England, but when the British refuse to return the favor, an American embargo automatically goes into effect, ratcheting up tension between the U.S. and U.K. War might be coming, but William ignores the news as best he can; he passes the winter reading and drinking and working for his father:

> **February 2:** Went driving. Got nearly drunk on cyder. JC off the land trade. Snow.
>
> **February 4:** Went to help J Jordan roll logs. TP lost deed. Hunt it.
>
> **February 18:** Grub'd for TP. Flower calved.
>
> **February 19:** Hunted Flower all day. Vastly cold.
>
> **February 21:** Heard E. Gandy kill'd. Went after his father.
>
> **March 7:** Sowed oats for geese. J. Tyner come.
>
> **March 8:** Grubbed for TP with C Clark. Went H Gandy's after shoes. Drunk.
>
> **March 19:** Went court. Terrible noise heard by people.

The people of Darlington County know enough of the captured sailors and patrolled waters and embargos to feel on edge. Many of them remember the sounds of mortars from the sea, of gunfire in fields forty years ago. Any pop on a bright afternoon, any thud behind the church bell—*a terrible noise*—might be the call of war, might be the British coming back for what's theirs.

15

American masculinity is born out of revolution. Sociologist Michael Kimmel traces the roots of this manhood to battles for independence, to attempts to break free, fend off, and stand up to.

It is an identity formed from fear. Upon entering a room, a man sizes up the other men, Kimmel argues, always processing threats and calculating identity. The man may notice the women, and he may adjust himself accordingly, but more than any sucked-in belly or straight spine to attract a lady, he is most fearful of the manliness of other men, insecure of his own performance. He is forever measuring himself against the men within reach.

American manhood is built from a defensive footing, conjured in hiding, he argues. It is a constant battle to be seen as a man, not a boy or a woman. "Manhood," Kimmel writes, "is less about the drive for domination and more about the fear of others dominating us."

From this collective fear and anxiety, America crafted its myth of masculinity as William was courting MN in the early nineteenth century: the Self-Made Man.

Once we broke free from a tyrannical father across the sea, American men began to reshape the image of masculinity, leaving behind the previous English models of Genteel Patriarch and Heroic Artisan to aim instead at a template of bootstrap-pulling, strong-armed men. To be an American man is to do it yourself.

"The Declaration of Independence," Kimmel writes, "was a declaration of manly adulthood, a manhood that was counterposed to the British versions against which American men were revolting." We left home, broke free of our father, and set out to make our own way—on our own terms.

Of course, Kimmel allows that our history is one of *masculinities*, not a monolithic identity, but he contends that every American man must deal with the Self-Made Man myth that looms large in every dinner party and hardware store line. We claim it or reject it.

....

TP, William's father, was a teenager when he'd marched off to fight for independence: a seventeen-year-old private trudging through Black Swamp, ready to do battle with men who might have been his uncles. But when the British came for them outside of Purrysburg, they ran. TP flew through forests and along wagon roads, hoping to reach Charleston and be swallowed up into safety. He didn't make it.

Before TP's company arrived in Charleston, General Moultrie stopped them and ordered three hundred men to ride back and destroy a bridge. TP, young and wide-eyed, was an easy target. He went where he was told: to blow the bridge at Coosawhatchie just before being shot in the arm. Then he ran again, bleeding his way into Charleston, entering the city just before the assault began.

In Charleston, he lay around listening to rifle shots. The men kept up a "warm fire," he liked to say, on the British for a day before the redcoats moved south. A few months later, TP was sent home. His arm healed, a bridge burned.

It wasn't long before he was called up again, sent as part of Hezekiah Maham's Light Horse Company to rush along the roads near Moncks Corner: a ragtag bunch of kids ready to fight off the British empire. They came upon sixteen British near the Santee River and ran them down over the course of three miles. He shot. The other boys shot. Four men were killed. Then the smoke cleared, the war ended, and he married Nancy, the Coker girl from up the road, and tried to fashion a life all his own. William was born a few years later, in a brand-new country, with Patriots and Tories alike underfoot.

I wonder what William would have thought of TP as a teenage private, wrecking bridges and firing muskets and running for his life? Would he have recognized that boy as the man who made him, maybe recognize something of himself there? Would the explosions and dead bodies around him explain something of TP, of his gin still and beekeeping? Would he better know his father?

In 1811, when William is twenty-three and a captain in the militia and the threat of war hangs like a summer storm, TP is a forty-nine-year-old man who never surpassed the rank of private, a man who loses deeds and drinks past his fill and vanishes when works needs done. *I tell'd him one roof wou'd not hold both of us.*

April 26: Holp C. Cl. Split rails. Dissect a frog.

April 30: Holp CC make pasture fence. TP pouts.

The TP William has known is an unreliable, pouting man. A man William never intends to be.

....

As a boy, I was surrounded by men. Grandma and Granddaddy raised four boys in that little rock house by the apple orchard. Then those boys spread out, marrying and building houses across the Prestwood land. They each had a son. From my house, I could find an uncle at each corner of our land, Granddaddy bent over in the garden digging potatoes in the middle of us all.

On Thanksgiving mornings, Granddaddy released the beagles, and we went into the woods together. Our fathers carried rifles; we four boys trailed them. Those dogs flew around, noses to the ground, and we watched for rabbits to emerge from briar patches.

I only remember one of these mornings clearly. My dad rarely hunted. Granddaddy had given each of his sons a rifle when they became men, but Dad's stood in the back closet, unloaded and dusty. I remember the gun coming out once or twice when I was a boy, mostly to chase off woodpeckers hammering into our house.

But one year, he did take up arms and chase rabbits, and the rest of us boys stayed behind our dads and followed the dogs to the old Prestwood house above the creek. On the hill above the barn, an open field surrounded by brambles and blackberry bushes and high grass, a rabbit bounded out. The shot was dad's. And it was a clear one: the rabbit dead ahead, bouncing in a zigzag thirty yards from us.

He shot three times. The rabbit's back-and-forth escape made it seem like the thing had a superpower to dodge the bullets. Each shot missed, and the bunny disappeared into thickness again.

It was understood that Dad was out of practice. His brothers did this every year. Two of them had been army, one still a reservist. Dad rarely shot. I'm not really sure why he'd gone that morning—I may have pressured him, eager to slide through the woods with my cousins.

I should have felt embarrassed for Dad to miss. Or perhaps felt sorry for his atrophied skill. Or more likely, defensive: ready to fight anyone who said something about my daddy. Instead, I only felt glad that he'd not killed that rabbit. I was eight, maybe, and somehow I already knew that he was glad, too, even when he grimaced after blowing his open shot. I suspected he'd missed on purpose, the same way he did when he let me win playing basketball. I knew him to be good at nearly everything: as an athlete, an artist, a teacher. When he lined up the shot, I expected him to land it.

Maybe I should have thought him weak then. It was only a rabbit, one out of hundreds across our land. I played Vietnam in the creek with my cousins, shooting down unseen men without second thought; I watched *The A-Team* every chance I got, taken with explosions. But I didn't want to see that rabbit fall. I wanted to follow it as it bobbed through the grass, showing itself to us for only an instant, like a gift. I was learning then that I liked to charge into the lane for a layup, bodies colliding, and wanted to make my muscles sore running bases, but I didn't want to do violence. I was learning, even with each missed shot, where that line lay for me.

Dad's grandmother, Azalee Prestwood, had called him "the compassionate one" since he was a boy, and in that moment, I knew it to be true. I felt it in me, too.

But here's what I also knew: my granddaddy could hit a rabbit clean and never raise a hand to another man. My uncles who came back from basic training with shaved heads and bruises and weapons rarely grew mad. They laughed and sang on Christmas Eve. They prayed up front in church. These men could kill or not kill a rabbit on a chilly fall morning and still know something about what it meant to live in a crowded world without demanding too much space, without taking someone else's. I knew, even then, that I ought to aim to be any one of them one day, perhaps all of them.

Years later, I learned of an afternoon when my daddy was fifteen or sixteen. His oldest brother, Steve, had driven a girl home after school, and on that afternoon, the girl's boyfriend tore into the yard after hearing this news. He threw the car in park in front of the house and yelled after Steve.

Steve went out, creaking the screen door, and the boy socked him in the face—loosing his teeth, bloodying his lip. Steve stood there, dazed, unwilling to fight back as my dad watched through the window.

Dad went for the rifle. If Steve wouldn't fight back, he sure as hell would, so he made his way for the front door, rifle across his chest like an infantryman. There, Granddaddy stopped him.

Instead of shooting him, Granddaddy brought the boy inside, sat him down on the couch beside Steve, and talked them through it. Later, he sent Steve's dental bill to the boy, but no one else threw a punch or pulled a gun.

I wonder about Dad's anger once he'd put the rifle back on the wall and come into the living room. He must've been seething, watching his pacifist brother—who would later become a preacher—and his quiet daddy sit there with a boy who'd come up on their land and spilled blood and was fixing to leave scot-free. He should get what was coming to him.

But in Granddaddy's world, in the world he laid out for his boys, this talking-to on a sagging couch in a tiny rock house across from the apple orchard *was* what was coming to him. Granddaddy was a letter carrier who'd returned from World War II and fashioned a discreet life of honeybees and church baseball and rowdy boys. He was a man who'd lost his parents as a child and then been taken in by this land and by a Prestwood family. He was a man who believed in grace, in the movement of even the smallest undeserved goodness through the world.

I wasn't in that living room, where Steve bled on the couch and Dad stalked in the corner. But it has made me. Whatever Dad took from that afternoon, whether then or later, he passed it to me. And on Thanksgiving, I was glad to be the son of a man who couldn't kill a rabbit.

16

In May, Uncle William—TP's brother—dies. He goes quickly, is in the ground by the middle of the month. Young William drinks whisky. Then he drinks brandy. Then he plows his field and writes his opinion of his life: "short." He and Watkins try to kill a dog, and he dreams that he murders children and flees to Georgia. He hunts livestock, and he, of course, chases women:

> **May 19:** Went home. Went with T. Coker cow hunting.
>
> **May 26:** Went to see Red Hill Meeting. Court'd Miss P. Hawkins.
>
> **May 29:** Planted peas and corn. Holp J Cl. hunt his horse.
>
> **May 30:** Plough'd cotton. Stay'd Cl's. Hugg'd Peggy and felt her cunt.
>
> **June 1:** Went after horse. Killed a terrible rattlesnake.

In June, some men come to employ William. He has been cutting wheat all month. Just yesterday, he went to the mill and returned with flour. Then he "cut a girl's toe nail off." But now, these men have come to hire him—men sent by the lawyer King—and William can see his future taking shape.

> **June 20:** Went Esqr. King's. Saw my old woman make curtesy.
> Didn't get employ'd.

So, unemployed, he goes back to the wheat, starts plowing cotton. He pulls A. Jackson's tooth out. He hears that Mr. Gandy dies. He helps dig a grave. An enslaved man named Frank runs away from Powell's.

William is sorting out just who he is. Who he will become. He is a man who hides Cato when he runs away and who wakes Binah at any hour he wants. William is a man who cuts a girl's toenails and pulls a man's tooth and dreams of murdering children. He is a man who feels cunts and eats honey and digs graves in June.

Near the end of the month, another death and another strange noise sets everyone on edge:

> **June 25:** I. Ganey dead. Heard an uncommon noise about half after one A.M.

Meanwhile, Napoleon now has a son. At first he was sure the boy was dead. "She screamed horribly," he wrote of his wife during the childbirth. "When I came in the room he was lying on a coverlet as if dead." But then the baby cried, and Napoleon was a father.

Or, a legitimate father anyway. He has twenty-one mistresses and children scattered across the countryside, but this screaming baby carries his name, Napoleon II, and has been christened King of Rome.

Cannons fired after the birth, and Parisians counted the shots, waiting for news of the baby's sex. Twenty-one shots for a girl, 101 for a boy. When the twenty-second shot erupted so did the city. Three cheers for a Y chromosome. For a new Napoleon.

Those ships still circle, and those adopted sailors, the Brits-turned-Americans-turned-Brits, still keep the cotton away. But all remains calm on the Western Front, and it will be a year before Napoleon changes that, marching off into Russia. For now, there is a boy who will follow him, who will rule the world.

For William, July is full of liquor and women. He beats juniper for his father's gin still. He beats apples for cider. He funs with P. Kelly and hears Betsy wants him. He finds her. He beats peaches for brandy. He's elected captain in the militia. A spider bites him, and he cures it with lye. He writes a letter by moonlight and learns HM has been telling that William has a letter from MN. "I am done with H. Moore," William writes. He eats watermelon, and Jo Jordan brings his razor. And then, the threat of British invasion hanging forever like a summer storm, he sets out again on horseback.

> **July 24, 1811:** Warned people on road.

....

Thomas Jefferson let the military dwindle. His administration liked to think and talk and occasionally invade, but the military's strength didn't occupy much space in those executive conversations. In 1802, 2,873 men constituted the U.S. Army—.05 percent of the population.

Jefferson envisioned an America where citizenship meant taking up arms as soon as William Prestwood came flying down the road on horseback, hollering to ready yourself. Jefferson's ideal America wasn't one of a massive standing army, stowed away and ready to snap into position, but instead a place where every man, woman, and child was ready to fight back for the sake of this strange new idea.

When James Madison came into office, the military's numbers had risen slightly, to six thousand army men out of more than seven million people. But Madison's newly appointed secretary of war, William Eustis, sold most of the army's horses and didn't supply many regiments with uniforms. He did not command a war-ready force.

It wasn't long, though, before Madison came to understand that war might be inevitable. Those vanished sailors across the ocean rattled everyone. *Impressment,* it was called—a made-up word, this practice of capturing American sailors in open water and reminding them that they would now and forever serve the king. They'd been brought back home, by force, and remade as British sailors. Or perhaps, their Americanness had simply been undone, washed away, and now they'd returned to natural form. They'd been impressed into service.

It wasn't impressment alone that pulled Madison toward war. It was also that far-off ever-growing frontier. Out there, British troops lazed around in forts they should have left three decades prior, at the end of the Revolutionary War. And as the country pushed westward, the Brits took up arms with the indigenous tribes being pushed around in the process. The Shawnee chief Tecumseh had seen the tribes of the Great Lakes killed and removed as these once-Europeans grabbed up more and more land, and so he mounted an army—a confederation of more than twenty tribes—to keep these new Americans from feeding their ceaseless hunger for new land. The lingering British troops joined in, and fights broke out along the creeping border.

Madison felt squeezed. The king from which the country had emancipated was coming from both sides, pushing back on the frontier and reclaiming the waters. Madison scrambled to build an army. He intended to grow the army to ten thousand before declaring war. He vowed to grow the militias. Volunteers were recruited. New militias were formed. But he couldn't do it. In 1812, the country could only muster 6,600 army men to pull on a uniform.

17

I took Abe down to the bottoms a few weeks after we moved to North Carolina. We passed the barn and crossed the bridge where Dad proposed to Mom, and then cut off the dirt road onto a path splitting the creek and a cornfield. We found my grandfather—my mom's dad—on his tractor there. Abe perked up at the sight of that; he'd learned quickly after we'd come home that he could perch up there and Papaw'd let him take the wheel.

Dad wasn't far behind us, and soon cousins and aunts and uncles and Sunday school teachers and childhood friends would follow, unloading coolers and casseroles for the Fourth of July. Adam and Andrew would show up with fireworks. Mike was coming with wood for the bonfire. Uncle Danny had the cornhole boards. But it was early yet, and so Abe and I made for the water.

We descended the bank of the creek in a slide, and he was in before I could suggest we change shoes. I'd conjured for this moment in those sleep-deprived hazes of his infancy, and here he stood, hunting flat stones in Clear Creek. It felt good but also cold. I remembered a photo I'd unearthed from Grandma's all those years before: my cousin Isaac and me in this creek, not much older than Abe, and our dads standing, arms crossed, on the bank watching. I didn't doubt the same scene had played out a generation before: my Uncle Tim and Dad and their brothers, throwing rocks in this water while Granddaddy stood in the sand. And a generation before then. And then another yet.

When we climbed onto dry land, both my grandmas had arrived. My mom's mom spread tablecloths, while Dad's mom had settled into her chair, more or less in the same spot where she'd been when I laid William's diaries on her lap two years prior.

"How do?" she called when we emerged.

I nudged Abe in her direction, and we sat down beside her.

She filled us in on who had taken her to the hairdresser, who she saw at a recent doctor's appointment. *And you know they took my keys.* We updated her on our settling in.

"Oh my, how I do love that red hair," she said to Abe as he squirmed in my lap, ready to be back on his feet and chasing something.

"It never fails to surprise me," I said, putting him down and watching him march toward my dad across the field.

"It reminds me of Mother's hair," she said still watching Abe.

I'd known Azalee Prestwood for the first six years of my life, and from those memories I somehow imagined she had worn white hair her whole life—born in black and white and a housecoat in 1903. I never knew she'd been a redhead.

"I sometimes wished I'd gotten that gene," Grandma mimed fluffing the back of her hair like she'd just received a permanent.

When Abe was born, the young ob-gyn who waited to catch him called up to Sarah and me that she could see his head. It was early in the morning, and we'd been in the hospital since the night before, waiting for this moment.

"He has a lot of hair," she said between contractions. I chanced a look, still in disbelief that a human baby would soon be in the room. "At least it's not red," she joked.

I smiled politely. Sarah had other things on her mind. Then the next contraction came. And so did he.

Once Abe's cord had been clipped, the nurses dried his headful of hair to find it the color of a pumpkin set ablaze. The doctor wisely decided not to comment on this surprise before leaving us to our new red-headed son.

His wet head and our dark hair might have made the joke seem safe, albeit weird. As we cradled the tiny, five-pound thing with his toupee of fiery hair, I summoned the little I remembered about recessive traits from high school biology. Where did this come from?

A few months after he'd been born, we drove to North Carolina for a family reunion hosted by my other grandma. Her people, the Maxwells, swarmed her yard, and within minutes of arriving and meeting second cousins and great-aunts, I understood what lay buried in my DNA. Any one of those Maxwell women could have walked off with our baby and looked more like his parent than Sarah or I did.

The MC1R gene is an autosomal recessive trait, requiring both parents to be carriers. Abe couldn't have popped out with this hair only because of Scots-Irish Maxwells or Azalee Prestwood. Sarah, too, had to carry this gene somewhere in her body so that the buried, inactive genes in our DNA could together make this fair-skinned kid, our ancestors cooking him up and sending him into the world.

Sitting in a camping chair beside Grandma, it felt preposterous that I could look around that patch of earth off Townsend Road on the Fourth of July and find most of me there—my mom and her parents, my dad and his mom. I was just a bundled-up package of those people shuffling around under a tarp by the firepit. And yet. We, each of us, carry markers of previous generations that could awaken at any moment, springing up red hair or enciphered texts in trash bags.

I went to fetch Abe some dry clothes from the car. My cousin Isaac pulled his hemi-engined truck to a stop as I did, parking it beside other trucks in the field.

"You going to an Indigo Girls concert, Jeremy?" he hollered as he climbed out.

"Yeah, man, you can't get in without driving one of these." I patted the hood of my Subaru, but the joke was on him; I'd been to an Indigo Girls concert. Twice.

We walked back toward the tables and creek together, and I wondered if I stood out among these men, like my car among the trucks—I'd washed away most of my accent and spent my days talking about figurative language with tattooed young people in college classrooms. Isaac spent most of his days alone in a field.

The masculinity of this place I was raised, the place I'd now planted my boy, is one coded in big trucks, tobacco-ringed back pockets, and mumbled conversations away from a crowd. The guns and mufflers are loud, but manhood in the mountains often takes the form of a quiet man who'll smile without teeth and look anywhere but your eyes when talking about the weather or God. It's perched up as gruffness and stoicism, but I've known it often to be an unexpected softness, a desire to get out of the way. A smallness.

But I didn't own any overalls or Dickies. My hands were soft. The only pair of boots in my closet were for hiking. What's more, I'd been known to gobble up attention—I managed at least one concussion acting a fool in front of a crowd at a college party. I wasn't sure that I carried my manhood like these men. And yet, as the sun sank lower behind Huckleberry Mountain, I was happy in a folding chair at the edge of the creek talking to my uncle about fiddle music. My accent sometimes crept up from somewhere in my gut. Abe and I made our goodbyes quietly.

At home, I woke around midnight to the sound of fireworks somewhere through the woods. I listened for stirring from Abe's room as the booms resounded. I heard none. He slept on, and I felt a rush of relief—and then a rush of privilege—to know that if Abe woke to the sound of explosions in the dark of night, he'd not think of war. He couldn't think of war. Nothing in his short life could have supplied him with the images or knowledge or language to know what war is, to know that war exists. I took the comforter and wrapped up the body that was becoming my father's while the empty sounds of independence rang on.

....

William can't sleep. War draws closer in May 1812, and when he tries to nap, he tosses and turns: "tho't I was under fire." He doodles on his notebook, trying out his new rank on the cover—Capt. Wm. Thomas Prestwood. Rumors spread: War will come in June.

But the next week, nothing happens. William replants his corn, reaps his wheat: "The Great Destruction didn't come." William's days are filled with kids, "the scholars," he calls them:

> **June 21:** Went school, 6 scholars. Went TC Jr's meeting. Saw M. Smith's wife's cunt at piss. Stay'd all night.
>
> **June 23:** Major Edwards come. Went to warn volunteers. Had discourse with Wm. Bennett. CC's horse throwed me. Come home.
>
> **June 24:** Went CC with horse. Maj. Wms. come.

And then, as if from nowhere, the British are coming:

> **June 25:** The Express of War.

Madison declared war on June 18, but word finally reaches Darlington County a week later, and now William is a captain at war. Any day now, he may be aiming a rifle at a charging army or standing stock-still behind a tree out by Powell's, praying himself to age twenty-five, praying he might one day be a father, praying he might become a man to crowd around after Sunday dinner.

He musters every week. He goes to Society Hill, "rendezvous of soldiers," and receives brigade orders and starts for Georgia before they're called back. A volunteer militia has been organized, and William must command a company of young men who've never marched in step. But between the musters and court martials, he teaches and sleeps with Binah and "devils" Amelia Jordan and drinks whisky and writes a pass for an enslaved man named Tarlton. The community raises a new school at Seedtick, and William courts Tabitha and Delia on the same day. He carries on.

There is fear, of course. Every passing noise might be the British creeping up the shoreline at any moment. The people of South Carolina expect the Brits to cut through Charleston and come calling for their prodigal sons and daughters, to impress everyone back into the service of the king any morning now.

And so, without warning, William is thinking of Mary again. How long has it been since he saw her? What is her life like now, married? He walks to Mr. Norwood's that morning. "Dodged about to see MN Sellers." Why does he think of her now, on July 27, war at the edges? He writes nothing of death on his pages in 1812, but surely it creeps into his day while he cuts oats or hoes corn. Once a week, he is preparing for something he's never seen, for men who want him dead. Then it rains, and he looks for Mary, just a glimpse of Mary Who Would Be His Life.

He finds her there, in her daddy's store—with her husband. He leaves before speaking. Why did he come here? What did he hope to find? Once home, in his tiny notebooks, he scratches down a rare moment of recorded emotion: "Sorrow Sorrow!!!"

The next day, the volunteers under William's command desert the militia. He ignores this news and goes to the schoolhouse to teach, to carry on with his life. But Major Edwards comes by school to order William to track down his runaway men. William doesn't. Not yet. He gives them a day to run off and then finds the deserters near Powell's the next day. They surrender without incident, and William goes home, mad that Major Edwards sent him after the men in the first place, mad at this new identity of commander.

For most of William's life, the militia has been a social club. A social club with its own dress code: most militias design their own uniforms, tasseled and dandied up, flashier than the regular army. They mustered and trained; they fired weapons and rode horses, but they also drank and wrestled and talked of Pruny Kelly. William was elected captain by his men in 1811, in what was likely more a popularity contest than a decision about who could keep the men safe when under fire and undersupplied and underprepared. It's hard to imagine him as a natural leader, as a taskmaster in the midst of war. In an 1896 account, one of William's former students says that "Prestwood would sleep and sleep during school time, and eat roast turnip peelings, and we often went out and played when he was asleep. Of course we learned little. I think I got through the ABCs."

I want to imagine him as a strong-jawed captain, whipping young men into fighting shape so that this young country might be saved from the oppressive king, but instead I see him sitting around, his shirt untucked and a fiddle in his lap, talking about philosophy and women while orders come down to prepare to fight. He is twenty-four, heartbroken, and afraid to die. When the first frost comes, William writes Mary "a consoling letter" and is sent out on horseback again.

18

I've never been in a fight. Not really. I've been bloodied by cousins and teammates, had five concussions, two knee surgeries, but I've never stood, fists raised, across from someone with fire in his eyes. I tried once, in a snapshot of the frantic insecurity that is middle school. I had in my mind—planted there by someone or by everyone—this notion that I needed to fight someone to be the right sort of twelve-year-old boy who'd forever have friends and girls and fast cars and money. Who would become a man.

I was wearing short purple shorts at the time.

The locker room had cleared out mostly, and I still sported my gym clothes, APPLE VALLEY PE across my chest, those purple cotton shorts hiding only half my thighs. I can't reach back to find the triggering event, to some conversation that urged me to create a fight from thin air. I had no enemies, no grievances. I knew to hate bullies, knew to hate the kids who stoked tension with their *I heard you said something about me* volleys in the hall, their crew fanned out behind them. And yet I came into the locker room and aimed myself at Nick Carver.

During PE, I had been thinking about how to create this fight, about the best sparring partner. I settled on Nick. He was solid, square-shouldered, a little tubby. He was bigger than me, but he wasn't especially athletic or brazen, and I spent Friday nights watching *Walker, Texas Ranger* and perfecting my roundhouse kick in my bedroom. I knew I should fight someone who wasn't so small that I'd be an obvious bully. It should look fair, if not a little skewed against me. This was, after all, a performance. So I went at him.

In the memory, I can feel another boy or two behind me, smell the sour sweat soaked into the tiles. I push him, say something too literal as he stumbles backward: "Let's fight, Nick." He lands in a squat by his locker, looking up at me.

"No," he says.

"C'mon," from one of the boys behind me.

"C'mon, Nick." Another one. "Don't be a pussy."

I can't push him again while he squats. It's too easy, too ridiculous. I try to tower over him. I wonder if he can see up my shorts. "Get up, pussy."

"No," he says. "What the hell, Jeremy?"

"I don't like you. Let's fight."

He wouldn't stand back up; he just squatted there by his locker and said he didn't want to fight. I tried to muster up something to launch at him—anger? greed?—but nothing workable would come. I finally gave up and left the locker room. On the way out, I turned back to see him hunkered down, pulling clothes from the locker.

I'd forgotten this until we moved back to North Carolina. Sarah was at work and Abe was napping—a rare, touchy affair—when the man showed up at the door to install our internet. We tiptoed around, scouting for suitable spots for a modem, before landing in the basement looking for a power source. "Hey," he said in the dim light before I made to go back up the stairs. "I think we went to high school together."

It'd been fifteen years since high school, and I'd been mostly gone since then. I had no social media accounts, had been to no high school reunions, and I hadn't seen most of the people I threw graduation caps into the air with since 2000. I smiled and said maybe so, but I couldn't place the face in front of me. I was sure, suddenly, I'd be stuck in this same awkward exchange over and over at grocery stores and gas pumps now that we'd moved back to our hometown after a lifetime away. *Your face looks so familiar.*

"Nick," he said. "Nick Carver."

Then, I saw him there, behind the goatee and years. In truth, I don't think he'd recognized me at first either—I'd lost my hair, gained some weight—but he had the advantage of my name on the service ticket, and so it must have clicked somewhere along the way. Before long, we were standing around in the kitchen, talking about marriage and old teachers and where everyone had gone. He was thinking of moving to Chicago. I had just moved back home. Once the modem was up and running again, he left, and I remembered the locker room.

I wondered if he remembered it, too. I hoped it had been a throwaway moment, one of a hundred strange middle-school-locker-room moments to forget, but I worried that it might have been the first scene he recalled when he saw me there in the basement—maybe he'd recognized me and then seen me towering over him in my purple shorts.

We'd gone to school together for years, had hundreds of nonthreatening interactions in our small, rural high school, but for all I knew, that one middle school scene sat at the top of the pile.

He'd left a card, and when the memory came back to me, I had half a mind to call the number and ask him if he remembered, too—to apologize for picking a fight over nothing after playing volleyball in Coach King's class. But I didn't. Abe woke up crying not long after the door had closed, and I went to get him.

I wondered if I'd ever tell Abe this story, if it might prove some teachable, parenting moment to discuss power and peace. In college, studying theology and reading poetry, I'd decided I was a pacifist, but after becoming a parent, I found that position harder to hold. Climbing the stairs to Abe crying, I considered what I'd do if someone came for my son, if someone made him cry like he was crying then.

I felt in my chest, at the mere thought of this possibility, the power to kill. I'd not had to work hard to live out that classroom pacifism—I didn't need violence to eat or survive. I'd not been called to war or threatened. I lived a comfortable, middle-class life with a literal white fence out front of our new house. But I tested my brain in moments like those, wondering how I'd react if confronted, if my blood boiled or my muscles twitched—if I stared into the face of hatred. I asked myself how I would stand down then, how I would live out that belief that I don't deserve to live any more than anyone else.

All I knew that afternoon was that I wanted Abe to know he didn't need to fight Nick Carver in a locker room in middle school to become a man. So much of life, I was learning, was deciding when to let the body lead and when to slow it down. When to lose control and when to take it.

19

Napoleon, wreaking havoc across the world, likes to get down in the floor with his son. He covers him in kisses. "I do not see how anybody can kiss a child," his wife says, but Napoleon ignores her. He likes to make faces at the boy in the mirror. When the child cries, Napoleon dances around, saying "How, sir, you are crying! What! A king and crying?" When Junior begins walking, Napoleon drops his hat on the boy's head and fits his sword around his waist. The kid toddles around the room, dressed for war, as Napoleon doubles over with laughter.

He is giddy. There is still war. Forever there will be war. But Napoleon has a boy, and together, they will rule. In those cheekbones, Napoleon sees the future.

The Americans search for enough wool to outfit a ramshackle army and stand up to their father; Napoleon makes his son a ruler and sets his sights on Russia. He sends fifty thousand troops to Smolensk and orders a small palace built for his boy, the King of Rome.

....

The British do come. As do Tecumpseh and his United States of Native Americans. Madison decides it's a good time to invade Canada. Napoleon goes for Russia. Everyone is invading or defending on the whole of the Western Hemisphere, it seems. But no one comes to South Carolina.

May 7, 1813: Rain. Went muster. Got drunk.

In 1813, William continues to teach his scholars and shave his grandfather and chase women. He goes to cotton pickings. He gets a sword. His friends marry while he stacks hay for his daddy.

Being elected captain should have laid the groundwork for a career, for politics. He should have mustered once a month, shooting the shit and shaking the right hands before firing off a few rounds. He should be married to Mary Norwood. But William's luck is to become an officer before an actual war. To need to court-martial law-breaking militiamen and prepare for buckshot wounds and train like his life depends on it.

As 1813 draws to a close, he meets a new woman, Sally Spence. Amid the potato digging and Paul Revere-ing, he gives her a ring.

October 1, 1813: Went muster ground. Didn't hold court martial. [He] resigned.

October 5: Went meeting.

October 6: Cut grass. Warn people on road.

October 7: Warn'd people on road, etc. Went to CC's shucking.

October 10: Had fuss about boots.

October 11: Split rails. Col. Edwards come.

October 12: On road.

October 15: Dug sweet potatoes. Martha come. Went fort.

October 16: Shav'd grandfather.

October 17: Stay'd home. Found bell.

October 23: No court martial. Met Sally Spence.

October 24: Sold boots.

October 26: Went court house to court martial.

October 29: Went shop. Powell and T Coker's wines.

October 31: Come to Spence's. Give Sally a ring.

But it doesn't fit.

November 17: Fuck'd Nancy. Hunted hogs.

November 19: [Sex with] Biner, 5 AM. Got 2 hogs.

November 28: Fucked Nancy. 8 AM. Went to Chesterfield.

....

Napoleon leaves his men. They're dying. He returns to Paris, sure he can calm everything back home, can maintain power even as his armies are defeated. But he can't. The political tides have turned in his absence, so he abandons the throne. He leaves it to his son. The new king of France is four and work has yet to begin on his palace.

When Napoleon flees, he's sure that little boy teetering with a grown man's sword on his waist and a hat pulled down over his eyes will fill his throne eventually. He must have told himself, as he tried to set sail to the runaway nation of America, that it had all been worth it—that it was worth the piles of frozen bodies and torn-up maps to leave the world wide open for his son.

But, within a few weeks, the boy king is overthrown and Napoleon is captured before crossing the sea.

....

It might have been night when William left. Maybe he took off in a rush, TP laid up drunk somewhere. Or it may have been long-planned, a detailed itinerary and well-rested horses waiting one morning, the family lined up to say Godspeed. It's impossible to know. What is clear is that sometime between William's last entry on November 30, 1813 ("Come by Raynold. I. Hawkins, etc. Home") and his next recovered entry on November 10, 1814 ("Kept school"), he leaves his father for good.

William gives no indication about why. Why he and his mother and his little sister and Binah might leave behind the status and security of the Prestwood lowlands, of TP, of his mother's wealthy Cokers. Perhaps the war had changed something, was changing something. Maybe William no longer wanted to ride the road, shouting warnings. Maybe he realized he wasn't a captain in his heart; he wasn't made to return warm fire for years on end. Maybe he feared the family land being taken by raiding British troops. Maybe his mother had reached her limit with TP, and William had always been a mama's boy anyway. Or maybe William was ready to leave home. To find a new world, a world without reminders of Mary Norwood at every corner—*sorrow, sorrow!!!*

William sits to write a list of all of the markers of his master mason status:

Master's Sign: Draw the Right Hand edgeways across your belly.

The Grip: Forefinger Wrist, Foot Foot, Knee Left Hand Back

Word: Mahabone or Macbenach

Pass Word: Tubal Cain

Clap: Both Hands Above Head. Striking Apron. Lord Our God. Fellow Crafts.

Then he leaves his father and the only place he has ever known and makes for the mountains.

Dear William:

I haven't looked at your diaries for weeks now. It's not that I haven't thought of you; in fact, I imagined you just yesterday as I drove deeper into the Smoky Mountains and wondered about the stretches of time you spent wrapped up here making a map in the 1820s. I tried to think like you, like a surveyor, tried to plot the dot of my car on a square, to see the rising green wall of mountains as circles of all sizes, drawing in closer and smaller like two-dimensional nesting dolls. I tried to see the world from above—everything as equations and lines. Easily arranged and divided. But the truth is everything seems a mess. A perfect mess, mind you. Arranged chaos, intentional haphazardness, a place that seems to spring forth from the earth and the cement every night.

For you, though, on horseback bending these ridgelines, the world must've been snapping soundly together, each mark on the land a line on your map. The murmur of the stream as a curly hairline leading somewhere else, somewhere bigger—Hanging Dog Creek, Lick Log Branch. Every indention moving into another: the streams piling up until the ocean would eventually take them over, the worn paths of settlers and renegades and Native ghosts running always into other trails and wagon roads. Everything as progress, as a piece of a whole.

The irony doesn't escape me, William—from here I envy that vision, that perspective, but I'm the one with your whole nineteenth-century life splayed out before me like a crude map. I'm the one connecting dots, sorting what's left of the code of your existence. I'm the one with a GPS in my lap. But rushing down that four-lane road at 60 mph, I admit to longing, some days, for a mathematical brain and slow-moving horse.

I want to tell you about the plains of the West, about the never-ending prairie of the Midwest. If you can imagine it, nothing stands in a man's way out there, save wind. No impeding mountains like you and I grew into, no forests—simply land stretching forever. Consider the possibility those pioneers must have felt at casting their future forward into land that opened wide before them. If only their eyes were stronger, sharper, they could have seen further into the future, the whole expanse of time waiting there atop the planed board of earth.

When you left home, you could only see as far as the mountains allowed. In your wake was everything you'd ever known, and all that waited ahead were rolling, imposing mountains like blurry walls. Did you see them rise, as you neared the Catawba River, and feel pulled into them, or did they reach up like a bad omen, like a closed door? When you saw them there, did you long for the wide-reaching plantations of Darlington County, of rushing down the roads lined in cotton at dawn? Did you wonder what Mary Norwood might make of mountains claiming the horizon?

Imagine this, William: The towns in the west are set down in perfect squares. A man like you could have dropped into a place like that with your plummets and wye levels and compass and created a whole society of perfect blocks. Everything measured and exact. Not like here, where the roads stay straight only for a breath, where the houses cling to any flash of flatland. There, the buildings huddle together amid the wide open, finding comfort in the closeness and order.

And the storms, William. You can watch them tearing up the soil, sending down the rain from miles away. They're beautiful, really—even when the wind and rain curl into a black funnel and connect heavens and earth. But in awe and miles away, you know that the storms will soon be upon you. And where does one hide when you're living on a blank page of earth? It's the inescapable future, William—just at the edge of eyesight.

But not here in the mountains. Here, everything is just behind the ridge. Just out of sight. For better or worse, we don't know what's coming until it's here.

PART IV

ς488|4ϭ478

Settlement

♐♒ *Advice for My Sons* ♌♒

January 5, 1823

My sons court not popularity but always rise by your virtue and merit.

20

By chance, I stopped at the Caldwell County Heritage Museum driving across the state one afternoon. I decided I ought to at least look around the historical society in the place where William moved after leaving his father, where he lived out the rest of his life. So I took the exit.

What was once the gymnasium for an elementary school, and before that a nineteenth-century college, now served as a museum documenting life in the county over centuries: photographs of old baseball teams, lists of injured Confederate soldiers, displays of railroad equipment. Upstairs, the former classrooms were lined with relics: desks from long-ago buried schools, wooden dolls from centuries-old playhouses, a "Permanent Wave Machine" from the 1930s that looked more like a torture device than hair salon equipment.

I rambled along, alone. No one else looked at the faces of dead soldiers or beauty apparatuses on that morning. Two women, volunteers, sat at a desk on the opposite side of the gym, so I asked about looking at family history documents, to see what I might stumble upon. They led me into a back room of binders and books and pointed me to a file cabinet of family names. They gave me coffee. I started digging.

It's easy to search when you don't know what you're looking for, and I pulled anything that struck me from shelves: a book about old schools, a pamphlet about a Native burial mound. Finally, I found a folder for the Prestwood family in the cabinet. It directed me to a binder. On a bottom shelf, beneath a handful of other fat binders, I found it. Inside the binder, tucked into a pocket before the family trees and birth records, waited a manila folder, so I pulled it out first and splayed it across the table. It was stuffed with dozens of loose pages, and it didn't take much flipping before I realized those pages were Browder's pages, the cryptanalyst's notes stashed there in a folder within a folder in the back room of an old elementary school.

Some of the pages were neat lists hammered out on a typewriter: census data, estate records. But everything else amounted to scribbled-on notebook paper. What was clear immediately amid the scattered pages, however, was that Browder was meticulous. While his elderly hand may have spread shaky cursive across the pages, the sheets had clear headers and dates, the margins firmly laid out. I found re-created census tables with measured, straight lines dividing the categories. They reminded me, in this way, of Prestwood's tiny notebooks themselves, carefully laid out and plumb.

The folder held correspondence with masonic temples in North Carolina and South Carolina, trying to confirm William's membership and status in the nineteenth century. There were letters to distant descendants of Prestwood, asking about genealogy. One of these letters had fallen from the copy of his transcription I bought online years ago: a note Browder had written to a woman named Jacqueline Baird. He had been trying to track down history of the Baird family, trying to fill out related family trees.

But as I looked through everything, I realized that the inscription in the front of my copy of the diary wasn't Browder's note at all. "For Jacqueline L. Baird with warmest regards" wasn't the same squared-off cursive of the pages in the historical society. The note in my book was smooth and clean and steady. Before long, though, I found its match on other pages in the folder, and then I understood. Much of what lay before me in that back room wasn't the work of Nathaniel Browder, but the work of his daughter, Betsy.

Betsy became his out-of-the-house assistant as he approached his eighties, in the 1980s. Browder had moved in with her in Raleigh after his wife died. Betsy went to courthouses and archives and tracked down what he hoped to find while he worked with his magnifying glass and typewriter. In some cases, she left notes for him on these pages: "Unfortunately, Joanna was not on the list. The writing varies from just readable to awful." Mostly she copied, word for word, any records that seemed relevant, tracing family connections and recorded events.

Reading the Browder duo's research notes, I realized I was out of my depth. I saw in their approach a system, a professionalism that was absent in my own notebooks. The Moleskine in my lap was a compilation of half-finished sentences, one-word maps, and questions without answers. Boxes were drawn around anything that might be important; circles showed up when I wanted to connect two bits of shorthand, sometimes across pages. Browder's pages were numbered, his lists bulleted.

Eventually, the women came to check on me. More coffee? Some water?

I told them about what I'd found, about what I was doing. (What was I doing?)

"We're Prestwoods!" one of them said. They were mother and daughter, it turned out, and, it turned out, we were cousins.

They ticked off their lineage like we were reading Hebrew scriptures. They didn't get as far as William, but I already knew that would be where we'd meet. He was the only Prestwood man to move here in 1814, and so he had become our North Carolina forefather.

When I connected those dots, and showed them William's decoded diary, they were surprised. They'd known nothing of him, didn't know about his diaries or his code or his womanizing or his road-riding or his heartbreak. They hadn't known a copy of his life waited back there in that room, some twenty steps from their desk.

I expected them to be more thrilled to know about William than they seemed to be, to be grateful about his recorded life in full view on this table. But then again, there were days when I read through the pages and wished I didn't know. I wished I didn't see Binah's symbol (ה) appearing in the morning. I wished I could simply dream I come from a stock of Scots-Irish immigrants who were too poor to be slaveholders or too pious to engage in the system of it. Or perhaps a people who comingled with the Quakers somewhere in Pennsylvania before coming south, lighting lamps and providing sanctuary for Black lives on the run through the North Carolina mountains.

But I knew better. I was from the mess of William, and, for better or worse, I'd now opened these women up to him.

In estate files and pension requests and court documents, I saw William's last name misspelled many different ways in North Carolina: Presswood, Prepwood, Preswood. Back home, I was used to spelling it for friends and deliverymen when I gave directions to our house on Prestwood Lane. I knew no other Prestwoods in Fruitland. We weren't even Prestwoods ourselves anymore really: Grandma married a Jones, and so we Joneses lived on Prestwood Lane.

Priest of the Wood, I'd learned when I dug into genealogy after college and found the Prestwoods in England. The name fit us, I thought then. Asbury, my great-great-grandfather who moved into the house above the barn in 1906, had built the Methodist Church and planted our lives in the forests of Fruitland. Until I met William, with his symbols of women and days plowing drunk on whiskey, I thought I'd come from Appalachian woodland priests.

But there in front of me in a retrofitted elementary school were two flesh-and-blood Prestwoods. I didn't need to spell the name for them. And what's more, there were Prestwoods everywhere in the county. I Googled and found lawyers and doctors and surveyors and electricians scattered across the town of Lenoir. All of them William's children.

Of course, when I'd taken the exit off the interstate to come dig through these papers in the museum, I didn't expect to find any buildings to tie me to William, no two-hundred-year-old houses with a sign on the door—*Billy Prestwood was here*. But I had wanted to set foot on land where he might've walked, where he might've lived. But finding it proved difficult. Names then were not names now. I couldn't find the oak tree to send me enough paces toward the bend in the creek. So I asked these women.

"You ought to ride out to Prestwood Hill," the daughter told me.

She drew me a map of boxes and lines—it looked like my notebooks—and pointed me toward two churches and a cemetery. "That's where the Prestwoods have mostly been."

I wondered then, but not for the first time, why my great-great-granddaddy left this place to move to Fruitland at the turn of the twentieth century. Grandma always said it was for the schools, that he wanted his daughters to have a good education, so they'd come to Fruitland. But I'd just passed through the whole history of Caldwell County on display in the gymnasium; I'd seen active schools everywhere here. What was the real reason to uproot and settle farther west?

When this new cousin of mine handed me the crude map and smiled, I felt a ridiculous and unexpected loss at being disconnected from these women 120 years ago, removed from all those Prestwoods in the houses and gravesites sketched on the paper in front of me. But I let it pass. I thought of the woods back home. Of Asbury's house, of Albert's house, of Betty's house. Of my own.

Then I packed up my notes and set out to find a grave.

21

Grandma died in the fall. It was expected and it wasn't. She was eighty-seven. And yet she was living on her own and had entered the hospital because of a treatable infection. The day before she died, she'd been up and about at a rehab facility, mostly herself but a little loopy on drugs. She was ready to go home. We expected her to.

But then she went to sleep. It's cliché to say that she seemed like a girl like that, alive but at rest, curled up on the hospital bed. But when I placed my hand on her head and stroked her hair, she was, for a moment, my child. Then she was gone.

Months later, when I walk through the woods, I wind up at her house. *She's not there*, I tell myself, but my legs lead me into the fields above her house anyway, windows dark. I can't shake all of the memories folded into my muscles, of bounding out of the woods past the beagle pens, of creaking open the back door after I amble down the hill.

Her house is mostly the same—her bed made, framed photos of grandkids on the mantle. It is as her grandparents' house is above the creek: vacant but full. This is what we do here. We leave these Prestwood houses distilled like museums and carry on. The structures of five generations stand like gravestones to mark the passing of time.

I'm a grown man who ought not feel so uprooted by his elderly grandmother's death, a woman who lived a long, robust life. But when I drive past that empty house or walk toward it like a sleepwalker, the world feels somehow off-balance.

After her funeral, we crossed the creek to the plot where our people lay. Uncle Danny opened a hole in the ground, beside Granddaddy and Albert and Azalee Prestwood, and we dropped flower petals in with her ashes. It was cold and spitting rain, and we spoke memories of her kindness or brashness with each petal. It was my cousin Isaac, back on this land after tours in Afghanistan and Iraq, who spoke of her house.

"Don't worry." He dropped his flower. "I'll still wave when I pass your house."

In her later years, rocking by the picture window, she complained once or ten times that Isaac never waved as he passed by on the way to his house. These conversations, bickering over his saying hello, were ready-made, like Grandma's and mine were about the birds. So Isaac took his greetings to the extreme: sometimes rumbling his truck directly into her yard, a few feet away from the window, to swing his arm like he was landing a plane, other times stretching his entire torso out of the window to flail his arms in the air as he drove by. Every time he left home, he performed this exaggerated ritual before her.

Isaac prefers to be in the woods. He didn't speak at the funeral like the rest of us—he hasn't worn a tie since he was eight, and he never quite mastered the art of the "inside voice." He's never one for sentimentality or vulnerability, and this one-liner in the cemetery landed as a joke, but I understood its sincerity immediately. It gut-punched me there in the rain above the creek: though her body is gone, her house lives on.

....

Unsurprisingly, people die all across William's pages. The nineteenth century means lots of grave digging, for babies and mothers and mares and dogs. People are hanged and shot, taken by fever or nothing at all. William dreams people to death and, sometimes, conjures them back to life:

> **Nov. 22, 1808:** Dreampt Malcom M'Quange was hung by TP and come back to life again.

Awake, William does his fair share of killing: of hogs and snakes and possums and "beef" and bucks and squirrels. And I must assume he grieves, but I have no real record of this. His diaries log death with firmness and flatness. His mother's passing in 1841 receives the same space and directness as a goat's in 1826 ("Mother died"; "Goat dead"). Only hints of emotion reach up from the code—hearts sketched in the margins. His mother's death is annotated with a tiny heart. His wife's death in 1858 receives two, one filled in, the other empty.

To me, the whole of William's record speaks of loss. The diaries themselves ought to have been lost. Fate or chance led them through generations and hands of relatives once-removed to finally be cracked more than a century after William's death. But even what's here, saved by kin and passersby and an old cryptanalyst, leads me to what's missing. Not only emotion and reflection but also whole years—104 months of lost books. What happened just after the War of 1812 to send William and his mother into North Carolina, leaving his father behind? The months between November 1813 and November 1814, like the years of 1824 and 1834 and 1840, have vanished.

Even beyond these disappeared books, the cipher within the salvaged pages leaves holes, due mostly to water damage and script too curled to decipher. *June come night. Said MN would have me if she could get [unreadable].*

These open spaces read like black lines in a redacted file—the needed information unreachable, covered up. Browder, the cryptanalyst, wrote that what's missing is far less remarkable than what's been saved—"the percentage of words lost is very small compared to the total entries that survived"—but I can't help but get caught in the absence.

To look at the decoded transcript—two columns of justified, typewriter-hammered words per page—is to see text overrun by white space. Many of the 231 pages are scant with text. For some months "Do" (ditto) hugs the edge of each column, leaving wide oceans of whiteness.

Sometimes I come to his pages as if to an image—seeing the sprouts of black and fields of white at a distance. I think of those black-and-white silhouettes in psychology textbooks where one's brain must choose which image to see and which to ignore—the faces or the vase, the old woman or the young one? I wonder, sometimes, what is foreground and what is background on William's pages. Is the minimal black text the story and the whiteness the backdrop, or the other way round? Is what's unsaid—what's undone—more representative than any recorded action? Is what I can't know more revealing than what I do? What William do I see when I foreground the silence, the absence, the negative space instead of the text?

Gestalt theory, the twentieth-century psychology behind those black-and-white mind-tricking images, suggests that we come to images always making wholes from parts—that we conceive of individual pieces as collective images in order to make sense of the world laid out before us. Our brains—our "active minds"—are forever working to make meaning of patterns, of the codes. No matter the empty spaces, the absence, our minds find connections and fire synapses to create a whole from parts. In German, *gestalt* translates roughly to "unified" or "meaningful whole."

The broken headstone of Delilah Prestwood,
daughter-in-law of William Prestwood, near Lenoir, NC

From a page of minimal text and floods of white space, I piece together, I find patterns. I perceive a meaningfully whole man. Gestalt theory is, after all, about perception—not about *what* we see, but about *how* we see.

....

I found buried Prestwoods covering a hill in a community called Cajah's Mountain. To stand in the middle of the cemetery was to be surrounded in Prestwood bodies, all of them descendants of William. On the edge of the land, near a parcel being cleared by an excavator and front-end loader, waited a smattering of unmarked graves.

There was nothing left to read on those headstones. They'd been smoothed back to mere stone, but it seemed likely one of them was William's. I had a half a mind to lie down there and call out to him through the dirt—*it's me, from the letters*—but instead I walked among the graves and imagined his life here two hundred years ago.

I'd driven here to Cajah's Mountain, with my long-lost cousin's map in hand, by following the curves of Gunpowder Creek and Lower Creek. When William moved to North Carolina he lived along Lower Creek, but I couldn't find where exactly as I rode toward the graves. Still, I knew I may have driven over places where he snuck off with women who would become symbols.

But William's world, a settlement then called Tuckers, had faded away just like William's headstone and body. What waited now across the road from this cemetery was a used car dealership called Three Guys Auto and a handful of nondescript houses. There was nothing to mark his life there, nothing remaining from it on that land. Save me. And the women in the repurposed elementary school. And my son. And every life that followed after those buried around me.

Before long, I spotted—then heard—the rain swallowing up the trees on the mountain behind the church, so I jogged back across the resting ground of my far-off family just as the sky opened and covered us all up.

22

It has rained all day in the North Carolina mountains, in the place where the Spanish built a fort in 1567 and where William has taken up residence since leaving his father behind last year. War is over, the White House is still smoldering, but William makes no mention of any of this. He has seen three terrapins and is, today, in love with a new Mary, Mary Earnest:

> **June 19, 1815:** Saw 3 terripins laying. Nt. Very much affected in love with Mary Earnest. Suppose by kissing her with love root.

William doesn't know that love root will only increase his urine flow. He simply knows that Mary is the woman for him.

He has been in Burke County, North Carolina, in the shadows of the Blue Ridge Mountains, for over a year. He's teaching again, surveying some. Gone are the family plantations, the constant work for TP. Gone is the rank, the power of his last name. Here, William has a modest life. He is twenty-seven years old and living with his mother.

Still, he has managed to meet plenty of new women since arriving to the settlement of Tucker—two of them sisters—and to each, he fashions a special symbol:

> **February 6:** Kept school. Went CS with mare. Lay Betsy.
>
> **February 23:** Went to B Massingale. Sleep. Hug PM.
>
> **March 7:** Kept school. Nt. B Massingale's. Peggy murdering herself.
>
> **March 9:** Went Setzer's. Hugged Betsy.
>
> **March 12:** Come Raders. Went see MM, went on mountain. Ale. M cried.
>
> **March 15:** Kept school. B. Massingale's. Emission on MM.

Of course, as always, he writes of Binah (ה). ה at 4:00 am. ה at 4:00 pm. ה at noon. In this new place, gone are the cousins and uncles and aunts. The family land. Here, the Prestwoods are four: Nancy, Nancy Jr., William, and Binah. A mother, her children, and the woman they've taken.

William doesn't often sleep at home. Some nights, he's at Cobb's. Other nights, Rader's or Boone's. Sometimes at Jerry Clark's. He's not Captain William Prestwood of the Darlington Prestwoods; he's a couch-surfing twenty-something, playing fiddle and chasing girls in a new town.

He might be homesick. Or he might simply be sick. He has been "dull" and "sluggish," generally "not well" in North Carolina. One night, he dreams of Boggy Swamp back home. His grandparents are all living. Everyone is there. "Abundance," he writes. Then he wakes in this new life.

Since leaving home, William has let emotion leak into his diaries only twice. In April, he tried to ford the Catawba River. The water was frigid; it had been "spitting snow." He fell in and later punched down eight exclamation points to document the injustice.

In November, Mary Norwood appeared to William like an apparition one rainy day at his desk. At school that morning, he had whipped two children, and in the evening, he read two verses of Goethe, from *The Sorrows of Young Werther.* Without warning, she was there before him, her memory real enough to touch. On his pages, she is now forever attached to that word, *sorrow*. "Thought MN," he wrote and then sketched a tiny heart.

But, in April, this new Mary appeared for the first time:

April 17: Clean'd pistol. Hugg'd Mary.

Then he fell in the water again:

April 18: Fell in the creek at ford. Rain.

And now it's June, and the plums down at Settlemire's are ripe, and last night he courted Mary at the edge of the property in the dark, and today, he feels the effects of the love root as he lies in bed. He might be whispering the name *Mary* like a prayer as he falls asleep in a house that isn't yet a home.

....

Home was always the rhododendrons. Between our house and Grandma's, huge patches of them rose up like caves in the woods. To enter them was to disappear, and I spent much of my boyhood inside, wrapped up in those giant leaves, spying on the world around me. I liked to be still long enough for the woods to forget me, to watch everything come back to life: squirrels racing up trees, cardinals zipping in, rabbits poking out from nowhere. More than my bedroom, more than the house my parents built when they married, more than Grandma's house below the garden, those stretches of forest held me closest.

When we moved back, that piece of forest was gone. My sister's house sat where the rhododendron stood, where the trail to Grandma's cut. It was a nice spot for a home, surrounded in that bit of woods I liked to surround myself in, but when I drove to my parents' renovated house and found the rhododendron vanished and Granddaddy's tractor shed leveled and Grandma's house empty, everything felt shaky.

Of course I knew that moving home would not be home exactly. Trees fall, people age. But I'd always been bad at change, a sucker for nostalgia. I fought my parents when they wanted to trade in the woodstove for gas logs. I was eight. Back home now, I was thirty-five and I hadn't lived on that family land for seventeen years, and yet I expected it to never change—to wait patiently for me to return, as if the nature of home is one of stasis.

Meanwhile, in our twelve-year marriage, Sarah and I had lived in eight different houses, scattered between Central America and the Midwest. Since moving off that Prestwood land half my life ago, I'd not stayed in any one house for more than three years. We'd stopped hanging art on the walls, already preparing to move before we unpacked.

It was unsettling. Sarah had been raised in a 150-year-old family house off Main Street. My family had holed up on the same plot since 1906. Neither of us was built for transience, and yet, we kept moving.

We weren't alone of course: This is the nature of American life in the twenty-first century. But suddenly, there we were: outliers coming home to live among our extended families, send our children to the same schools we attended, and chat with the mailman because we played basketball together decades ago. On any Saturday afternoon I might see my prom date at Target.

We'd moved into a house in town that had been Sarah's grandfather's. It was too small for us. Every month or so I'd drive to a storage unit to climb over dusty furniture and winter clothes to dig around for a pan we needed or an end table we'd now made space for. My instruments—a banjo, a dulcimer, some guitars—slept in my childhood closet at my parents'. Most days it felt like we were camping out in someone else's house, whittled down to our bare necessities. Other days it felt like we had too much stuff and ought to light it all aflame.

But then Sarah was pregnant, and so we were preparing—like always—to move. We wouldn't go far this time around; we were settled in our decision to be back in the mountains, but we were still rooting around for a place to call our own, a place where we might fit our furniture and my banjo and a brand-new baby.

The incoming baby was a boy. Abe was four and mostly thrilled, but I was a mess. Not because of the baby but because of a soccer-induced concussion. If I stood too quickly or turned my head sharply or bent over, migraines set in. I was spending lots of time lying flat in dark rooms. I was also worrying about my brain, about my memory. Some days my head hurt to think, to read, to open a computer. Words felt blurry when I spoke, hard to hold on to.

The brain, my neurologist said, is elastic. It heals, it changes. I tried to picture it up there—whirring away but sputtering occasionally, then mopping up blood. Then that made my head hurt, too, so I stopped.

I made more notes than usual—lists of tasks to complete, emails to send when I could stomach it. I considered keeping a log of my days like William—to remember what I'd quickly forget, to test my brain. But I was too inconsistent, too disinterested: *Made oatmeal. Drove. Taught. Lay down.*

Mostly, I became acutely aware of how everything was always moving, always changing. My head was set off by Abe spinning in the room, by sunlight flashing through the trees, by swallows falling and rising. It was impossible to freeze everything without going into the dark and lying down. But lying down in the dark was no way to live, so I moved slowly and let my head hurt while Abe twirled a ribbon on the porch and a new son stretched out in Sarah. I readied myself to pack up yet again, to mourn the rhododendron and Grandma's house, and settled into my chair to let my brain take a new shape as the world moved on.

23

Figure and ground, the first principle of Gestalt theory, suggests that our brains have a natural tendency to separate whole figures from their backgrounds. Upon seeing an image, our heads immediately search for the central figure, pull it closer, and then relegate everything else to the background.

In his introduction to the deciphered transcription of the diaries, Browder writes that William "never put himself forward." It's a brief critique amid the otherwise objective translating of code. Browder can't help but insert an editorial comment after William's advice to his sons: "Court not popularity but always rise by your virtue and merit." Browder came to see William as a gifted man who never took his shot, never lived up to his potential. He was a man who preferred to fade into the background of the little life he created in the North Carolina mountains.

When I first read Browder's words, I wanted to push back. William had recorded his life day after day, after all, holding it out for the world to see. But, of course, my next thought was that he'd buried this life in a cipher, intending to push it, too, into the background forever.

Now, with Browder's help, I bring him into the foreground, finding in him the figure to separate from the ground of nineteenth-century muck and scattered symbols. But even with him out in the open, I have to admit that he was an anonymous figure in the sweep of history. An everyman who lived a small life and then faded away in a cemetery across from Three Guys Auto.

In the days before Grandma's funeral, I sat in my office and stared at a photograph. I'd gone there to consider what I might say about her in that church where she ran the kitchen and drove me to Vacation Bible School, where I learned about sex and God, where my parents and grandparents married. Instead, I stared at the wall. I'd hung there the image of Asbury and Clementine Prestwood and their young barefoot children around the turn of the century, but alongside that picture, I'd taped another, this one a couple decades

Asbury and Clementine Prestwood (seated middle) with family, circa 1927

later. In this shot, Asbury and Clementine no longer stand at the edges of the frame, keeping their wild kids in place; now they're seated, all white hair and surrounded by adult children.

The photograph marks a generational shift in picture posing. The sons and daughters, all in their twenties and thirties, smile and smirk while Clementine and Asbury stare stone-faced at the camera, like they'd done in the earlier photo. They come from a time when one focused grimly on the photographer like determined, resolute prisoners. *We're not going anywhere*, the gaze seems to say.

In the decades between the two shots, Asbury has traded in his giant beard for a close-cropped goatee, his hat and workman's vest for a three-piece suit. His dusty boots still betray his farmer's life. But sitting at my desk that afternoon, my eyes didn't linger on Asbury. Neither did they survey the bald, round-faced men in the back row—my great-grandfather and his brothers—and see in them my father and his brothers. Instead my brain pulled forward my great-grandmother Azalee, now picturing her hair red, and for the first time, I thought I saw the contours of something in her dress, a baby bump reaching out of the black and white.

In the photo, she and Albert stand immediately behind Asbury and Clementine, and her long figure rounds slightly in the middle, her dress seemingly pushing out from the background. The wornness of the photo had left a lightness there, like a flash of a light atop her belly, and while I had no idea about the precise year of the photograph, I somehow knew then that Betty was swimming around in there—my grandmother taking shape in the womb as the photograph was snapped.

So I grieved Grandma in that old image on the wall. How strange to sense her loss before she had even appeared on this earth, in the body not yet formed, the body we would soon put into the ground. Sitting alone in my office, I had pulled her forward in my brain's search for meaning, made her whole out of a blur of negative space.

Of course, everyone in the frame had passed on by then, nearly ninety years later. All that remained from it was the backdrop, the house overlooking the cemetery and creek. When I finally put pen to paper, I started there, with what stayed behind, what lingered in the background. I thought of the empty houses across our land and pulled them into the foreground. I lifted up Grandma and Granddaddy's home out by the apple orchard. I thought of those empty structures not as headstones but as extensions of lives lived—welcomed hauntings.

What I realized, and what I said later in front of my youth leaders and Sunday school teachers and cousins, was that the simple life my grandparents fashioned in that little rock house had meant—had become—the world to me. That striving for smallness, a life poured into the land and people around us, a life in the background, was about the holiest thing I knew.

....

Father is here. *Father*, William writes. Not TP but Father. "Father come Wednesday." Uncle James has come to the mountains to visit, and he tells William Father is on his way.

But then William writes nothing more of it. On the Wednesday in question, William spends the day and night at Setzer's. His father makes no appearance on his pages. Perhaps he makes no appearance in the flesh. In any event, William carries on with his scholars and his women, with no recorded concern for TP, for Father. He doesn't need him here. He's finding his footing in these mountains. He goes to a shooting match; he plays cards all night. He visits his friends, Boone and Cobb.

And yet, something unsettling runs under William's entries in North Carolina. He dreams of being banished from South Carolina. He gets a toothache. He writes of nearly being arrested one Saturday after muster when he "tries to creep" with Biner. He's sick and puking again.

And he's already moved on from Mary, despite the love root. He's got his eyes now on Sally:

> **November 28:** Went B. Shell's. Kept school. Nt. Mitchners. Set up with Sally til cock crow.
>
> **January 22, 1816:** Nt. Mitchiner. Set up Sally, 3 am.
>
> **February 5:** Kept school. Nt. Mitchiner's. Court Sally.

Or maybe E. Setzer:

> **January 1:** Shav'd. Boon's. Tried to fuck E. Setzer.

Or maybe Susy:

> **January 24:** Kept school. Nt. S Cl. Set up Susy. Slow. 2 am.

Or N. Woods:

> **January 26:** Kept school. Nt. At cotton picking. Courting N. Woods. Curs'd D Rader.

Or Polly Emmons:

> **February 14:** Kept school. T. Book's. Polly Emmons' my valentine.

Then, near the end of February, William takes leave from his teaching post. He packs up and sets out on his own.

He camps on the Little River that first night, and then travels south, pitching a tent most nights and ambling slowly back into South Carolina, back home. It's cold, but he's in no rush.

When he arrives, he stops to see his Grandmother Coker first. Caleb is there. It's been years since he last saw his cousin, since they talked about women while shooting squirrels. Now Caleb has taken over the thousands of acres in the

Coker plantation, and William lives in his mother's small house, but how much William must want to tell Caleb about his new life, about Sally and Betsy, about the shooting matches. About his new friend John, the great-nephew of the infamous Daniel Boone. About the deep cut of a mountain winter.

He doesn't travel to see his father while in South Carolina. He doesn't visit his sisters who stayed behind when he and his mother took off, doesn't brag to Martha about all the mistresses he has now. Not once in his time back in the Cheraw District of South Carolina does he write of any Prestwoods; he avoids the lot of them. He writes only of his mother's people, the Cokers.

He stays for two weeks there. Then in mid-March, with a new mare freshly shod, he says "adieu" at the bridge, and then, for the second time in as many months, William is running from the law:

March 24: Fled Sheriff.

As he escapes, aiming back into those mountains, I wonder if he feels like he's leaving his home or returning to it. Does he long to see the tip of Grandfather Mountain rising up from nowhere as he pushes north? Or does he think on those green fields, the wet heat behind him—of Caleb, of his father, of Mary Norwood? Maybe nowhere feels like home anymore. He spends his days with children and his nights poking around looking for a sleepover. He has a bag always packed, items strewn around the county. Women at every corner. He's nearly thirty. He ought to be married, a kid on his knee, a wide fireplace at his feet. He rides on.

....

We said to people that we'd come home after a decade, but I wondered if that was quite right. What of all the homes we'd tried to make along the way, each of the handful of partially filled houses we occupied? If I was honest, I never truly gave myself to those places, always held something back even as we registered cars and made friends. Our return to the Blue Ridge felt permanent in a way that I'd never experienced, tempting me to give it all over to this place.

Were we settling down? A second child would soon arrive; we were weighing school districts. It should have been terrifying, but somehow it wasn't. It wasn't seamless or comfortable: resettling the place that we were from was like hearing a song we couldn't quite remember the words to; so much was familiar, but enough had changed that we didn't know it by heart anymore. But the process of hunkering down, of considering the rest of our lives in one place didn't rattle me like it would have a few years before.

Part of what might have shaken me in the past was the anonymity of digging in. Something about *settling down* suggested a disappearing, like sand sinking to the bottom of a stream, lying there forever camouflaged—faded into the background. But when we returned, what I wanted was a way to disappear into the world around me. "Home," the Egyptian writer Naguib Mahfouz wrote, "is where all your attempts to escape cease."

In Charleston, I often answered the door with a gruffness that surprised me. I flung it open to Girl Scouts and Jehovah's Witnesses with the suspicion and narrowed eyes of a hermit. I never quite understood what came over me as I moved from reading comfortably on the couch to an angry old man at the door, a beat away from growling *get off my lawn* to wide-eyed eight-year-olds.

Eventually I realized there was never an unexpected knock in my childhood. In that Prestwood forest any car crunching down the dirt road could be heard long before it was seen. Sitting in the rhododendron or my bedroom, I perked up at the sound of a far-off approach. If no one was expected, we waited at the window to see who—or what—appeared. As a man off that land, I never acclimated to a world where someone might walk quietly up to my front door and put their hands on it.

I didn't like that about myself, didn't like that muscle memory tensed my body at the knocker, but I never quite unwound it. I didn't like, either, the way my body tightened when we moved to Iowa. I couldn't shake the strangeness of being so exposed in that ever-reaching landscape. No matter where we moved, my body missed the forests and the folds of mountains, places where one could vanish.

As boys, my cousins and I painted our faces in greens and browns and loosed Granddaddy's army coats from the closet; we practiced lying in ways to fade into the woods. We toyed with designs on our faces that might call to mind shadow and leaves. We worked at becoming nothing but earth.

Camouflage is itself a kind of code. It unsettles the brain's tendency to separate figure and ground in its deliberate attempt to hide any shape, to erase any clues that our brains ought to bring anything forward. Successful camouflage vanishes the contours of the object so that there is no figure to make whole. Everything within view is of a piece.

After the second baby was born, we bought a house in the woods, a few miles from Prestwood land. Just around a bend in the road waited the grave of my great-great-great-great-great-great-grandfather, Abraham Kuykendall—the first in my family tree to settle this county. Of all the houses we'd lived in—from the adobe box in cobblestoned Honduras to the drafty farmhouse in Iowa—the new house felt the most comfortable, not because of the bathroom design or bedroom layout, but because we were surrounded in forest. We were hidden, and that, finally, felt like home.

24

Not long after William returns to North Carolina, he sees Andrew Baird at Flanagan's. That's when he learns that Andrew has asked Nancy Jr. to marry him. Nancy is only eighteen—the little sister who packed up with William, who refused to stay behind with Martha and Ruth and TP, and now she has said yes to Andrew Baird and will be married next month. She'll leave this house they share with Mother and start her own. "Hell Hell Hell Hell Hell," William scribbles when he's back where he's comfortable, at his desk alone.

He doesn't leave the house for three days.

The wedding is big, at Colonel Baird's grand house on May Day. Little Nancy Prestwood becomes Nancy Baird in front of what feels like the whole settlement of Tucker. William must smile as the couple looks at one another. Andrew is, after all, not a bad man. A little too sure of himself, a little stiff perhaps, a little too reliant on the status of his uncle—the colonel, the former state senator, the iron works owner. But he works the field like anybody else. He'll treat Nancy well. And, surely William is thinking of what this might allow him, this familial connection to wealth and power after leaving it all behind in South Carolina. But he must also feel it as he sees his little sister suddenly as a woman, as a wife. He feels his age. His aloneness.

So he drinks. The hope of the wedding takes him over. He decides he's in love with Andrew's cousin, Elizabeth. He lets loose.

> **May 1:** Wedding, Col. Baird's. Love Eliz. Baird.

He sets out to find her the next day.

> **May 2:** Went Phebe Baird and Elisha. Had pleasure walking with Eliz. Baird. Nt. Binah.

But at the end of the day, he is where he always seems to be—using Binah in secret. Seeing in her claimed body anything he wants, everything he wants. A means to an end. A quick release. An escape. Control. His sister is married, he won't call on Elizabeth again, and he falls asleep in his mother's house alone.

....

I'd heard over and over that pregnant mothers nest: painting nurseries in the dead of night, buying a year's supply of toilet paper on a whim. But none of this happened to Sarah. When she was pregnant with Abe, she didn't line up DIY projects every weekend or pile the closet full of baby clothes. In fact, we had just ordered a car seat when her water broke.

This wasn't supposed to happen. Abe wasn't due for over a month. But one evening, the day before the spring equinox, I made a joke. She laughed. And then a baby was on the way.

I walked circles around our small house. "We should go," I said over and over. Meanwhile, while she waited for the doctor to call back and confirm that the wet spot on the couch meant a baby, Sarah squeezed months' worth of nesting into an hour: she washed towels, changed the sheets, cleaned the kitchen. That morning, she had decided to load up on groceries, including bizarre impulse buys: Lucky Charms, Rocky Road ice cream, Oreos. I came home wide-eyed and giddy at the abundance of food and sugar. Then, her water broke, and I wondered if she knew something I didn't.

As she packed snacks for the hospital and threw away expired items from the fridge, I wondered to myself how she could be doing chores when a flesh-and-blood baby inside her body was working its way into the world. I'd come back from a run before the couch incident, and I hadn't stopped sweating since. She finally suggested I take a shower instead of completing my ninth round trip through the house.

I obliged, but I wondered if the world had gone upside down. In our marriage, I am the calm one, the one who falls asleep without flinching while she worries about tomorrow's work assignment. I'm the everything-works-out, hand-patter in the relationship. So as I allowed her to usher me into the bathroom with a steady hand on my back, I wondered just who was out of sorts, which one of us was in our right mind?

She cranked the timer on the dryer while I continued to pace, only now in the confined space of the bathroom. Before leaving me, she had turned on the water, so as I flitted back and forth in front of the mirror, my reflection was consumed by steam. Finally, I moved myself to the shower and stood still.

I wish that I could say I was worried about the weight of fatherhood, worried about broken promises and broken arms, worried about adolescence and male-pattern baldness, worried about the mind-blowing process that sends a human from inside the belly of another human. But I only thought—over and over—*we should be going; we need to go.*

The sound of the towels now flopping around in the dryer seemed to say, *we should stay.*

In the shower with a too-small baby coming for us, I felt my whole body pulled up, blurred past the present moment into somewhere else. It wasn't an out-of-body experience, exactly, but a fleeting eternal awareness, a calm too big to fit into the word *calm.* Nothing mattered, and yet I knew it would all be okay. As the water hit me, my body, from veins to brain synapses, settled into a softness. I don't know how long I stayed there, wherever there was, but I eventually returned. I dried off and surveyed the nursery, thinking about this house—with its freshly laundered towels and clean sheets—as the home of a child. Then we grabbed the Lucky Charms and left.

....

William is courting Peggy Franklin in 1817 when Binah has a child. He isn't there. He's been gone for days, surveying land and sleeping at Boone's. When he finally comes home on Monday, he hears: Binah had a child four days ago, the same day that Beache's old mare died.

He writes nothing of the baby's sex or size. About its parentage. Of Binah's health. No hearts or exclamation points. Only that he hears she had a child. Then he goes back to Boone's to help with the harvest.

The next month, in August, his sister Nancy loses a child.

William does not become an uncle. William is probably a father.

His mother moves out soon after. William helps her haul her things to the Baird land, where Nancy now lives with her husband. And suddenly William's got his own place, by virtue of sheer stuckness. Squatter's rights. He starts sleeping at home again.

Back in South Carolina, William's cousin Caleb has inherited the Coker plantation, pulling all that land and power into himself, all that land and power that William left behind. With his small inherited house, his modest garden out back, William has shaped himself a new world far in the mountains. And yet, most days after school, he walks to the Baird land to help his new brother-in-law, Andrew, split rails and pull fodder, just like he'd done with Caleb years before. And that Baird plot must feel something like home, reminiscent of the lowlands of South Carolina: wide fields of Black bodies forced to work. A place of terrible wealth.

The Baird land is the world of the colonel—an ironworker who came to North Carolina from New Jersey in the late eighteenth century, sucking up land in the vacuum of the new nation. He held more than half a million acres across western North Carolina, much of it wrapped up in a landholding company then. In 1795, he sold off four hundred thousand acres of the land "east of the Blue Ridge Mountains," to Tench Coxe, assistant to Alexander Hamilton, the then-secretary of the treasury. This was how, only a few decades after the Declaration of Independence, Colonel Baird opened the region to land speculation and grew rich. A self-made man.

His nephew, Andrew, may as well be his son. He calls him "Junior." And now William calls him brother. Overnight, William, the unmarried schoolteacher who left the power and money of his family to live in his mother's abandoned house, has become a part of the wealthiest family in Burke County. For a young surveyor crashing on couches, this connection to a man with the ear of the government and an eye on everyone's land could be life-changing.

Everything's looking up. William has his own place. He kills a possum. And, then, a few weeks after his mother has moved out, he meets ɜ.

....

Nowhere on William's pages does it say it in 1817, but Binah's boy's name is X3||3Ϛ. Willis Prestwood. I thought a lot about that name given to a baby on July 3, 1817, while I taught in Charleston. I thought a lot about the burden of names. The seats in my classrooms then were filled with old Charleston names—names William would have recognized: Ravenel, Calhoun, Aiken, Pinckney. But the bodies carrying those names weren't the white descendants of plantation wealth, but the Black men and women branded with a name centuries ago. And there they came out of the same Southern soil their descendants had been forced to turn to discuss Faulkner and Hurston in my class.

I wondered if Binah chose the name Willis or if that was taken from her, too. Was it her way of nodding at William, of letting everyone know the boy was his, the young white teacher and his enslaved mistress? Or was it merely a name, plucked from nowhere?

As I uncovered his pages—and what was left from his pages—I wondered about a lot I'd never know: Where did Binah have the child? Who attended to her? Was Mother there, watching over her shoulder, proud as the summer rain fell? Did she think of money when she saw the baby was a boy? Did William? Or did Binah deliver Willis to the world alone, screaming in the woods until another voice joined hers?

But mostly I wondered if that boy was William's. And what that would even mean if so.

25

Celia. ɜ. Celia. ɜ. Celia. ɜ. Even though William has been courting CR for some months and took a short-lived run at Jenny Wiseman, in March 1818, Celia becomes his everything. He visits her at home most nights. He takes her to cotton pickings. He sings to her. She sings back. ɜ becomes a mark of punctuation closing out nearly every day.

> **March 20:** Kept school. Hail. Lingle's, Bean's. Nt. Mave Clarke. Saw Celia.
>
> **March 24:** Kept School. Nt. Mave Clarke. Celia.
>
> **March 30:** Went Rader's. Nt. Mave Clarke. Celia.
>
> **March 31:** Went home. Come by AB. Home. [Sex with] Byner.

Even the appearance of William's father in mid-April doesn't shake him.

> **April 14:** Lingle. AB. Nt. Home. Saw my father.
>
> **April 16:** Went Celia.
>
> **April 19:** Cold. At singing. Celia.
>
> **April 24:** Celia. Home, work'd.
>
> **April 25:** Celia. Settled.

Settled, he writes. And he might be, settled in his decision to make this twenty-one-year-old woman the last woman he courts, settled to worry over his father no more. When Celia's around, he might consider the change in the air in the house—how he wants to breathe it, wants to keep breathing it.

> **May 5:** Home. Nancy had a daughter, died.

May 6: Child buried. Nt. Celia & home.

When he watches Nancy's second baby go into the ground, it's Celia by his side. When he goes home, steeped in grief, it's Celia there, holding his hand.

May 31: Rain. Celia.

June 4: Kept school. Celia.

June 5: Kept school. Celia pinch'd my nose.

June 15: To singing. Rain. Nt. Celia. Brot Celia to tears nearly.

He's not "trying a fuck" or "deviling" Celia. She's simply there, flirting, crying, comforting him. Once summer's here, their courtship speeds up:

June 21: Singing. Nt. Celia.

June 26: Kept school. Nt. Celia. All nt.

June 28: Celia. Nt. Celia.

August 16: Went singing. Celia. Sucked her bubbies.

Ten years ago, a young William dreamed of sucking bubbies, Rebecca Williamson's. He then only had love for Mary Norwood. He whined that he'd become a neuter if she didn't give him an answer. He waited, chaste, sometimes dreaming of other women. Then, he moved on, took off on a decade of womanizing. He writes nothing of regret, writes once of sorrow, so this confession to Celia one September night seemingly comes out of nowhere.

September 13: Celia. Told I wish I were a eunuch. She cried.

Is William ashamed of his sex life? Ashamed that he sucked the bubbies of the young woman with whom he hopes to settle, the woman who's still living at home with her mother, the woman he hopes might become the mother of his children? Ashamed, perhaps, of his body, of his urges? Does he think of *flesh*, of words he's surely read from Paul and heard called from pulpits from South Carolina to North Carolina: "the flesh is death" or "the flesh has desires against the spirit" or "the spirit is willing but the flesh is weak?" Does he long for a life of purity?

It passes. When the wind picks up a few days later, he finds Binah.

September 17: Wind. Celia. [Sex with] Biner. Nt. Home.

But he writes no more of Celia's bubbies. Only that he courts her at singings and frolics and cotton pickings. Jonathan Clarke has a battle royale. William gets a loom and a new watch. And then, on January 1819, TP shows up again.

January 7, 1819: Home. TP there. Went Boon. Nt. Biner.

Last time his father appeared, William disappeared to Boone's too. And as he seems to do at every difficult turn—Nancy's marriage, Mary Norwood's rejection, telling his girlfriend he wants to be a eunuch, the appearance of his estranged father from nowhere—he goes to Binah. He goes to Binah like someone might go for a run.

On Friday, he stays home with TP all day. Celia doesn't come over. Maybe he keeps her from TP. Maybe he has decided to simply spend time with his father, to reconnect. After TP leaves on Saturday, William fills his days with Celia again.

January 9: TP exit.

January 10: Celia. Nt. AB.

February 14: Went singing with Celia.

February 16: A.M. Felt Celia's cunt. Nt. Home. Windy.

And after Celia's brother's wedding on February 25, William is overtaken.

February 28: Went singing. Celia. Nt. Celia.

March 1: Come home. A.M. Felt Celia's cunt. She touched my prick. Snow.

March 3: C. Coffey's. Nt. Celia felt my prick.

March 7: Nancy sick. Nancy's child died. Nt. Celia felt my prick.

March 12: AB's. Nt. Celia. Cunt. Prick.

March 14: Celia. Nt. Celia prick.

March 27: Boon's. Nt. Celia. Pr.

April 1: AB's. Celia, etc. Home.

....

I never proposed to Sarah. She didn't propose to me. We'd been dating since high school, and after returning from a life abroad after college, we realized that we were ready. "Should we just get married?" one of us said. A few weeks later, we did.

The future waited blurry and unreachable. We were applying to graduate schools, and the competitive nature of MFA programs and law schools had revealed the real possibility that we'd wind up in different places just after saying *I do.* Making a home across multiple states didn't make sense, but we didn't care. We'd gone from kids holding hands in a gas station parking lot to adults navigating Salvadoran streets flush with automatic weapons and flowers. We'd broken up and been together, and now we knew we wanted the rest of our lives together.

Sorting out this togetherness would be the work of a lifetime, but in the very decision to start that work, we'd already come to understand something of the push and pull of independence and reliance in a marriage. Being together might mean moving apart. Love might mean being alone.

In the end, stars aligned and we landed in Iowa together, buying a century-old farmhouse in which to start a life. On our first Thanksgiving as a married couple, we burnt the turkey and dropped the dessert, leaving a shattered, sticky mess across the kitchen. We took a frigid walk into the wide-open, alien land just beyond town. It was perfect.

I still thought of home, of the crowded living room at Grandma's, of my cousins throwing rolls when our parents weren't looking, of the same jokes being trotted out just after lunch. But after cleaning lemon bars from the tile and taking Sarah's gloved hand in that sepia fall light, I knew this was home. Not the drafty house or persistent cornfields, but her nose turning red above the edge of a smile I could already see coming. It was too cliché to bear, certainly too cliché to say, but I warmed in that Iowa cold knowing that wherever we landed, from now until gray heads, we'd be okay.

Back in our house, we went our separate ways: Sarah upstairs to resume the never-ending studying law school required, and I sat down at my desk in search of words to tell myself what I'd learned.

....

In May, William sees an elephant. A week later, he sees a horse with gears. He visits a place called Turkey Cock. He's thirty-one years old, readying fields, recording nights of *etc.* with Celia. Life is good. Until C. Coffey puts him "in a jealous fit."

In a flash, he surely thinks of Nancy Powell, who vanished out from under him after months of courtship, who married the Husband boy before William could act. And, of course, he remembers Mary Norwood. Mary Norwood who waited for a year for something he couldn't give before marrying Abe Sellers in a flash. In William's wake are dozens of women, now married and settled down. And yet, even with his blood pressure raised and after a year of courting Celia, he makes no mention of marriage.

> **August 11:** Home. Lazy.
>
> **August 14:** Went store. Home. Joanna Clark's. Wilson's. Saw Lowdermilk court Celia. I was bad. Nt. Celia, etc.
>
> **August 15:** Celia, etc.
>
> **August 29:** P.M. Went Celia. Nt. Emission in her blessed body.

In September, the week after William kills a rattlesnake at the school, his mother lectures him. He's been here before: Mother telling him what to do with his life, to sell his land, to teach, to stay in his books. Surely she's pushing for marriage, for William to make an honest woman out of young Celia, to bring her grandchildren to love on. To do like his sister. Instead, he goes back to Binah.

> **September 8:** Pulled fodder. Binah, 7 P.M.
>
> **September 10:** Mill. Stupid.
>
> **September 12:** Home. Fuss Mother. Cut wood for Jer Cl.

During the next few months, Celia is scattered across William's pages—"Nt. Celia," "Lay with Celia," "Celia etc." "Celia etc." "Celia etc."—but less frequently. Yes, Mother, he's thinking about marriage, about the rest of his life, but he's also been sleeping away from home again, considering the world outside of his small place. He's been housing corn at Woods's, working for Colonel Baird. One night over at Baird's, he sees E. Raby. Maybe it was the way she smiled when she came in or the way she laughed at his usual lines, lines Celia no longer has need for. He has a go at her, wonders if she might be the one for him—or at least the one for tonight.

But he goes back to Celia the next day. *Celia etc.*

It might be cold feet, his hugging Peg Taylor at Hiram's one night in April. How long has it been since he smelled another woman? But it passes by the next day. Then he comes back to Celia, goes home with Celia, "Lay with Celia, etc." He will marry her. Next month, she will become his wife.

May 5, 1820: Miller's. Biner. Celia.

May 8: Plow'd (most drunk).

May 14: Went Bean's meeting, etc. Married.

26

I not only remember Grandma writing in the spiral-bound notebook open on her lap desk, framed by the window; I also remember her reading back through those pages like she was burning through a novel. It struck me odd then, this act of reading the past recorded in your own hand. As a kid, memory seemed too obvious to fret over. *Yesterday* was always within reach but never important. But now, even without a diary, I understand the urge to drop back into a moment, to find its mood and detail captured by my own eye, to pull myself back into the feeling of a day. "Remember what it was to be me," Joan Didion wrote of her notebook-keeping. Maybe it's why I'm writing now.

"Why are you reading those?" I asked her once when I was young.

"To remember," she said.

I wonder if William did this, too, reading back through his coded lines to remember what it felt like to be courting any pretty little thing who walked by. If he sometimes read to wrap himself anew in anger with his father, returning briefly to moments when TP barged in without warning or disappeared into his gin. To remember why he left everything he'd ever known to start over in a tiny place called Tucker on the edge of hazy mountains. To me, two centuries later, his short lines are flat, but to him, each word carved on his pages was layered, wrapped in clues to moods and smells. Every coded line was a wayback machine.

After she died, I read through Grandma's pages one afternoon. On the first page I open I find echoes of William; one of the entries simply reads, "Lazy." Overlaid across her page, I picture the transcription of William's life: "Home. Lazy."

She stopped writing in the diaries a few years before she died. I suspect her hands couldn't keep it up. In one of her last entries, she writes, "Have had a good time with many things after my last writing—wish I could read what I write."

I flip back to the previous entry—a month earlier—and find the handwriting shaky and small. She'd been sick. The power had gone out during a snowstorm.

But in this good-time entry, it's March, the weather is warming, and her hand is steady: "Abraham Ray was born March 20." My boy.

At her words, I'm thrown into a panicked shower, into Sarah's calmness after her water breaking, into Abe's tiny, yellow body in my arms in the middle of the night once we returned home. But I try to imagine this news from Grandma's chair, to learn of a great-grandson born hours away, on the coast. To know he's carrying her late husband's name as his middle name. To know he was small, redheaded like her mother. She records Abe's stats—length, weight—but she writes nothing else of the news. Only that he'd come and that Tim is taking her to church tomorrow.

I work my way into her diaries—starting in the 1970s, their quick capturing of everything: her father's death, my dad's basketball games, my birth. Eventually, I find my grandfather's death on her pages, and I weep on the floor in my office, her diaries in my lap.

As the words hit me, I feel my own grief again, from twenty years before, but I also feel hers—a woman already gone herself. By intercession, I feel the loss of that man, a husband. I also transpose the moment into my own life and imagine Sarah dying. Then, I'm mourning not only for myself, but also for my sons' loss of her, for their future children's loss of a grandmother.

Like William, Grandma records only the events, not the pain: times, who was present, what the nurse said. Granddaddy had gotten a haircut the day before he died. They'd eaten breakfast at Hardee's. That night, he took a turn after supper. An ambulance came, "the infection was in his blood."

In my memory of his death, he had gone into the hospital while I'd been playing in a basketball tournament an hour away. We'd driven straight to the hospital after the game, and he'd died not long after. Then I drove aimlessly through town. But Grandma's diaries make it clear that Granddaddy had entered the hospital the night before, that it hadn't looked good by 1:00 a.m., when they'd found the infection and the pneumonia and the dropping blood pressure. And yet, Dad had driven into Madison County to watch me play basketball that Friday night. I didn't know how bad things were then. He did.

The choice rises up in my head: my son's basketball game or my dad's death. It's a false dichotomy of course—in the end, he made it for both—but I'm washed over again flipping the pages, now in gratitude and grief for my father, who cheered in the stands while his dad faded away. *Let the dead bury the dead*, Jesus was fond of saying, and it's on an ever-growing list of bits of the Bible I can't wrap my head around. But knowing now that Dad had come to a gym in the middle of nowhere while his father was in the hospital feels instructive somehow, a life lesson that I hope I'll never have to unpack.

"He was having a hard time breathing—he passed away about 3:00 a.m."

The days that follow are filled with planning, taxes, eating. Granddaddy's family doctor calls and cries. His brother Leonard arrives—a moment I still remember vividly: an old man I'd never met walking into the yard as if from nowhere, and he looked so much like my grandfather that I felt certain, for a breath, that he'd been resurrected. The church was full, people sitting in the choir loft and the wings. "The service was wonderful. Linda taped it. Everybody come for supper."

....

On May 14, 1820, ⊐ becomes *Celia* on William's pages. He drops her sex symbol and instead gives her a name, her name, his name: Celia Prestwood. Not only that, he suddenly becomes one of those maddening newlyweds who refers to his new spouse as "my wife" at every moment in every conversation: the words charged with a grown-up shiver.

May 21: Brot Celia home.

May 24: Plow'd with my wife.

May 27: Yadkin. Nt. with wife.

June 5: Plow'd. Nt. Wife.

June 6: Ditto.

June 12: Twice got wife.

June 16: I and wife went her mothers.

June 20: Went after wife.

June 22: Went after Celia's bed.

It takes a month before the marital bliss begins to fade and for life to grow domestic and routine.

June 26: Plow'd

June 27: Plow'd

June 28: Plow'd

June 29: Plow'd

July 1: Plow'd. Went Celia's mothers.

July 2: I come home. Pouted.

July 6: Went after Celia.

July 7: Fuss.

It's also in July that William first writes of Binah's son, Willis. He's just turned three. The day after the boy's birthday, on the Fourth of July, William writes, "Willis scar'd by Man."

Of everything William leaves out of his recorded life, this detail stuck up enough to find a place. But there's nothing more—no mention of who the man was, about the stakes. Was it someone who meant to take him? Someone with a strange face, a menacing gait? Someone with a whip at the ready? What has Willis already learned about his place in the world, about whom to fear—men who look like William?

William goes back to plowing, planting corn, hauling wheat. He's trying to learn to be a husband. So far, it means farming, fighting, and taking Celia to see her mother. He's learning about Celia, too, of course. He learns, for example, that she's clairvoyant:

August 1: Sow'd buckwheat. Wife saw my spirit.

In October, William stops to see Willis. He writes nothing more of the visit, only that he'd gone to tell Clark his cows were out, eating up the corn, and he'd seen Willis after. The boy's steady on his feet now, talking. A miniature man, really—with expressions he'll wear his whole life. Maybe William sees the boy and imagines him as a man. Maybe he sees the boy and regrets his existence. Maybe he sees the boy and doesn't know what he feels, only that there's a Black boy before him who has his eyes, and there's no place in the world for that. Maybe he only nods at Willis and goes on his way.

When he leaves, he must see that Binah is again pregnant. When he arrives home, he doesn't know yet that Celia is, too.

....

The world was on fire when the new baby stopped breathing. Ezra, four months old, a replica of Sarah—olive skin and dark hair—was sleeping on the night of the 2016 election. Meanwhile, down the mountain in Chimney Rock, wildfires snaked through the forest.

I'd gone to bed, too. Sarah and I were sleeping in shifts, trying to string together enough stretches to not collapse in the daylight, so I closed the laptop with the map of states changing colors, more turning red than should be turning red, and let the guest room go dark.

When Sarah woke me hours later, Ezra was limp in her arms and she was frantic: "He's not breathing! He's not breathing!"

The wildfires didn't threaten us really. Lake Lure had been evacuated, but we were ten miles away; we breathed smoke when the wind turned. Firefighters from all over the country had set up camp around the burning mountainside, watching it, tending it. Ash fell like snow, and they said it would all die out soon. But across the border in Tennessee, where more than seventeen thousand acres would burn, the fires came with such a quickness that fourteen lives were taken in a flash.

Not long after I took him in my arms, Ezra came to. The light was on, and I was sitting up, my woozy head pushing me into an ocean. Sarah was pacing, spinning my head faster, and Ezra was smiling at us like nothing happened.

In the emergency room, with Ezra hooked up to a roomful of monitors, I couldn't help but hear about the election, about the now inevitable result. Couldn't help but hear the man through the thin walls saying, "I voted for him, but hell I never thought he'd win. I hope he knows what he's doing."

The doctors found nothing wrong. They diagnosed the evening as a BRUE: brief resolved unexplained event. A UFO.

When we left the hospital at 3:00 a.m., Ezra was asleep in his car seat, and Sarah couldn't believe I was thinking about a presidential election. Our son was alive. He'd stopped breathing and now was alive, and I was thinking about politics.

I might've been distracting myself from this taste of death, distracting myself from the inconceivably out-of-control nature of life by watching the states fall and commentators grow perplexed. Distracting myself from the brief glimpse of a life without this new baby. A life, too, without Abe. How could there be a world without these boys—these boys who hadn't existed a few years before? It felt—as it must feel to all parents—that they'd been here all along.

And yet, in the same breath, I was shell-shocked, torn down by the world we've brought these boys into, a world with white supremacy and pussy-grabbing masculinity exalted. As I carried my still-alive baby to the car, I was suddenly afraid for him—and he'd be the safest of us all: a white, middle-class boy. In the artificial light of the hospital parking lot, I wasn't afraid he'd be deported or called slurs at the grocery store. I was afraid for the world he'd see on display as his eyes took in more distance and color in coming months, for a world that would freely offer him so much power.

27

Hi All I am Virginia Presswood.

I stumbled upon this 2001 post on a message board one afternoon on Ancestry.com. She continued:

> *I am looking for the direct family connection between the African American Presswoods/Prestwoods living in Alabama and Mississippi and North Carolina to our Presswood/Prestwood Line. I have been trying to find the link and have had no luck!!*

In the two decades since she posted, a handful of other Presswoods and Prestwoods had responded to her request: their posts like flares shot up over time, sporadic and sparse.

> *i am a presswood with my fathers roots being from mississippi. i know that my grandfathers name was aaron. not much other information.* (July 12, 2002)

> *I am also a descendent of Cullen Presswood, through his son Robert.* (Nov. 24, 2002)

> *My father is Robert Presswood as well. Who knows we may be related.* (September 18, 2008)

The exchanges connected only a few dots for people. The theme of the board was absence. There were few, if any, records of Black family members in the antebellum South. Most people could track their family two generations back, and then there was nothing, only the black hole of slavery. In the posts, Great Migration stories took shape, families leaving the South in the '50s and landing in Chicago. One of the participants tracked the Prestwood family's entrance into the colonies from England in 1666, following their movements south in the seventeenth century, noting their ultimate slaveholding. He ended his post with these lines:

Unfortunately since we as slaves were never allowed to be family orientated we may never know. Love from your possible family in Chicago. A black man born in Mississippi. (April 4, 2010)

I could guess at those Prestwoods-turned-Presswoods. I knew William's aunt Ruth moved to Adams County, Mississippi, that some of his cousins and two of his sisters moved to Alabama. But Virginia's original question—how to connect the North Carolina Prestwoods with the Deep South Prestwoods—had to come back to William. He was the answer. Binah was the answer. Willis was the answer. Abraham, Hagar. A lost history.

I couldn't find a way to contact Virginia. The post was nearly twenty years old, and she'd left no information. Her account was inactive. She might not have been alive. Still, I browsed through social media uselessly, not sure what I'd write if I did find her. *Hi. My ancestor enslaved and may have impregnated your ancestor.*

Meanwhile, a House subcommittee held hearings about reparations on TV. I heard the usual arguments against: *I didn't do it.* On the other side, scholars and thinkers laid out the numbers of how slavery and Jim Crow—the systematic breaking of lives—shaped this country. "It was 150 years ago," Ta-Nehisi Coates said before the committee, "and it was right now." I thought of Virginia and Binah, of the lines that connect one generation to the next, of inheritance. Of forgiveness. Of punishment.

William had died in 1859 with nothing material to pass on. He left this earth in debt. His only belongings sold for $11.94. I was grateful for that, grateful no enslaved people were affixed forever to his will, that he had lost the power and wealth (or, maybe, for the love of God, the will) to enslave another person. But I knew that the land he'd sold his boys before he died, that the very words he stuck to these "pathetic little books" were held up by the short, tortured lives of Binah and Willis. Lives that couldn't leave behind land or pots and pans or diaries: lives that could only be lost, lives that were gone before they started. The little William passed on—some land and a cipher—was fashioned out of a system that took and took and took. And now I was left with his words—and one hundred acres of family land. And the descendants of Binah may never know her name.

So I wrote the little I knew on an old message board probably no one would read. "I am a white Prestwood in North Carolina. My ancestor had an ongoing sexual relationship with an enslaved woman named Binah. Her son's name was Willis.

"I'm sorry I don't know more."

....

The Gestalt principle of *continuity* claims that our brains relate objects arranged on a line, no matter their differences. When I tick off the names leading from me to William, I see a populated timeline in my brain, each person a dot on a straight line running from my body to his. A constellation of other lives waits in my past—babysitters, Sunday school teachers, family friends—but I connect the dots from William to me by a taut line of DNA, tracing the cause and effect from one life to the next, no matter the differences among us.

When I meet people with no sense of their genealogy—adoptees or immigrants or people whose histories have been taken—I second guess this continuity I'm imagining from one generation to the next in my life. Perhaps my active mind is merely inventing connections because we're all standing in a line, not because those people have shaped me any more than my third-grade teacher or a middle school crush.

I often hear people talk of their "found families," of the people they've chosen to be surrounded by, of the lives they've decided to share. Sometimes they have few useful connections to their biological families; sometimes they've had to sever every single one to stay healthy—or alive. That long table lined with food in Grandma's house felt necessary to me for most of my life. But now I know that it is a luxury born mostly out of luck—the fact that we have stayed put for generations and don't hate one another is downright miraculous.

I'd be a fully fleshed out man without that table. I'd not be the same version of me writing these words, but I'd find another table and manage another life. But when we gather in Grandma's house on Thanksgiving the year after she's left this world—the small space feeling both too empty and too tight for the tables and small children and growing bodies—I force myself to recognize the privilege of it. I don't *need* that rock house and those uncles and aunts and the land reaching toward the creek, holding my ancestors' houses and graves. But I have it. And few Americans will ever inhabit a space so haunted and alive.

Most Black people in America will never know their families beyond a couple generations, slavery still taking lives more than a century after emancipation.

They cannot sit down for dinner on land held for five generations, cannot walk to a cemetery across the creek after clearing the table to read headstones stretching back centuries. Everything that has shaped me or that I assume has shaped me—the lives and land under my feet—is absence for many Black Americans. The privilege I was born into waits in everything, even the dirt.

We left Grandma's spot at the head of the table empty and never spoke of her sentimentally, only made jokes about what she might have said, what she might've misheard. We passed corn from generation to generation down those folding tables borrowed from the church so that I could fill my sons' plates.

Of the classical principles of Gestalt, *closure* is the strongest, according to many psychologists and designers. More than our tendency to match objects by their likeness or proximity or symmetry or continuity, our brains work to fill in missing spaces—to complete the contours. More than any other unconscious work, it is this finishing the unfinished that primarily guides our brains toward the whole, that most easily brings the figure forward and pushes the ground back.

Reading William's pages, my brain does this work daily. I trace over all the empty places, all the lost entries and unrecorded acts to complete him (*Got 9 turkey eggs. Shall land and marry MN*). I connect the scattered dots of his life so that I might make him whole. I do this because it's natural but also because I want it. I want to know William as well as I can; I want the closure of understanding who he was and what he's done so that I can know what I should do with him now.

But I'll never know the lives around him that made him who he was—Mother, Celia, Binah, all the women he relegated to symbols. I only have what he's left on his recycled pages, and so I trace those dotted lines, no matter how erratic, to see who steps forward once it's filled in. Then I'll move on.

On Thanksgiving, we made our table whole by skipping Grandma's empty seat when Uncle Tim handed Uncle Danny the sweet potatoes. We left the space open but closed it off with each passing dish to keep everyone together, to keep everything moving. As we ate, the shape of our family held even as part of it passed away.

28

In January 1821, the arguments begin; Celia and Mother are both on his case:

> **January 1, 1821:** Went OH Powell. Wife and mother both give me lecture.
>
> **January 22:** Home. Fuss. Mother at me. And Celia.
>
> **February 19:** Sow'd wheat. Nt. Celia mad.

William is teaching and surveying most days. He's bought more instruments for his work, and business is coming all the time: Shell, Braswell, Harshaw, Fogelman, Coffey. He's measuring and making maps most weeks.

Binah has a child on the first of April. This time, William records the event on the day. He was teaching. He does not write the child's name.

(Her name is Sylvia.)

> **April 8:** Home. Fuss Mother.
>
> **April 9:** Rain. Home.
>
> **April 10:** Home.

Celia delivers a baby in June, at 1:45 pm. William writes the child's name in his cipher: Evander. He drinks whisky.

He doesn't know Evander won't make it past his forty-second birthday, that he'll die in a Union prison and be put in the ground hundreds of miles from here. He only knows that there's a baby in this house, and he's a father.

(Was he already a father?)

A month later, William sees tumblebugs fucking. He writes that Evander rolls over, but that doesn't seem possible for months yet. Just as having sex with Celia the next month ought to be impossible, barely a month after childbirth. But it's here, set in ciphered stone.

William sees a solar eclipse in August, on a day when he's writing a letter for Miller. Then the rain comes on, and William stays home to take more time to read. He bottoms a chair and breaks his watch.

The other women in William's life have gone. No other symbols appear at night, only Celia's name amid the plowing and teaching and corn shucking. William has a mother-in-law who is around more than he wishes, but he is faithful, and his life has slowed to a predictable pattern:

> **December 29, 1821:** Sow'd & Survey'd. Nt. M. Cl. [Mave Clark, mother-in-law]

He farms, measures, and takes Celia round to see her mother in the evenings, their new baby boy in her arms. He settles down.

> **June 22, 1822:** Made easy chair.

....

I first felt the allure of settling down on a late bus from the coast in Costa Rica. It didn't make sense. I was twenty-one, far from home and responsibility. A pretty girl had taken the seat beside me, and the bus rumbled through pastureland toward the shiny lights of a capital city. The whole world waited.

As the sun began to drop and wash everything in sepia, I watched the "living fences" fly by. I was obsessed with the audacity of those Costa Rican fences. The soil was so rich that farmers had learned they could simply lop off branches from a tree, stick them in the ground and string them with wire, and the branches would continue to sprout, despite being separated from the trunk.

The girl beside me was studying to be a teacher. I was reading a novel by a Costa Rican writer she liked, Fernando Contreras Castro, so we chatted in my nascent Spanish as the country blew by. She was returning to her small town along the route, and I was on my way back to San José, where I studied.

At some point, I turned back to the window to watch those stubbornly alive fences and was surprised to feel her body leaning into mine. We'd made polite conversation for an hour, but I didn't know enough Spanish to flirt. I don't remember having any interest to flirt. We talked about books and teaching and landscape, but then, she crossed the invisible line between our seats and fell asleep on my shoulder, her leg pressed perfectly into mine.

I liked it. Yes, she was pretty, but that wasn't the point. The point was that I relaxed my body so she could sleep, softened it to hold her better, and then I imagined this girl and I were on our way back to her small town, where she'd one day be a teacher. Her mother would show me how to make tortillas and tease me about my accent. The girl and I would sit on a porch—in just this position—after a not-so-long day, talking about nothing as that very same sun dropped behind those cows and displaced branches. We'd go inside to our small bed in our small house in our small town and fall asleep until birds called us up. Then we'd start all over.

I was young and free and on my way to a city of clubs and museums, but suddenly I wanted nothing more than to climb off that bus when we reached the dirt road to her town. To carry her bag for her and never look back.

We didn't walk hand in hand into the sunset. She stood, collected her bag, and disappeared. But once the bus rushed on, I somehow knew I wanted to fashion a life rooted in staying put. I wanted to graft my branch back onto the trunk instead of enjoying whatever small buds on the road, alone. I knew then that I would come back home—not right yet and not for some years, but I knew I would. I wanted a settled life; I wanted that Prestwood land. I wanted to marry Sarah and sit on a porch and watch the sun fall. I wanted to adjust my body just so and wait for the world to grow up around us.

29

Cicero McAmy is born just after the new year, William and Celia's second boy. He comes into 1823 at 11:25 a.m.; the next day, William sits to write a second entry in a new notebook—written in plaintext, under the heading "Advice to My Sons."

My sons court not popularity but always rise by your virtue and merit.

A family of four: William and Celia and their two young boys in 1823. It's barely two weeks after Cicero's birth that William records sex with Celia—"Went Mother with Evander. Fuck'd Celia." And so it is that William's family grows and grows. With this insatiability.

Robert is born the next year. Celia has a daughter, Polly, two years after, in 1826:

> **January 30:** Kept school. Celia had a girl (9 PM).
>
> **February 5:** Home, etc. Woods.
>
> **February 7:** Kept school.
>
> **February 8:** Kept school.
>
> **February 9:** Kept school.
>
> **February 16:** Fuck'd Celia.
>
> **February 17:** Survey'd for Tomson
>
> **February 18:** Survey'd for Rader
>
> **February 19:** Home. Rain. Fuck'd Celia.

William and Celia are amassing a brood. He writes little of them. Evander (now almost five) is sick in April. Otherwise, the children fade into the background of William's recorded life. He notes that his ax has been fixed, that

Boone's dog bites him, that his goat dies. But mostly, William's life is now filled with "Dittos" (T^2), tracking endless days of keeping school and surveying. And amid it all, he and Celia fuss. A baby is crying somewhere. Evander has a runny nose. Robert and Cicero won't keep their hands off each other. The corn is already gone.

July 15: Fuss Celia. Fasted till nt.

July 16: Home. Children sick.

July 17: Kept school. Sick. Puked. Setzers blow'd up.

In August, William writes a letter to his father. He may simply be telling him that he'd seen an elk that week. Perhaps it's a laundry list of updates: new baby, great storms, a fixed watch. But the letter comes after a week of fights with Celia. "Hell fuss," William writes two days in a row. Perhaps he sees his father for the first time that week, and in a flash, he understands as much as he can what it might have been like to be a young Thomas Prestwood thirty years ago: fresh from war, an army of small children at his feet. Maybe Thomas's disappearing to the gin still over and over, his scatteredness, takes an understandable form in that week, and William writes to him from a place of empathy, surrounded by small children and a wife who just won't leave him be. Or maybe he writes desperate for advice.

As he scratches the letter to TP, he might wonder just what will come from the rest of his life—decades of ditto, weeks of hell fusses? Is this all that he has to look forward to? He sees a meteor the next month; he drinks jars of whiskey. He fusses. Then he goes after apples to make his own cider. His father's son.

....

In the summers, I disappeared for handfuls of days to teach in different parts of the country. Out there in the world, I slept past 6:00 a.m. and ate dinner later than 5:00 p.m. I changed no diapers, read no bedtime stories. I was alive.

I was also shrouded in guilt. I felt guilty when I woke at 8:00 and realized Sarah had already fed the children and readied their backpacks. I felt guilty when I called them to say good night just before I set off into some city to eat whatever I wanted. I felt guilty when I ignored the text message about a tantrum at home before I walked into a classroom to teach.

Even though I took the far-flung teaching gigs to help make ends meet, I couldn't figure out how to shake the guilt. That didn't keep me from laughing in a bar or turning off my alarm, however. I lived, for stretches of time, as a man without a family.

When I tried to calculate the balance of domestic duties in our house, I couldn't help but drop tasks onto a scale as if all items are created equal. I did the dishes. Sarah cooked. I did the laundry. She shopped for kids' clothes. When I piled up everything and stepped back, I thought we'd managed an even share of the load, but even with balanced scales, I couldn't shake the gendered packaging I still wrapped certain tasks in. When I cooked, I expected a gold star. When I cleaned the bathroom, I waited for someone to notice.

The agreed-upon arrangement of our house was that I got up for the nighttime wake-ups and handled mornings—breakfast, teeth-brushing, school drop-offs, and on and on. I fared better than Sarah on little sleep, so it was good for everyone involved that I stumbled into the kitchen at 6:00 a.m. to scramble the eggs. But no matter my education and the feminist writers standing on my bookshelves, I sometimes found myself feeling like I was doing Sarah a favor by tending to *her* children in the wee hours. Not that I was caring for my own kids because I'd brought them into this world. It was a recipe for resentment, and it was cooked in patriarchy.

What's more, I got the praise of the world for this work. Walking into a grocery store with a kid in my arms and another holding my hand brought with it shouts of my bravery, as if I'd just tiptoed through a minefield to save a bunny. In checkout lines and public libraries, I was forever told I was a good dad by older women who saw me doing the basic duties of parenthood alone in public and fawned. The smallest tasks brought with them a Purple Heart.

Neither of us came from families with so-called traditional gender arrangements in the home. It was true that the women did most of the cooking in my family, but they made most of the decisions, too. My grandfather did all of the laundry, all of the dishes. My mom handled my parents' money. I learned early on that being in a family meant pulling weight, no matter what it was.

And still, wired into me somewhere was a notion that some of the work of raising children and fashioning a home was women's work. It was hard to recognize the presence of this thinking until it was too late. I'd grumpily throw the dirty diaper into the bin because my brain had been tallying everything, calculating that this was the third dirty in a row that I'd handled.

If nothing else, being together since we were eighteen meant Sarah and I hold little back. We don't put on airs; we don't have to wonder what the other is thinking; we shoot straight. Most of the time. Somehow, after Ezra was born, the work of rearing children and not living in squalor increased fivefold. With two kids in the house, she and I found ourselves alone less and chores always waiting. As our already busy lives found ways to grow busier, these everyday tasks grew sharper edges. I felt passive aggression rising in my body, noticed a new ledger my brain created to count the number of times I changed the toilet paper rolls or mopped the kitchen.

This means that I, Modern Man—progressive, feminist, baby-strapped-to-my-chest-at-the-farmer's-market dad—had to work daily to slough off the sexism in my skin. And, simultaneously, to ignore the admiration launched at me precisely because of it. My body wanted to tell me I was a victim and the world wanted to tell me I was a hero, and I was only a man trying to keep his kids alive.

So I tried to ball up the scorecard in my head. I tried to be honest about my feelings. I tried to say *thank you* more. But I also left town to teach in a writing festival and bask in the temporary freedom. Then, in a blink, I was missing the dirty faces of two small boys eating oatmeal in the bleary morning light, and I was ready to wake at the crack of dawn and change a diaper and give more of myself away each day. I was ready to raise our boys into men who'd be better husbands and fathers than I could be.

30

In August 1827, William leaves. In his wake is Burke County and the noise of five children stretching out the walls of a small house. William is sleeping under the stars. "Mapp'd," he writes for days on end. Or, sometimes, "plott'd." He's on horseback, winding into the mountains with his wye level and a man named Reuben Deaver. Deaver is a boy, really—a twenty-one-year-old with little surveying experience, but he's ostensibly in charge of this operation, a government contract to survey Cherokee land. William is nearly forty, with two decades of surveying experience, but is listed as the boy's assistant as they set out farther west—*always rise by your virtue and merit.*

Even if he's the more talented sidekick, William needs this job right now. No hell fusses. No sick children. A steady paycheck. As they near Ellijay he may think about Evander and wonder if the boy has healed up from falling off his mare last week, wonder if he's curled up under that tree out back, out of view of the house, scratching away bark with the knife he ought not have. Or William may simply think about those ever-opening mountains and the whiskey in his bag. About open space and no one underfoot.

The land he's riding into is another country. Or was another country. A decade prior—and for centuries beforehand—the rising mountains had cradled the heart of the Cherokee nation: Nikwasi, the Mother Town. In 1819, the Cherokee people ceded the Mother Town and all land east of the Nantahala River as part of the Treaty of Washington. Then, as they'd been doing for decades, they shrank farther into the Smoky Mountains and watched white men carve roads and pastures out of their villages.

When the surveyors and settlers arrived in 1820, the state allowed them four hundred acres to claim and make something new. They argued about where this should be—the Watauga plains or a flat ridge. But in the end, they voted to simply set their new town down upon the Cherokee people's old one. Mother Town became Franklin, named after a white surveyor named Jesse Franklin.

In the middle of Mother Town stood a flat-topped mound. For at least a thousand years, the Cherokee people had built upon that mound in an architectural practice the anthropologist Christopher Rodning calls "emplacement." Atop the built-up land, the Cherokee people constructed townhouses and meeting places, only to later tear them down and build new ones on the same plot, a process of forever raising up new structures by founding them on old ones. But in 1819, they were forced out, and not long after, white settlers arrived to lay claim to what they felt sure was theirs.

In 1827, William and Reuben ride into a frontier town built around an abandoned ancestral mound. Two of the scattershot of houses have recently been converted to hotels, so they clop up to the newer of the two, owned by a man named Jesse Siler, and get to sleep. The next day, the men meet with Captain Love, the man who oversaw the original survey of Nikwasi in 1820, to make their plans. They're here to measure and map all of the land surrounding this burgeoning town. Love's original survey divided up the four hundred acres of Mother Town to create Franklin, but the state now wants everything else surveyed before being sold. Next year, the land will break free as its own county, a place named after another white man, Senator Nathaniel Macon. So William and Reuben gather their equipment and set out to find the edges of the ever-expanding America and pin them down.

Back home, Celia is pregnant, but out here, William is a man of the land. Every day, he and young Reuben stand in wide open spaces and consider the shape of the earth. He's happy about this isolation. When they decide to move hotels, toting everything into a hewn-log house erected by Irad Hightower, William finds himself bothered by the clatter there. People are drinking, townspeople want to discuss the map and the coming world, and William only wants back outside: "Plagued by people," he writes.

Then, he's back in the woods: "Work'd hard at mapping." For weeks he stares and makes notes; his diary is a long list of "mapp'd" and "do" (ditto). Only four times during the month of September does this pattern break: twice he writes about being "pester'd" by other people. But once, in mid-September, he shows a flash of missing home: "My dear wife heard from," he writes. A week later, he tries to head home, but he's met on the way by Baird, who sends him back to keep up the work.

William doesn't write about how he landed this job. It may well have come from the connections his sister's marriage to a Baird man has allowed. But William might have also landed here because of his perpetual experimenting and dreaming. Two years prior, William invented an instrument for surveying. News of this creation pops up briefly in newspapers through the region in November 1825: "Mr. T. Prestwood of Burke County has invented a *Mathematical Instrument*, by which he can take inaccessible distances!!!" The entry describes briefly how the device—something involving two sights, one of which is movable—works to quickly calculate distance. Maybe it's this invention that earns him his place mapmaking in Cherokee country; or perhaps it's simply the news of it across the state that catches someone's eye.

When I discovered the newspaper entry of William's invention, I wanted to call up Nathaniel Browder—now forty years dead—to tell him that William did sometimes *rise by his merit*, that this advice he gave his sons wasn't, as Browder called it, "a flaw'd philosophy." Then again, William put no patent on the invention; there's no surveying tool called a Prestwood. All it got him was a paragraph in the newspaper and a job on the frontier, where he's an overqualified assistant who'll receive none of the credit. "Thus," Browder wrote in his introduction, "an unordinary man went through life with modest notification."

It's cold when William and Reuben finish the work—210,552 acres measured and marked—early in October. On the second night of his journey home, William stays with his uncle Jonathan, who has also made a life in North Carolina, leaving South Carolina to build a house in Reems Creek, near Asheville. None of them knows then that Uncle Jonathan's neighbor will soon raise up a boy named Zebulon who'll be the governor of this state in its darkest, bloodiest time. It takes William five days to descend to home. Once he's back, he writes nothing. And then, six days after his return, Celia has a son at 4:00 a.m. They name the child Fabius.

At 4:00 on that morning, it is inconceivable that this baby will die in a faraway prison, captured by other Americans at Gettysburg, fighting in a war overseen by the as-yet-unborn Zebulon Vance. It's equally inconceivable that this baby will one day father a boy named Asbury, who'll raise a son named Albert, who'll grow up a daughter named Betty and a stray named Ray, and together, they'll bring a houseful of boys up from the dirt, one of whom will be my father, so that I can sit at this desk on a bright summer day and contemplate Fabius's birth because of symbols scratched onto a tossed-away page: ϟ4|35 [5ſ5ς27.

In 1827, when William holds the boy in the dark of morning, his mind might still be flooded with equations of rising land and his skin still taut with that mountain chill, but with a baby in his arms and children at his feet and corn to put up, he's home.

Dear William:

I took my oldest boy to see the eclipse. I wasn't expecting the chill. I knew to wait for darkness, but the sudden coolness in August shook me.

We lay in the grass, Abe and I, alongside college students and English professors, waiting for the sun to be swallowed up. We were on my campus—a place you might have known, once the Cherokee village of Two Sparrows Town, within Cullowhee, but now covered up with buildings. Abe couldn't contain himself, hollering and running around as the moon squeezed the light out of the day. Thousands of students roared as the sun vanished. My skin bubbled. It was beautiful and apocalyptic.

I won't forget that image of him with a flashlight in the middle of a summer day as the whole earth seemed to yell in gratitude for astronomical timing, for darkness. Or maybe I will and that's why I'm putting it down here for you, for me. To keep it. But here's what else: all morning that kid was a grown man. He's five, but when we set out from my office to find lunch, he trotted off ahead of me, skipping through the students like he had the keys to the place in his tiny shorts. He trusted I was behind him. Trusted everyone around him. I couldn't, of course, escape the flash-forward image of him as a twenty-year-old strolling through a college campus across the country, far from me. It was beautiful and apocalyptic.

An eclipse like this won't pass overhead again in my lifetime. Maybe in Abe's, if he lives into old age. Not for nearly a hundred years had a solar eclipse been visible across the entire country like this, and our patch of the mountains stood perfectly beneath the many alignments that needed to take place for the sun to be swallowed up entirely. The Great American Eclipse, the newspapers started calling it because the path of its total darkness stretched across America. Not since 1776—since before you were born—has that happened, William. Not since this place was first calling itself a country and the piece of land where Abe and I lay was a Cherokee town with a townhouse emplaced upon generations of previous townhouses. We canceled classes; people drove here from across the country to wait for darkness.

I wonder what you might have told me about the eclipse as the moon crept in. Maybe it would have reminded you of the eclipse from 1822, when you worked in the orchard and the creek threatened to flood. Or of the one in 1831, a few days after Evander's mare died. You could have told me how I might calculate how quickly the moon could fall to earth, by multiplying the sidereal revolution by .176776 and subtracting .752575.

You saw so many eclipses, documented so many in your life. I wonder: were you lucky or prepared? Did you know they were coming or were you simply out there, digging potatoes, when the earth grew cold? What would it feel like to witness something so unnatural alone in a field?

But what I want to tell you is about the shared wonder. About walking into the eerie unknown with Abe, both of us aghast. About being unsure and shaken together. I thought of you, too. Not only of your many eclipses and your calculations, but of the days after Evander, your firstborn, came into the world. It was June. You were thirty-three and now a father. I'd like to think you cried, that you and Celia locked eyes and understood, if only in your bones, how the world had changed.

I thought of the eclipse you saw the next month. Had the world changed for you after that late night in June? Did you see it somehow fuller, notice more, think about it from the eyes of a baby who carried your DNA? Is this everything you wanted—a house with a wife and a baby, steady work?

But I know, of course, about Willis. About Binah. About Sylvia. I know of so much that's left out of your recorded life now, the black spots, the empty sections—everything you wanted to forget. I had some time to think about what's left unsaid in the middle-of-the-day dark of the eclipse. There weren't words to capture it, really. In fact, there was nothing to capture—it was an absence we'd witnessed, the loss of light. But that's something, too—loss—and so I'm putting all of this down here for you to know.

Because I read your pages while knowing much of your future, I know you'll lose a child next year. I'm sorry, William. It's an uncomfortable power I have on this side of history. It makes Fabius's birth bittersweet when I read the words in your diary and can only think of someone chiseling a headstone years later. But I hope for you that there was only joy at 4:00 in morning. I know how your other boys will die in the Civil War, how Celia will leave this earth before you, how you'll lose yourself to obsession soon. But for now I want you to be happy.

Having this future knowledge makes me greedy. I want what you've held back from your pages, what you've disappeared into white space. I want to know it all—to be the omniscient narrator of your life. What, for example, are you running from, William? Tell me, why did you flee the sheriff in South Carolina? Why do you dream the law is at your heels? What do you fear back home? What is catching up with you just as you start settling down?

PART V

7583γ4ς

Natives

♐♒ *Advice for My Sons* ♌♒

November 6, 1822

My son before you do an act consider our Savior's Golden Rule, viz, Do so you would be done by. Never do anything that would wound your conscience or you would be ashamed by afterwards.

31

William outran me just after my great-great-great-grandfather Fabius was born. He became a man in his forties, leaving me back here in my thirties to watch him ride into the final third of his life, children spreading out behind him and death watching from the shadows. Since cracking open his life, I'd gone from patting his lovestruck head to empathizing with his domestic adjustments. But when he returned from his mapmaking trip in the mountains and held my newborn ancestor in his arms, he outpaced me. He was finally my elder, experiencing stages of life I'd not yet encountered. Over the next few decades—or one hundred pages of transcript—he'd marry off his children, lose his mother, become a grandfather, and I'd still be here at my desk, with my two small kids and mortgage and vasectomy, typing away.

I found myself seeing what was left of his life like a montage—a sped-up sequence of images rather than the scenes that opened up before me during the first hundred pages. This was partly because William grows terser, his entries crisp and flat, the white space more pervasive. "Settled into routines," Browder writes of this period. But I also moved quicker through the pages because I related less. When he was living out a life I couldn't quite put myself into, he fell deeper into the nineteenth century, further out of reach.

Until that point, I'd imagined his diaries as a kind of lens through which to see my life, a code to tell me where I come from and, perhaps, who I am. But what remained of his life started to feel more instructive than reflective, like a guidebook for what was to come. A map. I flipped back to his plaintext list of advice to his sons and decided to count myself one. I took in his words, ignoring the bald hypocrisy undercutting many of them (*do not seduce young girls*), and wondered what I might learn by watching him live out the rest of his days in a country creeping its way toward Civil War.

I passed under the massive Confederate flag on my way across North Carolina on an empty-sky summer day. I was driving to Raleigh to dig through archives, flying down the interstate thinking about two-hundred-year-old land grants and wills when I entered Burke County, William's world. As soon as I crossed the county line it was there, towering over me like a UFO.

Only there was nothing unidentified or foreign about it: I grew up in a world of Confederate flags. No one in my family wore rebel flag t-shirts or slapped stickers on their trucks, but plenty of boys I went to school with did. Plenty of girls, too. Growing up, I understood the flag to mean Southern. It was Dixie—sweet tea and grits—and a battle cry of redneckry—muddy boots and camo. I sensed, too, the in-your-face undercurrent of the image back then, but that prickliness always seemed directed at the *damn Yankees*—at some city dweller trying to tell us what to do.

But then I grew up. And I figured everyone else did, too. I saw fewer Confederate flags year after year; North Carolina voted for Obama in 2008. When we moved back to the South after years of living in Latin America and the Midwest, I rarely saw the battle flag; sometimes it flapped on a back-road house or decorated a vanity plate, but it had mostly vanished in the decades since my childhood, and that seemed right. Then came the 2016 election.

A fake-tanned, silver-spooned New Yorker brought all the Confederate flags out of the closet—and not to tell him to go back home, but as a show of support for him. It boggled the mind. Flags appeared in yards, were affixed to pickup trucks. *The South will rise again* in the form of a rich New Yorker.

So finding a rebel flag flying along a summery North Carolina road in 2018 didn't shock me—I drove past at least two every day on the way to campus—but the sheer size and the pseudo-official placement of this flag along the interstate, exactly at the county line, set me on my heels. It stood higher than the trees and waited so close to the highway that it seemed sanctioned, like a welcome sign to the town of Morganton.

I tried to imagine how I'd feel if I were a Black man alone in my car on my way to do dusty archival research in the capital and crested a hill to find that flag dominating the horizon of a four-lane highway. Or if I were a Black man living in Burke County, passing under the flag's shadow on my way home every day. As white me, I felt confused and angry and sad. But I felt no fear. There was no threat waving above me, but I wondered if a Black driver wouldn't immediately hear in the flag flapping the threatening call of *you don't belong here*.

Twenty miles later, an identical flag took over the skyline. *Get out of here*, this one waved at the other edge of the county—my ancestor's home bookended by hate.

In Raleigh, before I opened up estate files from the nineteenth century, I read about the Sons of the Confederate Veterans aiming to fly flags across the state, about a group calling itself Old North State Flaggers, its simple mission to "erect Large flagpoles on hwy." So far only those two flags, marking the entrance and exit of William's county, stood on I-40, but they had plans to lay claim to more land.

They wrote that the recent removal of Confederate statues had spurred this movement: if the country was going to tear down a stony Robert E. Lee, they'd raise up flags in his wake. But the real battle, it seemed to me as I opened folders to travel into the past, wasn't about statues and flags and regional loyalties; it was about citizenship, about who has the right to be here, to be American.

....

William usually documents how he votes each election cycle, but when he goes to Tucker's barn to cast a ballot in August 1828, he doesn't record any names on his pages, only writes "Election." No matter his vote, the Jacksonians make big gains in Congress, presaging that the fall's election will bring Andrew Jackson to power.

The next day he travels to Morganton and writes, "saw 7 dead negros."

Two weeks later: "Byner and Hanna free."

Those words straightened me up when I found them. *Byner free?* I started digging immediately, looking for any record to indicate Binah's emancipation. I wanted desperately to find something, some scrap of something showing me William had the wherewithal to rise above his times.

William may be Binah's enslaver, but she hasn't lived with him for more than a decade. When his mother moved out to follow his newly married sister onto Baird land in 1815, she took Binah with her. "Binah come" appears across William's pages in the years that follow. When William and Celia married, they moved in with his mother briefly, and I wonder sometimes about Celia, a twenty-one-year-old newlywed living with her mother-in-law and the enslaved woman her husband has taken to bed for a decade. Does she know? Could she not? Did they discuss bringing Binah into their matrimonial home? They don't.

Binah stays behind with William's mother once William and Celia set out to start their family.

Now, William is forty, a father of five with a steady job, and maybe he sees the evil for what it is. Perhaps, he watches his daughter Polly grow each day and considers everything taken from Binah since she was born, all the lives she could never lead. Or maybe, as "Binah come" shifted to "Binah and Willis come," William began to wonder about what their lives might be if they could keep right on walking, never fearing a whip or locked door.

Binah is a mother of at least four in 1828: Willis, Sylvia, Eliza, and Ira. I don't know if any or all of them are William's. I know that he stops chasing women after he marries Celia; no more sex symbols appear on his pages. Except Binah's. He still goes to her and she bears children.

In 1828, North Carolina law required a petition and $250 to free an enslaved person, but I don't find anything easily amid the court records indicating William has paid up. The law also required that she leave the state within ninety days, but three months later, I find "Binah come" on William's pages again. If she hasn't left, does that mean she isn't free? And if she is free, what of Willis and Sylvia and Eliza and Ira?

Two years earlier, William had written that Binah had come by with Hanna and someone he called Free Poll, suggesting freed Black people might live in or near Burke County, despite the law demanding they leave the state, but the truth is I don't know if William has the money or power or will to free Binah in 1828. I hold out hope, but there's no evidence the line "Byner free" means anything at all.

Here's what I wish were true: William votes against the Jacksonian candidates, seeing the potential violence Andrew Jackson's presidency might bring, sees the dead Black men and women on his way through Morganton, and realizes he needs to free Binah and her children as soon as he can. It takes a couple weeks to gather the money and documentation, but he rushes it, pulling any strings he can so that come September, she's free.

That's the story I want to build from snippets of text he left behind in August 1828, but there may be no story here, only flashes of potential amid the "dittos" and "school." Lots of *what could have been.* Even if she were free, what would freedom mean? She can't move across town, build herself a small house and garden with which to raise her kids. This country hasn't made any way for her to be free.

32

William's life changes in May 1829. Celia delivers a stillborn son. "It buried," he writes—the pronoun and passive voice zapping the emotion from the event, as if William might be protecting himself from grief. He drinks whisky at Setzer's. He gets in a fight with his mother-in-law. He has sex with Celia. He has sex with Binah.

But just before any of this happens, William discovers gold.

May 5: Found 2 gold mines.

May 13: Sudderth gold mines. Gold. Distracted.

He welcomes this distraction like a warm bath, stepping back into the gold mine two days after burying his newborn son, tunneling into the earth to find a flash of light. On his pages, he still fences turnips and gathers corn and hoes potatoes, but gold—ζ2lſ—crowds in more and more.

October 5: Dug potatoes

October 6: Dug for ζ2lſ. Found none.

Before long, ζ2lſ reads like a symbol for a mistress. Something to sneak off to after taking Evander and Cicero to school. Something he can't stay away from, no matter the circumstance or season.

December 16: Hunt ζ2lſ. Rain.

December 21: Dug for ζ2lſ.

December 22: Dug for ζ2lſ.

December 26: Hunt ζ2lſ. Found none. Rain

After the new year, he hunts gold after Mrs. Moody's funeral. He comes home empty-handed and fights with Celia. Not long after, she miscarries. On the vernal equinox, they're laying another child into the earth, and it's cold, despite the promise of spring. "Like'd to froze," he writes.

William doesn't lose himself. He carries on surveying and hoeing stubborn ground. But more and more he slips away, setting off to the mines at every chance. On his anniversary, he's hunting gold. In the rain, he's hunting gold. In pain with a toothache, he's hunting gold. He hires men to plow his field so he can make for the mines. "Fixing for gold," he writes in June, and I imagine him as a junky, searching for veins in the land to make his life better.

....

Gold is a noble metal. It worked politely through to the surface in North Carolina in a slow-rolling process: deep in the earth, some incalculable time before William or me, magma shot through solid rock, unsettling everything. As the magma cooled, it leaked elements and water, and soon, like cracking glass, thin veins stretched toward the earth's surface. In this spreading and melting, gold stuck to the edges, was deposited along the fissures creaking outward.

Its discovery in North Carolina sounds like the spin-off to *The Beverly Hillbillies.* Or the story of William's diaries. It goes something like this: in 1799 a twelve-year-old boy named Conrad Reed found a rock in a creek. The rock was big and kind of yellow and somehow heavier than other rocks, so he toted all seventeen pounds of it home. When he pulled it out to show his family, his dad said it looked pretty and yes by God that was the heaviest rock he'd ever held. So they put the strange thing to use: they dropped it back to the earth and made it a doorstop.

For three years the nugget—worth around a quarter of a million dollars today—held their door in Cabarrus County wide open. Then the dad reckoned he'd show it to a jeweler in Fayetteville just to see what it might be. The man paid him $3.50 for it even though it was truly worth $3,600. Still, the sound of the money in his pocket convinced him to hunt for more gold along the creek. Before long, he'd stumbled upon more nuggets, setting off America's first gold rush.

Until 1828, the North Carolina mountains were the only ones in the country revealing their gold. At first, men caught glimpses in the seams or dancing in the light splitting through creeks. They stepped into the earth's open veins and pawed around for the heavy gold. It's not hard to imagine William like some hillbilly stereotype—corncob pipe and a pan for sloshing around stones and sediments, knee-deep in water.

But by 1830, when William is overtaken by obsession, the gold operations had mostly converted to hard-rock mines bearing deeper into the ground. Men no longer hovered around the earth's quartz veins in hopes of spying a flash here or catching gold loosed by erosion there. Instead, they opened the earth: William likely toted a pick instead of a pan when he first stepped into Sudderth's mine in 1829 and lit the spark that would send him burrowing into the ground day after day in search of something he could rinse clean and see flicker like flames.

....

In December, Hanna, an enslaved woman who might have been free, dies. She's laid into the ground at Cannon's Meeting House just before Christmas. The refrain that I'm growing more comfortable with starts every sentence about Hanna: *I don't know.* I don't know who claimed to "own" her. I don't know who she was to William. I don't know why he visited with her a few days before she died. I don't know how Binah felt to have lost this name that showed up alongside hers so often on these pages: "Binah and Hanna come, Binah and Hanna come, Binah and Hanna free."

It sleets, it snows, and a solar eclipse darkens the sky just after Evander's mare dies. A few hundred miles away in Virginia, an enslaved man named Nat Turner sees that eclipse, too. Only, he knows what it means. It is a sign from God, a signal that the time is coming to let His people go—the sky becomes a Black man's hand grabbing the sun. Turner buys muskets; he huddles up with four other enslaved men to make plans; he watches the sky. Come summer, they will free the kidnapped and trafficked men and women of Southampton County. They will bring God's kingdom to earth.

But before any rebellion, Binah dies.

It is March, and William makes no mention of illness, doesn't write of seeing her in the days leading up to her death. He only writes "Byner died. Mother's." Maybe it comes suddenly. Maybe it has been coming all her life. In a flash, she's gone just before spring. Willis is thirteen, Sylvia nine. Their mother is buried somewhere in Burke County on March 18, 1831, the same day my mother will be born 125 years later.

After Binah dies, William takes Willis into that ground in search for ζ2|ſ.

May 9: Work'd gold.

May 10: Do Do

May 11: Do Do & Willis

May 12 & 13: Work'd gold & Willis

May 16: Work'd gold & Willis

May 19: Work'd gold & Willis

May 25: Work'd gold & Willis

May 26: Do Do Do. Frost

May 27: Do Do Do

May 30: Work'd gold & Willis. Store.

William surfaces occasionally to survey or to hunt a lost cow. He spends a day helping Celia with the washing. But most days he's inside the earth with Willis, hunting for something to change his life:

June 26: Divine gold.

33

I didn't know many Black kids growing up. The rural part of the county holding the Prestwood land was very white—there were five Black students in my elementary school. Back then, I heard the N-word from children and adults alike, but it was rarely deployed to describe a person. Often it described a thing. A version of baseball where we threw the ball at the person for an out was called N—ball. If something rundown was fixed up in an unorthodox way, a bumper reattached with wire or a treehouse doorknob made from a coat hanger, it was N—rigged. All these connotations of brokenness and backwardness I took in even as the father of one of my Black classmates coached my soccer team.

I might have once said we didn't really see race as kids, that those Black classmates weren't treated differently. I never once heard a racial epithet thrown at them; we didn't hesitate to play together. No one complained about Mr. Pepper coaching the soccer team. But, of course, I realize now that that version—my version—is an easy, privileged rewrite of a time and a place. That's me looking back on my life like I might look back on William's, cobbling the limited pieces together for the best, making of it what I want to be true.

As a young kid, I couldn't or wouldn't see any of the racism, casual or overt, around me. I somehow knew I should never say the N-word with any of my family in earshot, but I knew other kids could speak it freely in their yards. Like the Confederate flag, it floated around the county, and I accepted its presence.

When I look back on those early years, I realize my mom's sense of justice may have shaped me more than anything else. It surprises me now, in fact. Mom grew up across the creek from where I did. Her daddy drove a forklift at the textile plant; her mama taught in the same elementary school I attended. Mom and Dad married young, and she took classes at the technical college to become a dental hygienist. They built their house above my grandparents' and started a life.

After the 2016 election, in the scramble to understand what had happened, it became clear that the most predictable marker of a Trump voter was a white person living in relative racial isolation. Not far behind was not having a college degree. From a distance, that made sense: these voters feared everything they'd never seen—immigrants, Black Lives Matter protesters—would come take whatever they had. Mix in the delusions of a steady stream of cable news fearmongering and you can conceive of plenty of reasons to pull the lever for Trump, most of them driven by a sometimes subtle white supremacy.

Mom should fit that profile easily: she lived her whole life along Clear Creek in rural, white Fruitland, North Carolina. She didn't go off and take liberal studies classes in college, sitting alongside students from all over the world and complicating her worldview. She married her high school sweetheart, moved into the woods, and started cleaning teeth.

But nothing about her—especially her progressive, vegan life now—fits into a profile, and the memories I carry of her standing up to 1980s racism surprises me now. In one, I've gone to get a haircut at my favorite barbershop in town. I always walk away with bubble gum and a crewcut, usually after a soccer game at Jackson Park, and I like the smell of it there—the shaving cream and aftershave. But on the day in question, she marched me out the door before I could get my Super Bubble or my neck brushed.

I hadn't been paying attention inside, likely reliving moments from the soccer match earlier, but while I waited my turn, a Black man entered the shop looking for a cut. The barber, through gritted teeth, told the man to leave, saying he wouldn't cut a Black man's hair. So Mom snatched my hand and we left, too.

The more I sit with that scene now, the more I learn from it. The barbershop stood on the end of Seventh Ave., a traditionally Black portion of Hendersonville. Maybe the white barber didn't know how to cut a Black man's hair, but a Black person coming in looking for a cut couldn't have been a surprise. The bite in the barber's words revealed more than his unwillingness to give a haircut: the man he ran out that door wasn't really a man to him at all.

What's more—and more instructive, looking back—is that the barber was a man Mom had known her whole life. He lived not far from us, out in Fruitland. That small stand she took on a Saturday morning in Nowhere, North Carolina, wasn't her leading me out of an anonymous store to make a point. This was a neighbor: she would see this man for the rest of her life. But doing the right thing mattered more to her than saving face or niceties at a cookout, so we left and never came back.

The other moment that my memory filed away is on the land of a family we knew, not far from us. I've slept over, and when she comes to pick me up, she points at the lawn jockey by the house—the small statue of the Black boy holding a lantern—and says to the father's face, "This is terrible. You need to get rid of it." He laughs it off, and they carry on talking, but in the car, embarrassed by her, I ask what's wrong with the statue. I've never thought twice about the lawn jockeys that lined many roads and driveways around us. "They're racist," she says, and I don't ask more.

This family we knew better than the barber—we saw them on Sundays, spent time at each other's houses often. The lawn jockey—Jocko, I later learned it's called—didn't end the relationship, but Mom didn't shy away from speaking her piece, for calling out what she saw to be wrong, even to the face of a friend.

Fatherhood is nothing if not ample opportunity to worry over how each and every one of my actions or inactions might shape my kids. This process often sends me backwards to consider how I've been shaped by my parents, by throwaway moments and teachable ones alike. I haven't asked Mom if she remembers either of these two events, but they stand out to me: They retuned my eyes and ears to begin to notice the prejudice surrounding me, the prejudice within me.

More and more I wonder about how she arrived to this awareness and boldness without the two ingredients I presupposed most important: access and education. Her world had been a small, mostly white one, and yet she shook off the easy trappings of white power and bitterness. And then called them out.

The clearest through line I find is family: her parents insisting that everyone on God's green earth is equal no matter what the world sings. I think of my grandmother working her family's field as a kid, picking beans alongside the hired Black migrant workers in the 1950s, and I wonder how those long, hot days might have shaped her sense of the world. "Everybody worked," she told me, no matter if you were the ten-year-old daughter or the hired help. I think of my parents recently bumping into a Black classmate from high school and him recalling playing basketball at my grandparents' house on summer days and how safe it felt there, how my grandparents never treated him differently than anyone else. I want to think of that little Baptist church above Clear Creek that my parents grew up in, that I grew up in. And maybe I should, but some of the boys who were allowed to say the N-word went to that church, too, and I don't have to crack any book too far to see how the white American church has worked against racial equity for centuries, how many of its members are working against it even now.

Maybe tracing the history of my mom's decision to march me out of that barbershop doesn't matter. What matters is that she did, and now I have two small boys coming up in a world rippling with white nationalism. I have no excuse but to march them out of barbershops, too. To march them into the streets. But what's tempting is to protect them from it all, to bundle up the middle-class defenses and wrap our sons in them—to turn off the news in the car and avoid the subject of our broken country while we sing along to Raffi and roll into a Starbucks drive-through.

But this avoidance isn't protecting them; it's protecting me. I know in my bones I'd never call out a family friend about a racist yard ornament. I'd avoid the whole situation, maybe ghost the friendship. That kind of avoidance is making our life easier, but it's not preparing my sons to live in the world that's beyond our car, not preparing them to be men who'll help to change it.

....

I've been keeping myself busy rewriting William's life. In one version, he's broken by the death of Binah, by the life Binah couldn't lead, by all the contradictory feelings about her that he carried inside him: shame, desire, maybe something like love. He's broken knowing her children—his children?—have lost their mother so young. He'd be lost if his mother died, and he's forty-three years old, so he balls up all of the grief and guilt and fashions it into something useful. He aims it at Willis, thirteen years old—his voice changing, his body out of control, and his mother dead. William takes him out, thinking to busy the boy's mind with something else. The same way he does. Maybe he puts his arm around Willis as they walk into the dark mines alone, no one nearby to see this fatherly gesture with a boy he enslaved. Maybe he says something vague and comforting in this brief, tender moment: *it always gets better* or *she loved you and she's still with you* or *I'll free you like I did her.* Then they're side-by-side, wearing muscles out by smashing rock, busting up the earth so that his body, too, feels broken.

But, of course, just behind this version comes another, underwritten by my research into John Carson's mine, a few miles north of William in Brindletown. I know now that Carson's mine hummed along like a plantation, on the broken backs of thousands of enslaved men and women. When I first read ζ2lſ on William's pages I imagined it meant solitary work, something akin to surveying. I pictured him tramping through creeks, looking for cracks to open up. And maybe that was true early on, but in 1831, when Binah dies and he mines nearly every day, he's living amid a gold rush. Rich men like Carson have sent countless

Black bodies into the ground to make money. These mines are operations. So here's the version I fear: William takes Willis into the earth for an advantage. He can't compete with thousands of enslaved men, but maybe if he trains up Willis, he'll at least double his efforts. And, if it goes well, he'll be able to send Willis in his stead: Maybe Willis could dig all night while William sleeps, trading shifts in the morning with a bleary wave. Or maybe William wouldn't trade at all, maybe Willis works nonstop, upping the production until his young body quits. With Binah gone, what's another lost soul if it changes William's fortunes?

Both of these versions could be true simultaneously. He might genuinely want to comfort this motherless boy by taking him along. And he might genuinely want that free, forced labor. He might genuinely grieve for what is lost while he genuinely calculates ways to grow Willis's body stronger for future work. This can all be true at once, and this natural duplicitousness that we all carry in our skin makes the work of knowing—and loving—another person messy and dangerous.

Or maybe William thought none of this through when he walked to Sudderth's mine with Willis. With Binah gone, maybe he simply remembered those summer days of his twenties, rolling logs and digging fences with Binah back in South Carolina, talking about love, worrying over MN. Foggy with that memory and without any real planning, he winds up with Willis beside him in the mine, a misguided attempt to re-create what's lost. He searches for something to talk about while swinging the picks. He doesn't consider how he might be using this boy not only for mine labor but also for emotional support. He doesn't consider how his selfishness may have both brought Willis into the world and into this mine, trying to make himself feel better by reaching out for Binah and now for Willis. He doesn't consider that Willis, just like his mother, could never tell William *no.*

....

On August 13, something turns the sky nearly green. William doesn't write anything of this; maybe he doesn't notice while at the mill, but in Virginia, Nat Turner does. This strange sky is the sign he's been waiting for since the eclipse. He readies his small army of enslaved and free men, and they set a date: Next week, they will start a revolution.

William takes on some surveying jobs, traveling to McDowell County, where there just happens to be a thriving gold mine, for this work. But by Sunday, he's back home, sitting inside and watching the rain while Nat Turner steps outside and whistles everyone into action.

During the February eclipse, Turner heard his calling clearly: "I was told I should arise and prepare myself, and slay my enemies with their own weapons." So first they kill the man who claims to "own" him: Joseph Travis. They take his horses and weapons—and anything that might become a weapon—and scatter, moving from plantation to plantation to kill slaveholding families and to free enslaved people. After two days and fifty-five dead white bodies, the army and many militias descend upon Southampton County and exact revenge, first executing fifty-five Black people involved in the rebellion and then killing more than a hundred more Black men and women who have no link to the uprising. Turner vanishes.

The fear that takes hold in white people throughout the South after these two days in Virginia changes the country. Suddenly the math is terrifying—all those Black lives picking cotton and digging for gold and raising white children far outnumber the white men on porches, smoking pipes and watching the world come to them. White mobs take up arms for fear of Black mobs. They attack out of paranoia and anger, leaving lives scattered across the South. Floods of new legislation are passed quickly to make sure there will never be another Nat Turner—no educating, no gathering, no traveling. If the myth of the docile, content slave won't hold up on its own, they'll legislate it into existence.

The fears finally reach Burke County in October.

October 7, 1831: Alarm. Negro insurrection

Nat Turner is still in hiding. William has spent the past three days in the mines, but in a week, he's mustering with the militia, readying for whatever comes—not the British coming to reclaim what's theirs but the stolen Africans coming to claim themselves. He's at Tucker's for two days, standing in lines and awaiting orders, but then it passes and William goes back underground, alone. Work'd gold, work'd gold, work'd gold.

At the end of the month, Turner is captured in a cave, not far from where he'd lived. He's hanged days later in Jerusalem. "It's in God's hands now," he says before he dies. Then the executioner cuts off his head and war is coming.

Most historians agree that Nat Turner's two days of violence in Southampton County started, or at least hurried, the dark clouds rolling toward a civil war. It would be three decades in the making, but the storm was now forever coming.

34

Reading about Andrew Jackson during Donald Trump's first presidential term made for eerie research. The parallels between these two periods and these two men haven't gone unnoticed, of course—Trump even chose to hang a portrait of Andrew Jackson behind his desk in the Oval Office—but despite the bravado of their speeches and the xenophobia of their policies, the two men's histories couldn't be more different: Jackson came from nothing, rising in popularity and power after leading men in battle. Trump inherited everything, surrounding himself in gold, bankruptcies, and ever-younger women. And yet, both men entered the White House on populist waves, yelling about unfair, crooked establishments.

I knew little about Andrew Jackson before I started reading his biographies. I learned in elementary school he'd been born in North Carolina, so we proudly claimed him as ours. And later I learned his policies led to the Trail of Tears. Beyond those notches on a timeline, I only carried in my head that portrait of him with his strong chin and wild hair.

Naturally, he's more complicated. He helped to stop an early Civil War, pulling South Carolina back into the Union just as it threatened to leave. Unlike Trump's empty rhetoric about rooting out corruption and giving power to the common man, Jackson did enact corruption laws and flatten political power. He started a new political wing, which became the Democratic Party.

But like most men in power, Jackson was hungry. Trump hungered for attention, but Jackson craved land, a forever expanding country beyond his window. Trump's favorite talking point to earn applause became *the wall*—his steel barrier to protect our big, beautiful country. To keep what's ours, he wanted to keep everyone out. Jackson, instead, wanted growth, a country continually creeping west so that every white man could have land, a rifle, and a vote. Only, to do this, he needed to clear the way of the people who'd been living there for centuries. In the end, these different urges, separated by nearly two hundred years, produce similar results—removal of the "alien" to make way for the "real America."

....

"Hid Negro," William writes on April 13, 1833. It has been raining, and he has been sick, and the world is finally closing in.

If he knew this was coming, he wrote nothing of it. He dreamed about it plenty. He has dreamed about it since leaving South Carolina twenty years ago and fleeing the sheriff on every return, but nothing written in cipher in 1832 indicates that men with badges would soon come for Willis and Eliza and Ira and Harriet and John.

William spent 1832 working gold. A new baby is in the house, a boy named Sydney, born on New Year's Day. William spends the winter cutting wood with Willis, and then, like everyone else in Burke County, he's consumed by a murder trial in the spring. He sets aside the week to travel to Morganton to watch, but it's decided quickly: It only takes two days for the all-male jury to find Frankie Silver guilty of killing her husband with an ax, of dismembering his body, burning the pieces in the fireplace, and scattering his bones and ashes across their property. Frankie doesn't speak up. She makes no plea. She's eighteen, with an infant named Nancy waiting beyond the courtroom, and she's sentenced to death.

Sometime in the months that follow, Binah's daughter Sylvia dies. She was eleven, and probably William's daughter, but he writes nothing of her death on his pages. I wish that some pages were missing or water damaged in 1832 so that I could assume he documented Sylvia's life and death, that he sketched tiny hearts in the margins to capture what he felt—grief and shame. But every date is here and accounted for, and beside them, he writes that he killed a squirrel and fell in the river and mended his shoes. He gets drunk at Corpeny's.

Before the year ends, Willis gets in a fight with a white man named John Clonse. William offers no context, no details, only that he'd taught at the school and Willis had been in a fight.

Maybe this was it. Maybe it's this fight between an enslaved teenager and a white man that starts everything unraveling. Or maybe it's the demand for slave labor, the rising value of enslaved people. Or maybe it's astrological, stars aligning or eclipses passing by. Whatever the case, when 1833 comes, William knows the sheriff will, too.

35

I found the names of Binah's children online, on a scrap of a court record. Without that scrap, I would have never known Willis was Willis. I would have read his name on the transcribed pages and assumed him to be a friend or partner, not an enslaved boy. I wouldn't have been able to count Binah's children or know Sylvia died in 1832. I'd know little about the lives around William, the lives changed by William, if I only relied on his cipher.

But like all my digging around, I stumbled upon something unexpected one afternoon in my office. Online, I found the Race and Slavery Petitions Project—a multidecade effort at the University of North Carolina at Greensboro to collect and digitize petitions, to find and name enslaved people and their slavers. I typed that uncommon name into the search bar—Prestwood—and found William waiting there, though given the last name Presswood.

The snapshot of details on the page was largely empty, as is much of William's story. Most of the attributes—age, birth, plantations, literate, physical attributes—were blank. But some information was clearly listed: "white male" and "defendant." And beside the question "owned slaves?" I found a hyperlinked, as if emphatic, *yes.*

They were all waiting behind that click: "Biner, Willis, Sylvia (Silvy), Eliza, Harriet, Ira, and John," all listed by age on the next screen. In the farthest column, under the category Ownership Details, waited the same phrase repeated over and over: "In possession of. Disputed title."

That page was enough of a lead to send me chasing after a petition in 1833. I made phone calls, sent emails, and before long, I received a packet of pages in the mail—the longhand fight over the lives of Binah's children.

....

When the sheriff comes on April 24, he comes in the form of William's friend. In 1833, John Boone is the sheriff of Burke County, and his first year on the job has been rocky. Already he has arrested an eighteen-year-old woman for a grisly murder, and because of an inconsistent court system, she's been sitting in a Morganton jail for more than a year awaiting an execution date. And now he's arrived to his friend's house—the same man he trekked across the state with years before, who has crashed at his house too many times to mention—to demand he appear before a judge. And to take away his enslaved children.

April 24: Taken Negroes.

But John Boone doesn't take Willis. William won't tell John where Willis is. He refuses. Maybe John doesn't push, or maybe he threatens. Or maybe he doesn't care enough to ask. In any event, Eliza, Harriet, Ira, and John are taken to prison. Willis is a ghost.

....

It's William's sister Martha. She is, she claims, the rightful owner "of a certain negro girl slave called Biner." In her telling, her grandfather had given Binah to her, not William, and now she has the title to prove it. She's hired a lawyer and is suing her mother and brother for the rights to a dead woman and her children:

> Now at this time she has a good and valid title to the said negro girl with her increase which amount to six in number known by the following names Willis, Sylvia, Eliza, Harriet, Ira, and John that these negroes are in the possession of the said William Presswood and Nancy Presswood [*sic*] and are of the value of between eighteen hundred and two thousand dollars.

It's impossible to know what's brought this on after so many years. Maybe she needs the money. Her husband died a few years prior, and the price of an enslaved human is high in 1833. These children might fetch her $2,000—around $70,000 today—if she carts them back to Darlington County and sells them at auction.

Or maybe she's out for vengeance, betrayed by a mother and brother who left her behind in the South Carolina lowlands amid war. She was twenty-three and just married when William and their mother lit out for the mountains, abandoning her to a much older man with a stutter of a name: William Williams. In those early years, Martha had been William's confidante, his accomplice in luring Mary Norwood into his embrace, his late-night gossip partner. She was the one who had known back then, when she was eighteen and William twenty: "she hinted that Binah was my mistress."

She'd known all of William's secrets then, about MN and Binah and his forging passes for June. But when William left South Carolina, Martha disappeared from his pages and, it seems, his life. No more "Martha and I plotted." No more "hell fuss with Martha." No more twisted dreams that he'd married Martha. She vanished.

But in 1833 she's back, by proxy, coming to claim the children of William's "mistress": "to sue for and recover said negroes."

....

In the complaint, Martha claims that William and her mother are planning to take the children beyond state lines. I couldn't help it, but I felt—I still feel—a lift in my body at that line ("beyond the jurisdiction of the state and beyond the reach of the power of its courts"). Despite my best efforts and all that I've learnd, I'm still delusionally invested in filling any gap of information with the possibility that William might have been a man beyond his time and place.

Without meaning to, I'm already piecing together—again—this alternate narrative built of paper clips and chewing gum and shoestrings: William freed Binah. Binah died. Sylvia died. William didn't want the rest of the children, Binah's "increase," to live out their short lives as property, so he planned to free them. He can't afford to emancipate them all, so he and his mother make plans to take Willis, Eliza, Harriet, Ira, and John north. But Martha somehow catches wind. She sends James Mooney, Esq., into North Carolina to bring the children to her. In this timeline, there are clear villains and victims. A clear hero.

A more likely explanation is the attorney wants to convince the judge to send the sheriff to collect the children as soon as possible; the accusation, earnest or not, is that William will run with the children when he learns he's being sued. In this scenario, William is on the run not to take his children to freedom but to keep them all to himself. Greed squeezes in on their lives from all sides.

Or, maybe all of this is upside down. Perhaps Martha wants to free these children, has wanted to free Binah for years, but William took Binah by force in 1814. When he returned to South Carolina to visit, Martha sent the sheriff after him, but he always managed to evade capture and cross state lines. And now, finally, she has some documentation to gain ownership and emancipate this woman she grew up with and the children she's never met—lives held by her brother for so long. She doesn't even want compensation from her poor mother and brother, only "to recover the slaves specifically in as much as the said defendants are not worth anything."

Of course, there's no knowing any of this. What's irrefutable is that there are no heroes here. Only white people fighting over Black lives as if they're family heirlooms, a chaise lounge that every family member secretly pines for. There are young children without a mother, with a father who isn't really a father, and a whole country built to gobble them up.

36

When the children are taken by John Boone in April, William follows on horseback. He spends the night in Morganton, at the home of Jake Harshaw. He's not expected in court until September, but still he travels each day to Morganton, where the children are held, and every time lands at the Harshaws' to sit down with the men, Jake, Josh, and Jonathan.

The Harshaws are slavers. In 1833, they own more humans than nearly anyone in North Carolina. Soon, Josh will move west, Jonathan south, and they will stretch Harshaw plantations across the state, trafficking lives from end to end. William knows these men. He has done some surveying work for them, drunk whiskey on their porch. But these repeated visits in April and May stick out on his pages: His enslaved children are taken, so he seeks out the slavers.

He doesn't write why he goes to these men day after day. He may be asking for money, looking for a loan to pay the $2,000 bond to release them. The Harshaw men would, after all, understand the value of these locked-up lives. Or he may be seeking counsel, advice on legal strategy when navigating the slave trade. Or, perhaps, he's greasing the wheels, kissing the ring, going to the source of real power to try to keep what's his.

Meanwhile, he's stashed fifteen-year-old Willis somewhere in Burke County. The authorities can't find him; Sheriff John Boone hunts but reports back empty-handed to the judge: "[Willis] not found after diligent search & defendant William Preswood has refused to let him know where he is."

In early May, after his many sit-downs with the Harshaws, William "carries" Willis thirty miles to Bakers Mountain, maybe in a cart shrouded in burlap. Once there, he hides him—with a friend, perhaps, or in the woods alone, dressed in black. While he tries to disappear Willis there on Bakers Mountain, he could think of those nights back in South Carolina, peering out the window at men who've come to do him harm, urging Cato to stay quiet while the men demand him. Only, William shouldn't think of those nights. He's not on this mountain hiding a man escaping bondage, but hiding a boy he has bonded. William is, after all, what Willis should escape.

And, if he is going to think of those nights, he might ask what good did they do then? There was no camouflage or darkness complete enough to vanish Cato, no secret country into which Cato might be patriated. He was caught just after running from William's house, wrapped back up and strangled tight by this new country declaring itself free.

Days after William secrets Willis away on Bakers Mountain, Frankie Silver escapes the Morganton jail. Her father and uncle come for her, climbing in the basement window and opening her cell with false keys. They dress her in men's clothing and climb back into the night, riding deeper into the mountains.

All the while, William, too, descends into darkness: setting out into the mines day after day, chasing after the light that is ζ2|ſ.

....

"Interested readers may embellish it as they will," a 1984 *News and Observer* article about William's then-deciphered diaries instructs. It notes the "facts only" logging of his life, the lack of emotion or reflection. *Embellish* is a word that pains me as a nonfiction writer and teacher. It's launched at us, sometimes razor-tipped and other times sugarcoated, and the implication is always, "you make it up." If the fish in question isn't noteworthy, make it bigger. Make it a white whale. A tornado of sharks.

Maybe I'm overly sensitive, but the accusation seems to be that I'm inherently untrustworthy. I deal in half-truths; I write lazy fiction, fiction without imagination. But *embellish* in its roots has more to do with making something beautiful than it does making something from thin air. If I cling on to that original meaning, I happily claim the word: We nonfiction writers take the real world and make it pretty. *Making the ordinary extraordinary*, goes the call of the memoirist.

But with William's pages, there is, of course, my active mind at work making him "meaningfully whole." I imagine life into the negative space. I find his edges and erase his camouflage. I embellish, perhaps, but it's not making anything prettier.

Unlike William, Frankie Silver left behind scant facts, but her story has been embellished over and over since 1833. It's natural, the Gestalt principle tells us, this desire to make three-dimensional what is flat and unadorned. (Thirty years and thirty miles away, another convicted murderer will receive the same posthumous color treatment: Tom Dula, whose sung name is Tom Dooley, was hanged just outside of Burke County in 1868.)

The murkiness of Frankie's circumstances—rumors of her husband's abuse, her refusal to confess, public opinion that she should be released—leaves lots of gray for people to step into, to pour color into. Novels and songs and plays bring Frankie to life, reading between the thin lines. Tradition has long held that she recited a poem at the gallows, but it's unlikely she could read or write. What's left from court records and newspapers of 1832 and 1833 gives little. We know she was convicted, she escaped. She died.

And still there's the desire to make sense of it from nearly two centuries later. We're consumed by a need for understanding—not necessarily what happened but why. Or how. Or who. Something sends amateur historians and distant descendants back to that cabin on the edge of Burke County where the dismembered remains of Charlie Silver were found, burnt and buried. Is it mere curiosity? Too many true crime podcasts? Or something more essential, perhaps existential—a search to know just what lies buried in us, who we are or could be?

If we can find a flesh-and-blood Frankie Silver and know what she's done, what's been done to her, then we know something about ourselves. About our shared humanity. But not only that. We also learn something about this place we've created. She was sentenced to hanging without any evidence, without the legal authority to speak for herself, without any real deliberation. Like George Washington's cherry tree and Abraham Lincoln's pennies, this story, too, is our country: little Frankie Silver on her way to the gallows. Filling in her story, carving out holes for its justice and injustice, is an exercise in casting the narrative of America. Our nation of misfits, a people who fled our domineering father to make something on our own, has raised up systems robed in equality yet acting with anything but. How is it possible, the retelling of Frankie Silver's life usually asks, that a tiny teenage mother is sentenced to death like this?

....

Frankie disappears with her father and uncle in May. They make for the southern mountains, hiding Frankie in men's clothing, cutting her hair short, calling her Tommy. When I imagine them on the run, performing normalcy as they lead their wagon through towns, I always find myself settling on Isaiah Stewart, her father, as the central character. His little Frances, who'd been a squish of a thing in his arms only yesterday, is on her way to a hanging. A lawyer had assured them the court would never hang a woman, that the Supreme Court would reverse the sentence, and yet his child will be taken from this world in July, and there's nothing to be done.

But he has done—he's taken her through a window and toward those blue mountains. He will do whatever he can to save his girl's life. When I feel the pull into this story, it's there: a father trying to free his child.

Layer onto that the rumors that spin on now: that Charlie had been abusive, that Frankie had wanted to move closer to her parents, but he refused to let her leave the secluded cabin, that he came after her with a gun on that December night. If she killed Charlie Silver to protect herself, then good on her. If her tiny frame managed to get an axe across that big boy's neck as he came at her, then by God she deserves all the freedom this world has to give. If it comes down to it, it ought to be him, Isaiah, waiting on the gallows. He taught his daughter to take care of herself. Why should she be punished for being the woman he raised her to be?

So they run. Perhaps they're aiming as far west as the country spreads into North Carolina, pressing into the shrinking edge of Cherokee country, a place surveying tools haven't yet claimed, so that no one will ever know what they've left behind.

I do not think of William hiding Willis when I think of Isaiah and Frankie on the run. But I want to. I want to imagine the father of a biracial boy escaping into the mountains to keep him safe from a place that will never let him be free, but I know it's too easy, too selfish.

Still, William must fear Willis will be found when every sheriff in the region sends men onto the roads and into the woods looking for little Frankie Silver. Surely they'll turn up a teenage boy hiding on Bakers Mountain. William travels back to Morganton just after Frankie escapes, this time spending the night at Old Man Harshaw's house, the slaver patriarch. He's up to something.

Frankie is caught only eight days later. The story goes that as they passed through Rutherford County, her uncle said, "*Her* name is Tommy" to the inquiring sheriff. But "interested readers may embellish it as they will." All that's recorded in the newspaper in 1833 is that she had been captured passing as a man, returned to her cell, and chained to the floor to await the executioner.

A few weeks later, William writes, "Willis fool mother." Willis is back down from the mountain, perhaps still disguised and sneaking up on Nancy for a laugh. William and his mother stow Willis away somewhere nearby, content that Sheriff Boone is otherwise occupied, no longer looking high and low for a motherless boy. Then a summer storm comes on, and William sets off to see his brother-in-law Hiram, a plan hatching he'll not be able to undo.

37

It's not only the not-knowing that draws people to Frankie Silver, but it's also the claim that she was the first woman to be hanged in North Carolina. She becomes a societal shifting. A notch on a timeline. She wasn't, though. Black women had been hanged publicly by then, but no one is writing plays about those lost names; no one is embellishing those taken lives. There's barely an outline to fill in.

In my coloring, my embellishing of William's life, I find him in the flesh and blood. But the process of raising him from the dead is a constant reminder of the lives around him that are, too, our country and are, largely, vanished. There are so many lives surrounding him that will never be reassembled to be made meaningfully whole, will never be imagined into myth.

I know Willis is fifteen, that he likes to play practical jokes. He mines gold and fought John Clonse. But that's it. I don't even have enough lines to read between, not enough material to build him up, so he remains a haint of a boy, like his siblings, like his mother, floating around my ancestor, who is alive before my eyes. But maybe Willis was someone's father, is today someone's great-great-great-great grandfather.

What glares back at me while I pick through the past is the realization that, despite the shakiness of this new nation, no American system shifts unbalanced beneath William's feet as he passes his days hoeing corn and mining gold. All the other Americas—the Americas of Frankie Silver and Binah and Nat Turner and Tecumseh—fight for and against the country raising up around them, but it will never come after William. It will never come after me.

He may be sued. He may lose his enslaved children. He may not be paid his per diem for mapmaking in Macon County. But he slides smoothly through the machinery, just the right shape and color to glide along.

This is what I think of when I hear people around me complaining that we need to move on, that slavery was years ago, that they've never held slaves so why should they feel bad? Meanwhile, these same people obsess over Frankie Silver or whine about the removal of Confederate monuments. This is what I think of when white men cry over women in power or affirmative action or bathroom designations. Meanwhile, their histories are filled with people on the easy assembly line of American democracy, people like mine.

If building the narrative of William's life is to teach me anything about this country I was born into, it's that I come from a long line of ease. My people suffered and died and bled and went hungry, but they were never considered property. They were never kidnapped or forcefully separated from family members. They chose their lot and lived in a country made just for them, and I've inherited it all.

Maybe that's why when I uncover William's life, I want to find ways to make him into a man beyond his time, a man who takes a hammer to these unjust systems that benefit him, that will benefit me. I want to believe he saw these other Americas and fought for them, too. I want to discover him to be John Brown disguised as John Doe. But, I am realizing, I want this for me.

Finding William Prestwood to be a nineteenth-century outlier would make my life even easier. I could worry less about making myself into a good man, about fighting against injustice that will never affect me, about being a man beyond my time. I would be the son of a hero and wear his cape meaninglessly around town, stopping at Starbucks with my kid and ignoring the world burning around us. He would have done the work for me, and I could glide along that ready-made assembly line without a hint of guilt.

But he was not John Brown. He was a philandering surveyor who enslaved a woman and her family and started the long line of begets that became me.

....

I was zooming in on scans of nineteenth-century court documents on my computer when the technician fixing the internet tried to make conversation. "What kind of work are you doing there?" he asked to my back as the modem rebooted.

Outside the office, it was bright, a summer storm too far off to pay any mind. I stared out the window a little too long, fumbling for words to answer a straightforward question. There were dozens of answers, it turned out, but none of them was satisfying:

- Oh, this isn't really work.
- I'm looking for children.
- The thing is, I'm working out . . . something. What is it? Guilt?
- My ancestor probably fathered some children by an enslaved woman, and then his sister tried to take them away because they were worth a lot of money, but he and his mother fought her for ownership and so there should be a paper trail somewhere that might tell me where these children ended up.
- No, not exactly guilt. Maybe something more like unspooling the barbed wires of legacy. Does that make sense?
- What do you know about DNA?
- I don't know.
- You sound like you're from here. Who are your people? What do you know about them? About their pasts? Their sins?
- I don't know.
- I don't know.

Instead of offering any of these, I shifted the conversation entirely, the political pivot. I told him about the scalp laws I was discovering in the 1828 court minutes, about men bringing scalps of wolves and panthers "to open court" so that they may be paid for this work. Two dollars for a grown wolf; three dollars for a panther.

He told me about the foxes getting his chickens.

I went back on the hunt.

But after hours upon hours, I found only more empty spaces. Amid the court minutes and estate files and family trees stashed on microfiche and in dusty archives, I found no clear answers about Binah's children, only impenetrable questions. They appear in 1833, with names and ages, and then they're gone again from the record of American history.

What I do know is that Frankie Silver is hanged on July 12. "X2Ϭ57 [|7ζ," William writes: "woman hung."

I know that William and his mother respond to Martha's complaint. The long and short of their response is the legalese translation of *mine!* William's mother says the enslaved children are in her service but owned by William. That William never intended to take them from the state. That Martha has no claim to them.

William says he'd been gifted Binah in 1805 and that she is now dead, as is Sylvia. And, for what it's worth, Martha has known where he lives for years, so why now? Oh—and also—statute of limitations!

Despite these written defenses, William and his mother arrive in court on September 23, 1833. The children are brought, too, except Willis, "him not found." For five days, William writes "court" (ϟ2|L8). He often stays with the Harshaws at night. Then, on September 29, he writes "home," and it's all over.

But he gives no indication who won. No document I could turn up across the state does either. The paper trail dries up just before the September hearing. Or more likely, it was burnt up when many documents in Burke County were set aflame during the Civil War, and so William's fight with his sister in the Court of Equity over these five lives ends with an ellipsis. Fitting, perhaps, that even this bit of his life documented officially in black and white still manages to smear its way into a hazy gray in the end.

Did Martha haul Binah's children back to Darlington County? Did William cobble together enough money to satisfy her? Did the court side with him, a man known in the community, over this unknown widow from the coast? I have only guesses, only faint outlines to complete.

I know that William's cousin Caleb Coker dies back in South Carolina during the hearings. He was fifty-seven. I know that it rains on William on September 30. I know that a frost comes on October 3, just as William stacked the fodder. But the only hint of what might have happened to these children comes a week after the hearings when William travels to Morganton and then writes ζ28 74ζL24ς: "Got negroes."

The missing subject leaves something up in the air—*who got?*—but it seems that William collected Eliza, Harriet, Ira, and John and carried them back to his mother, back under his ownership. He has reclaimed these children of Binah's (these children of his?), but the event is barely a blip on his ciphered pages. If I hadn't stumbled across the names and the court records, I would have never known of this fight for these lives. I would have flown right by ϟ2|L8 because William is often in court, sometimes to testify, sometimes because he's been sued, sometimes to watch a young mother sentenced to death. On his pages, William carries on as if nothing has changed. And it probably hasn't:

November 1: Cut wood

November 2: Work'd bringing water to wash gold

November 9: Work'd fixing gold, etc. Rain.

November 10: Mother's.

November 11: School.

November 13: School. Stars fall.

. . . .

Only, there was this from one month before the hearings: [ϟ|. [4 ϟ2ϐ4.ς2|ʃ X3||3ς.

When I first read it, I wanted to find any other explanation for what seems to be there. I searched as many records as I could find. I reread the diaries in search of anything to undercut the most obvious interpretation. But I found nothing satisfying. Only those two damning words on August 13, 1833:ς2|ʃ X3||3ς.

38

A few years ago, Abe ate one of Ezra's puffs—a soft snack for mostly toothless toddlers. Immediately he looked up. He said he couldn't remember eating these when he was little and yet he remembered the taste. As the thing dissolved on his tongue, some sense memory pulled him back to his toddler years. Later, in his room, we found him looking through old pictures of himself and crying. "I'll never be that size again," he sobbed. He was six.

He's a sensitive kid and it was late and he was tired, but I get it. I feel it. I didn't know such an all-consuming empathy until these boys came into the world: Leaving a crying Ezra at preschool or seeing the fear in Abe's eyes when he's lost washes over me until I'm drowning. In some strange illogical intersession, I feel what they feel in my skin. It physically hurts.

Maybe some of this tidal wave of empathy is more particular to fathers and sons. I can find an access point to my sons' pain or fear or excitement in my own lived experience, implanted into my memory. The recklessness of crashing a bike into a tree or joy of throwing rocks into moving water for hours: I have these, too. They're filed away so that I'm momentarily shrunk and returned to some summer day on Prestwood land when my skin carried the sweet smell of sweat and my brain wanted only what it wanted in that moment.

From this overwhelming muscle memory, I try to find an empathy beyond my kids, too. I try to imagine being in the body of a stranger or friend the same as I feel the body of my boyhood when Abe hits a whiffle ball into the woods or Ezra skins his hands on the asphalt.

But the access points are often invisible, sometimes impenetrable in the lives of people who pass through the world differently than me. Perhaps the easy assembly line of my family history and the layers of privilege I embody will never situate me to feel the pain of someone on the margins, someone whose family was chewed up and spit out by this country. Maybe it shouldn't.

Maybe it's presumptuous to even want this access, to expect to understand something I'll never have to experience. And why should I? Is empathy a prerequisite for doing the right thing? For protecting the vulnerable and respecting every life?

"Empathy means realizing no trauma has discrete edges," Leslie Jamison writes. No one feeling is only one feeling. No one life is only one life. An honest empathy is one that is aware of its limitations, knowing you can't simply slip your feet into someone's shoes and head out for a stroll whenever you please. I'll never know what a Black woman in Burke County feels driving under those Confederate flags on the interstate every day. I can guess. I can ask. But I'll never feel it in my skin the way I feel the grass stain on Abe's knee. Maybe that's okay. Maybe living in a society means working for this awareness, this knowing that I'll never know, not truly. I'll simply trust that every life is complex and difficult and search for grace and justice at every turn.

But what of William? My study of his life has been a study in empathy. I've settled into his days as if one of Dickens's ghosts whisked me there, watching him grow old, worrying with him. Story does this naturally, of course. What is literature but a complex empathy chamber? The process of piecing together the narrative of his life has sucked me into it, but it's more than the sweep of story. I'm connected to him, even if by only a thin strand of DNA, so I pull up my experiences and ball them up so that I might somehow reform them into something resembling a nineteenth-century life.

But August 13, 1833, may be a bridge too far. I don't know why this is harder to wrestle with than so many other sins tucked away behind invented symbols, but it is. Maybe it's fatherhood. Maybe it's fear that it could have been me.

Maybe I don't need to empathize with William to watch him on his way to civil war and the grave, but when I sit back down to his pages, my head and heart lead me there anyway, trying to find a door in to understand him. But I smack into the wall of August 13 again and again and turn away.

....

From a random ancestry post that led to a newspaper article that led to a book, I tracked down Leslie Dula McKesson, the former dean of the community college in Burke County. She had retired from academia and then settled into genealogy, sorting out her own family trees and their roots not far from my own.

McKesson is a Black woman—a Black woman driving under those Confederate flags on the interstate—and her lineage reaches back to the Harshaw men William broke bread with day after day in 1833. Her great-great-grandmother Harriet had been sold by Jake Harshaw to a man named "Squire" Dula. In 1846, Squire's wife died at thirty-one, leaving him alone with six children—and an enslaved woman named Harriet.

Somehow, sometime Squire and Harriet come to live as something like husband and wife. Only, in this case, the "wife" was technically enslaved: "Of course, she could never be truly free," McKesson told me over the phone. Whatever it looked like, it's clear that the relationship wasn't the usual illicit affair—it was public and obvious, and it upset the community. Men conspired to undo whatever was happening in the Dula house. They took Harriet away and hid her.

Squire searched high and low, refusing to receive the message. He found her and brought her home, then built a separate house for her to live in, allowing that them sharing a house with their children might be too dangerous or too disruptive in nineteenth-century Burke County. He stayed in his house during the week and then went to hers on the weekends. They had more children.

After the Civil War, Squire, Harriet, and their children continued on together, and when Squire died, he left Harriet and the children land and money. McKesson, in fact, lives on that same land in Dulatown today.

The story McKesson pieced together was closer to what I wanted to find on William's pages. A white slaveholder with a heart, or some Hallmark special version of history. Of course even this story was more complicated. In her book, *Black and White*, McKesson steps into the gray, brushes away all the easy answers. But still, I would've taken Squire Dula over William Prestwood.

....

In a last-ditch effort to find Binah's children, I spit into a plastic tube and mail it away. I have just enough of a conspiracy theorist in me that I'd resisted giving my genetic code to a corporation, but I decided that if there was any chance a distant cousin could spring up, showing a connection to Binah, then it'd be worth whatever *Minority Report* scenario might be out there waiting.

Of course, to do any good, one of Binah's descendants would have to spit into a tube, too, and let 23andMe have its way with their double helixes. Still, it was worth it, so I spit and wait.

I wondered, too, about what else I'd find hidden in my body. A predisposition for some terrible disease? A variant that suggests I'd be a master fiddler if I took it up? I was curious about the letters in my skin, about the words written in me by the people who'd come before me. Who do they say I am?

....

On paper, Binah's children are lost after 1833. I searched everywhere I knew to search, but they were gone. Despite this absence, I learned a lot in archives. I know, for example, that Sheriff John Boone held eight enslaved people: Andrew, Dick, Elisha, Esther and her baby, Isaac, Lindy, and Wilson. I know that a man named James Murphy died, and his estate was settled in the year William went to court, selling 120 enslaved people in 1833. William's brother-in-law Hiram buys one: a woman named Mira. Plenty of lives were bought and sold in Burke County in 1833: John Avery sold a girl named Betsy. Avery Burgin bought a boy named Charles. A man named Avery was bought by Jeremiah Clarke.

I found names who appeared on William's pages all across the scattered records of chattel slavery in Burke County. Settlemires and Harshaws and Corpenings. Dirty hands everywhere. But I didn't find William and I couldn't find these children. There was some relief in that: He didn't buy more human lives.

Here is what I think I know, which is full of embellishment but void of beauty:

In the lead-up to the hearings, William makes plans with his brother-in-law Hiram Clark. William knows his sister is right: "said defendants are not worth anything." He can't afford to pay the bond on these enslaved children living with his mother. He can't afford much of anything. His back hurts, his house is overrun with kids, and he can't rub two nickels together.

Plus, his mother is aging. What good to her are five motherless children? And, out of curiosity, did the complaint say they might be worth $2,000?

In the week after Frankie Silver is hanged, Hiram helps to hide Willis from John Boone and the court. He takes him as far as Guilford County, one hundred miles away, as the hunt is on. William meanwhile surveys and threshes wheat, and once Hiram returns, they make plans, meeting multiple times a week.

Then it's August, and Hiram comes over and it happens:ς2|ʃX3||3ς.

Sold Willis.

William has turned Binah's firstborn into cash, his body little more than a machine. He's sold this baby he watched become a man and pockets the money.

Next week he'll hunt gold and beat cyder, and Willis will be someone else's property.

Naturally, he and Celia fight. They get into it on a snowy day in December when William refuses to wear the hat she gave him. Despite the cold, he longs for work more and more, to be in a field measuring dirt, thinking of those dances decades ago when he might slip off with Peggy or Pruny, feel the thrill of a new body, something hushed and hot. And MN. How she still comes to him all these years later, twenty years dead. When she does, she's twenty-six, and he doesn't know why, but she's walking that road by the cotton field with her mother and he's riding up on horseback and she has a glint in her eye that he can't quite read but is sure it's desire. She doesn't speak. He exchanges pleasantries with Mrs. Norwood while Mary walks along—disinterested? Aloof? Working as hard as she can to contain everything she feels for him? They don't speak, but he sees her and she sees him.

When Mary Norwood haunts William on a cold December day in Settlemire's freshly plowed field, she is all side-eye and open neck, and William is sure he's never felt more than he felt in Darlington County at age twenty, the world on edge and everything ahead of him. All he thinks of now is the word *plod.* He doesn't like his new hat. Celia never touches his prick. He will turn forty-six in a few weeks, his life trailing off behind him. He imagines himself like a snake shedding its skin, sloughing off what's not needed to make himself new. What can he let go of?

He sells the children.

After all, Hiram has plans, and William could use money. It's done in a day. "Settle," William writes in his little book, and the children are led off, only a few months after being released from jail. This man they've always been made to call Uncle Hiram is now their master, and the only life they've ever known is over.

He's not sure why he writes the little cross beside the entry, perhaps simply to remember it. He knows better than to feel too much about it. He thinks of crinkled-up snakeskin and counts his money over and over while his other children play in new snow.

But he has messed up. He was desperate and foolish, and he led the Harshaws on, promising them strong Willis and these young bucks who would soon be swinging an ax for gold. He took the Harshaw loans, took their advice, but once the hearings had come and gone, he sold the children away to Hiram, Willis off somewhere else entirely. The Harshaws did not get rich, did not amass a small army of enslaved bodies by being forgetful or soft. They sue William in April, demanding $4,000.

He doesn't have it, even after selling his children. But there's surely more gold to be found. More fortune just underfoot. He only need look. It rains for days.

Of course he sees the children. They're not vanished. He hasn't erased them from existence. They're okay. They'll be okay. Harriet has shot up, taller than any of her siblings, when William visits Hiram in June. She may soon outgrow him, a beanstalk of a girl. Hiram's wife complains that John is too slow-moving, always with his head in the clouds and forgetful. William will not wonder if that's a little bit of him in the boy, if there's something there to be nurtured not simply whipped away. He cannot make space for that thought because it will grow too large to contain, a drizzle becoming a hurricane.

Instead, he "hell fusses" with Celia and kills pigs. He takes more surveying jobs to pay his debts and disappear into memory. Another eclipse comes at the end of the year, and he wants to believe it means something, some sign that he's okay, that it will be okay, that there's more to his life, but he knows too much to allow it. He's calculated orbits; he knows Newton's Laws. There is only inertia, and only movement.

But in 1836, there is mostly death, which is both inertia and movement at once. William's brother-in-law Joel is killed in late October. William digs a grave. Four days later, his mother-in-law dies, and they're laying Mave Clark into the ground. Three days after her burial, Nancy Clark dies, the family shrinking by the week. The rain sets in, and a man named Stirs is shot. At school two days later a mad dog appears, threatening to bite the children.

William doesn't want to believe something's amiss, and yet he can't help but think of those children he's sold to Hiram and the death now chopping down the Clark family. He scribbles a black mark by each of the deaths, unable to sleep most nights for fear of something lurking, something of his own making.

But he turns forty-nine and life carries on.

March 3, 1837: Dug vein

March 4: Dug vein

March 5: Home

March 6: Dug gold

March 7: Dug gold

39

While the Israelites wandered in the desert, Yahweh called out to Moses—spoke his name—and so Moses set out up Mount Sinai to meet his maker. Atop the mountain, Yahweh appeared, enshrouded in smoke, and Moses must've felt as if he teetered forever there between the earth and heavens. After this encounter, he headed back down to the Israelites, full of eternal perspective and toting the literal words of the Divine. But in his absence, he found that his brother had cast God into a golden image of livestock.

Below him, his tribe—these resilient men and women pulled from slavery—danced and bowed down to a misshaped calf, forged of molten earrings. Moses *burned* with anger, throwing down the commandments. He melted the calf, ground it into powder, and forced his people to drink it.

At first, this act reads wholly cruel, nearly sadistic, but in the act of breaking down and then forcing down the gold, Moses reveals the ephemeral qualities of this so-called god: While gold may take centuries piled upon centuries to work toward the surface, it is temporary and worldly. Ultimately unsatisfying.

....

The discovery of gold doomed the Cherokee people and other indigenous groups in North Carolina and Georgia. Not long after Conrad had lugged that heavy doorstop home, the government set to moving Native groups from one corner to the next. With treaty after treaty, they were cut from one patch of land after another, opening up more and more gold-holding land to white settlement. By the time William set off with Reuben Deaver to make his map of Macon County, the Cherokee people had been pinned into the farthest west corner of North Carolina.

But not all of them left. One group of Cherokee people refused to move when that 1819 treaty tried to push all of them west of the Nantahala River, leav-

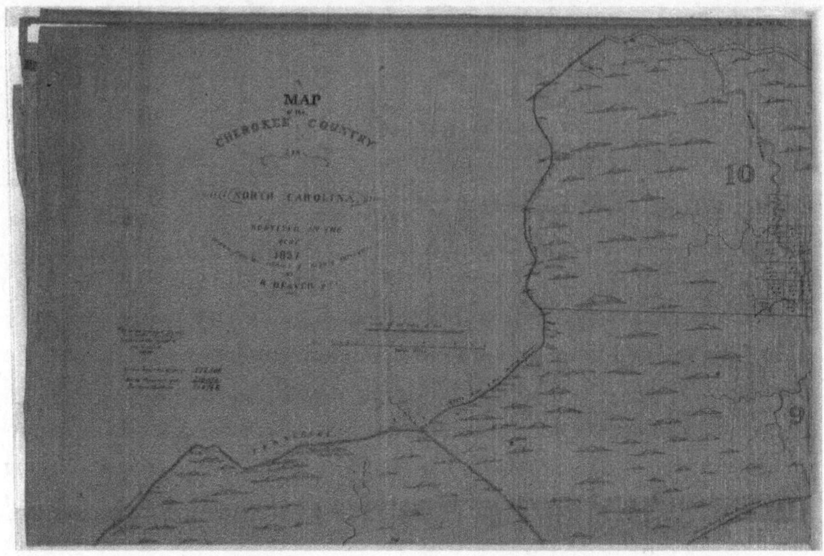

A portion of the map created from Reuben Deaver and William Prestwood's 1827 survey of present-day Macon County, NC

ing their emplaced histories to be surrounded or pushed over. When William came with his compass and wye levels into the former Mother Town, a leader named Yonaguska lived not far away with fifty other families, still going about their lives on ancestral land.

Yonaguska became head chief of the Cherokee people of the middle towns around 1800. When Tecumseh had come in 1811, urging the Cherokee people to join him in his alliance with the British as they set out to squeeze these new United States, Yonaguska convinced the other Cherokee chiefs to stay out of it, refusing to join this fight against the invaders. Eight years later, when the U.S. government came with treaty in hand, an offer to leave everything the Cherokee people had known and move deeper into the hazy mountains, Yonaguska built a side door into the agreement. He and another fifty or so families would leave the Cherokee Nation, become American citizens, and receive 640 acres each, not far from Mother Town.

I don't know how other Cherokee chiefs saw Yonaguska's decision, to leave his tribe and take on the name of the colonizer, but years later, this escape hatch would save his people from Andrew Jackson and the ever-opening maw of American greed.

....

Jackson isn't the first American president to want the Indians gone. Most of his predecessors pushed indigenous groups from one plot of land to another through treaty after treaty, threat after threat. "Next to the case of the [B]lack race within our bosom," James Madison said, "that of the red on our borders is the problem most baffling to the policy of our country."

James Monroe had drafted removal plans. John Quincy Adams had, too, but he hadn't acted on them by the time he ran for reelection against Jackson. When Jackson won the election and came to power in 1829, he approached the "Indian question" with urgency and without debate.

I'm reminded of the occasional fight over immigration that surfaces in our contemporary political discourse every election season, only to result in little action once officials have taken their seats. Like Jackson, Trump came to the White House single-minded about how to solve the issue, despite ideological or practical opposition to a wall running two thousand miles. Neither man wanted to work through—or see—the complexity or nuance before them, only to clear the way.

To do this, both Jackson and Trump framed their issues in terms of security, in terms of fear. Trump popped up around the country with families who'd lost loved ones to violence done by undocumented immigrants, despite the fact American citizens commit violent crimes at a rate double that of the undocumented.

Jackson, a man who spent much of his career fighting Native people from Tennessee to Texas, believed America wouldn't be safe living among these tribes. He comes to the issue in the first few weeks of his presidency after a white man is murdered by Creeks in Georgia. *This*, he believes, is reason for removal. Bad hombres. Rapists. Thieves. But not only this, also that Indians can't be trusted. They've aligned themselves with the British time and time again, and our country will only be safe if the East Coast is as white as cotton: "A dense white population would add much," he said about the South's security. Across two hundred years, the song is the same: We'll lose the country if we don't claim it for the "real" Americans.

....

One summer I was invited to teach in Kentucky. For a week, I moved into a house with so many writers I adore: Lee Smith, Silas House, Bobbie Ann Mason. Across the hall from me was Wendell Berry and his wife, Tanya. It was as if I stepped into a literary dorm from my dreams.

I carry in my head a list of writers who've unlocked something for me, books or poems that creaked open some clearer or bigger sense of the world. Wendell Berry is one. When I encountered his work in college, my sense of place and belonging shifted almost immediately. I read of rural life and attention to the breeze and of the intention to stay on land that raised you up, and something settled in me. I didn't know the term *emplacement* then, but I think about it now when I think of Berry: this living upon the lives and land that made you.

I trailed him like a dog all week. He was in his eighties and intended this to be one of his last public appearances, so I wanted every bit of wisdom I could cull. He wanted to tell stories and laugh. That right there should have been the wisdom, the lesson to learn, but the world felt on fire: Trump undoing every environmental protection, caging young children, sending ICE into the streets with full force. I wanted something to make sense of it. Someone to tell me it would be okay.

At dinner one night I put it to him while we ate green beans: "How do we remain hopeful in times like these?"

"I don't believe in hope," he shot back, and he must have seen the green beans in my open mouth as I waited for more.

"It's too easy to have false hopes," he said, or something like it. And then: "We're living in a cult of the future right now; everyone is panicked about what might happen, about all these hypotheticals and end-time scenarios. They're paralyzed. But what can you do about that? All most of us can really do is find the problem in front of us and get to work there. Find the need where you live. Hope can go wrong far too easily."

Someone shifted the subject, and I carried his words around for some weeks once I'd gone back home, trying to protect myself from the *cult of the future* and searching out the needs around me.

What I mostly realized was that I had few useful skills. But I could speak Spanish and I could talk about writing, so I worked with a nonprofit serving the Latino community in my county. I put together a memoir-writing class in

Spanish, with an end goal of collecting immigrant stories in a short book in order to display the diversity of experiences. There is no one immigrant story, was the idea. The executive director, whose background was in mental health, was excited about how the writing experience might allow people to process difficult and important material. I made photocopies; they promoted the classes.

On the night of the first class, I arrived to the building early and let myself in. I spread my translation of George Ella Lyon's poem "Where I'm From" on the tables, gathered up pencils and paper. Based on calls and social media messages, we expected around ten people for the first session, but I set up the room for more, just in case. Then I waited.

No one came. I checked the front and side doors. I listened for the phone. Silence. Eventually, I messaged the executive director to make sure I hadn't mixed up the times.

"ICE has been out today," he wrote back. Then I understood.

My county is a 287(g) county. This means the sheriff's department has signed an agreement to check the immigration status of anyone for anything, connecting its system with ICE's. The effect is that someone pulled over for a burnt-out taillight or jaywalking could be deported. In one of my colleagues' classes at the university, a student wrote about her father never coming home one night after work. They found his car along the side of the road the next day. They feared the worst, making phone calls and searching hospitals. Days later they learned he'd been pulled over and then deported back to Mexico as quick as a wink. He had no criminal record, and she feared she'd never see him again.

The 287(g) agreement also means ICE comes and goes as they please, and when they're creeping around town in nondescript vans or raiding restaurant kitchens, fear is seismic in the immigrant community. Messages are spread online to warn each other. The nonprofit where I intended to teach my class has become an online Paul Revere: *ICE is coming, ICE is coming*. People avoid work. Avoid the grocery store. They certainly avoid a memoir-writing class two blocks from the county jail.

If it hadn't been for the class, I wouldn't have known ICE was out that day, that people in the county were living in fear while I counted pencils. That impotent awareness that hit me then felt familiar. It felt like the process of uncovering and coming to understand so much in the unpacking of William's life, and yet not knowing what to do with it except simply know it. Here I was in real life, making a tiny effort to do something, anything, in the face of immovable injustice, and I failed. It left me with only a clearer sense of the injustice.

I locked up, went home, and put my kids to bed.

....

William is fifty when he's called up. The Ts are crossed, and America is coming for the Cherokee Indian. For any and all Indians.

Even at a half century, William is still bringing kids into the world. In January, two days before his birthday, Celia gives birth to Martin Luther, their eighth child. As 1838 takes off, William teaches and drinks brandy and surveys, but as summer approaches, the militia takes shape and he's mustering at Tuckers. This time around William is no captain. There is no threat of attack. This time around, he is the attacker, the one invading. When he hears the word, he'll set off west and leave behind his increasing family, ready to round up the people whose people were here long before the land was "discovered" by European settlers.

Elisha Miller is the captain of Company D, one of three companies marching out of Burke County to the far west. They expected to leave in May, but they're soon learning that Andrew Jackson's plan to rid the East Coast of Natives is pure chaos. It's June, instead, when William is heading along a path he's traveled before, to the Mother Town, to Franklin, to land taken by the government and mapped by him.

Jackson's 1835 treaty took Native land east of the Mississippi and "gave away" bits of Oklahoma. Go west and be free, he hoped to convince the Cherokee and other tribes. But when Van Buren comes into office in 1837, only two thousand have gone. He vows to finish Jackson's work, appointing General Winfield Scott to forcibly displace sixteen thousand emplaced people.

Enter William Thomas Prestwood, surveyor, gold miner, child seller. He writes, "start army" on his pages on June 6, 1838, and then leaves, keeping pace with Isaac Fincannon and Jacob Taylor, the musicians in his company. Then he writes nothing on his encrypted pages for weeks—the Indian Removal removed from his records.

....

As disorganized and rushed as Van Buren's removal plans are, they've been announced. Most Cherokee people know what's coming. They wait outside their houses, bags packed. Soon William or someone like him will arrive and lead them into an internment camp just outside of Mother Town. Then they'll go beyond the Mississippi River, into a place they've never known.

Yonaguska, however, won't go. He's no longer Cherokee, his people no longer Cherokee. They're Americans, and they're not going anywhere.

Everyone else will soon be carried away. Fincannon is playing the drum now as the Burke County men approach.

William writes none of this, but here's how it goes:

Along the way, word comes down from on high that the operation is to be delayed yet again. They move slowly, no sense in turning back to Tuckers. They arrive in Franklin/Mother Town, and it's hardly the frontier town it was when William and Rueben Deaver galloped in a decade ago. They meander on to Camp Dudley, eventually mustering out to begin work on June 12. William's company sets out down the new-cut State Road through Cartoogechaye, then up across Wayah Gap, and finally down Jarrett's Creek to Camp Scott. The Aquone Baptist Church stands nearby, but better not think of Christ on the cross as they prepare to imprison the innocent.

Once at camp, they await direction. Lt. Colonel John Gray Bynum orchestrates whatever can be orchestrated of the mess. He sends William and the other volunteers into Aquone, Briartown, and Nantahala to bring every Cherokee person they find.

But Bynum is already having second thoughts. When he first arrived, he wrote to his superiors worrying over the conditions of the facilities if "the Indians are disposed to be hostile." But now he has visited Aquone Baptist Church and many of the other churches in the Cherokee villages as he waited for men to arrive, and he can't find a rhyme or reason to any of this. These are upstanding people, he realizes quickly, and when he can no longer stand it, he writes to request delay: "If they are permitted to remain until further orders I promise to use my efforts to make them citizens. I have no doubt they will grant them the right of citzen-ship."

Deaf ears all around, so the men pull kids by the arms and drag women through the dirt. They huddle them within the walls and under the summer heat to wait and wait and wait. I wonder about the sounds William hears before falling asleep at the camp: crying? singing? silence? Does he long for the purr of a snore Celia has developed in recent years, miss the yammer of Fabius talking in his sleep? Somehow, despite the foreign terror he's created, he sleeps. Then he gets up and does it all again.

The work is meant to last two weeks. Two weeks of escorting families into makeshift prisons. But when time is up, no one comes in relief. No new militia, no new volunteers. The men wait for a day or two but the road down Jarrett's Creek is empty, and it's time to go home.

So they eventually throw their hands up and go. *We're off duty, mere citizens now*, they tell the imprisoned families, and then they leave the door open and Fincannon sets to drumming.

Many of the Cherokee people leave only to be rounded up again days later, this time by a company out of Macon County, a company that would ultimately lead them to Fort Lindsay and onto the death march to Oklahoma.

But some of those released men and women go into hiding, seeking out any dark hollow in the mountains that might swallow them up. The militiamen never find them, and they cling to the land until everything passes. Some of them go to Yonaguska, asking that they might join his rogue nation, his New Americans.

40

Today, the Anquone Baptist Church and Camp Scott and the footprints of Company D are all underwater. A 1942 dam left only Nantahala Lake here. But it's easy enough to imagine William and Elisha Miller and Isaac Fincannon marching off—dejected? homesick? drunk?—under that water. They go first to Asheville, to pick up their money, and then back to Burke County, where their lives awaited them.

Returned, William does nothing. For a week he writes only [264, *home*. Maybe he's depressed. Maybe he's exhausted. Maybe he's holding Baby Luther and making faces at Polly. Or maybe—and why do I hope for this affliction?—he's seeing the faces of all those Cherokee people he led from their homes in the name of country; they encircle him and arise in the faces of his children, or his mother.

Maybe this is why he copies down a poem in his notebook, "The Death Song of the Cherokee Indian" (written by Anne Hunter in 1784):

The sun sets at night and the stars shun the day,
But glory remains when the light fades away.
Begin, ye tormentors, your threats are in vain,
For the son of Alknomook shall never complain.

Remember the arrows he shot from his bow;
Remember your chiefs by his hatchet laid low;
Why so slow? do you wait till I shrink from my pain?
No! the son of Alknomook shall never complain.

Remember the wood where in ambush we lay,
And the scalps which we bore from your nation away;
Now the flame rises fast, you exult in my pain,
But the son of Alknomook shall never complain.

I'll go to the land where my father is gone;
His ghost shall rejoice in the fame of his son;
Death comes like a friend to relieve me from pain;
And thy son, O Alknomook, has scorn'd to complain.

William copies many random bits onto his pages: personal accounts ("This is to certify that I have impressed a Bay Mare praised to one hundred Dollars hard money."), astrological formulas ("Multiply the Planets Sidereal revolution by 0.176776 or subtract 0.752575 from the log of the time and the remainder is the answer"), and Mason handshakes ("The grip: Right hand thumbnail hard against the 1st joint of his Forefinger rt hand"). He copies selections from books (Hatton's *Mathematics*, Cumming's *Geography*, rules of navigation from Haselden's *The Seaman's Daily Assistant*). But this is the only poem I find in any of his sewn-together notebooks.

Yes, yes, I want this to mean something. I want this to mean he felt regret, felt shame. I want this to be another sign he sometimes floated above the moment, that he understood human dignity irrespective of human law.

But it could also only mean he liked the rhyme or the gore, had heard it set to music. It could mean nothing at all. Only inertia and movement, William might tell me.

....

Squire Dula would be a fine enough replacement, but there are other options in the mid-nineteenth century, other better substitute ancestors to claim. John Brown comes too late for an easy swap, but a quieter, older abolitionist would suit just fine. Really, any Quaker could do the trick. Of course, in 1838, Emerson is a top-round draft pick. As William mustered and fussed with Celia, Emerson pleaded with Van Buren not to "start army":

> The immortal question whether justice shall be done by the race of civilized to the race of savage man, [or] whether all the attributes of reason, of civility, of justice, and even of mercy, shall be put off by the American people, and so vast an outrage upon the Cherokee Nation and upon human nature shall be consummated.

Ignoring the "savage man" bit, this guy gets it: shared human nature. Civility, justice, mercy. Yes, please.

But obviously Emerson is a big get. The easiest replacement for William Thomas Prestwood is a man not far away, a man whose name is a mere word scramble away from being the same: William Holland Thomas.

William Holland Thomas is another white man living in the North Carolina mountains in 1838. Raised by a single mom on Raccoon Creek, near Cherokee land, William started working early. At thirteen, he took a job at Felix Walker's trading post among the Cherokee people and learned bits and pieces of their language. Wil-Usdi, "Little Will," the people called him.

Yonaguska saw something in Wil-Usdi, this fatherless white boy who sounded more and more like a native Cherokee speaker every time the chief visited the store. He invited William into his home to eat, told him stories, passed along advice. Before long, he became William's adopted father. But after some years, Felix Walker's trading post went under; he had managed it poorly and run out of money entirely. Walker, a U.S. congressman, couldn't even pay William as he shut down the trading post, so he rummaged around for anything of value to hand the boy. He came up with a set of law books.

So William read. He studied the books front to back and took the bar exam, needing only to pass it to call himself a lawyer. Maybe Yonaguska knew then what he'd sensed years before—there was use in this kid. Or maybe Yonaguska had merely helped raise a lost boy, and now his guidance and care had led William to make something of himself. In any event, Little Will was now a lawyer, and in 1831, Yonaguska decided he might just need one.

When Andrew Jackson and Van Buren and John Gray Bynum and William Thomas Prestwood come knocking in 1838, Yonaguska simply directs them to his lawyer and goes about his day.

Armed with paper and legalese, William Thomas comes to fight the American government on behalf of Yonaguska's band of Cherokee, now Americans, living in a place called Quallatown. He negotiates for them to stay put, to be passed over by the militias as if these sixty families have painted their doorframes to keep the plague at bay. They can stay. For now.

On his deathbed in 1839, Yonaguska names his adopted son, Wil-Usdi, the chief of these Cherokee. William spends years in Washington, DC, representing his people, fighting for their place. "The Indians are as much entitled to their rights as I am to mine," he said to the other white men surrounding him there and bought fifty thousand acres (the Cherokee people weren't allowed to sign contracts) for these passed-over Cherokee people to occupy in peace. In 1848, after a decade of lobbying and arguing, he won: the United States officially recognized the Eastern Band of the Cherokee. All hail Little Will.

……………

It was dark already when the Amber Alert buzzed my phone. My son's name was there: Ezra David Jones is missing, three years old. But he wasn't missing; he was upstairs in bed, surrounded by stuffed turtles and lions, his bear light shining on the wall. Wasn't he?

I stood up straight when I saw it. I started toward the stairs but told myself I was being ridiculous. Then I told myself I was being ridiculous about being ridiculous, and I climbed the stairs to make sure he was where I left him and not last seen in a 1990 blue Ford F250 headed toward Black Mountain.

He was there, balled up and covered up, but then the texts came from family. *Is Ezra missing? What's going on?*

He was fine; we were fine. I felt briefly guilty for the wash of relief that my boy's stuffed animals had him hemmed in when, a few miles from our house, another Ezra had been taken by his young father and they were running east. I wondered at whatever desperation or madness had sent a man to this; I wondered if he knew the whole of the state was on the lookout for his old truck.

I wondered, too, about that stingy empathy and if we could ever really know what led anyone to anything. So, naturally, I was in my kitchen reading an Amber Alert and thinking of my nineteenth-century forefather selling his children and imprisoning Cherokee kids.

It's lazy to settle on the notion that we can never judge anyone because we can never know their heart and head. I'm hung up on justice and empathy, wondering if those ideas are in conflict or complementary. Does empathy inhibit justice or does true justice require empathy?

In the end, I cop out. I'm no philosopher, no ethicist. I'm also no judge or executioner. No one needs me doling out justice. I can't condemn William Prestwood or the father of another Ezra David Jones. I'm just a man considering the misdeeds in his family tree, holding them up like strange fruit that smells somehow familiar.

41

While William wrote nothing of his time at Camp Scott, not far away a man named Daniel Butrick scribbled details daily about the treatment of the Cherokee people in the camps in Tennessee: "It is evident that from their first arrest they were obliged to live very much like brute animals." Butrick, a white minister serving the Cherokee, watches his congregants and neighbors carried away day by day, without mercy or reason. He is helpless to it, but he pleads with the militiamen and commanders as they come anyway. He visits the camps most days, reporting on the conditions and sitting with the families. He prays and preaches—and as everything grows worse, he fumes:

> How does the United States government appease a great nation, laying aside her dignity and with thousands of soldiers, and all her great men, and all her mighty men, and all her powerful generals, with all her civil and military force, chasing a little trembling hare in the wilderness, merely to take its skin, and send it off to broil in the scorching deserts of the West.
>
> O how Noble! How magnanimous! How warlike the achievement! O what a conquest! What booty! How becoming the glory and grandeur of the United States!

He cannot stop any of it, so he and his wife decide their place is with these people, marching into the "scorching deserts of the West." When the government is finally ready to send the Cherokee people away—after weeks of imprisonment and changed and failed plans—the Butricks fall in line on the Trial of Tears.

In his diary, he bears witness to devastating brutality: "15th death since we crossed the Tennessee River." As many as six thousand people die on the way, left scattered across the expanding country Jackson wanted. Butrick watches them fall, railing against his government and searching for hope on his pages. As the days stretch on, he begins to question everything, including his faith.

> Previous to starting on this journey, I determined to let it be a journey of prayer, and to devote much time every day to that sacred duty, but instead of this I have very strangely neglected prayer. . . . I know that all this cannot justify a neglect of prayer. I think my own heart is more peculiarly depraved, especially as respects impatient and angry feelings. . . . The little boy who died last night was buried today in a coffin made of puncheons.
>
> This year has been a year of spiritual darkness.

The depravity of the forced march of sixteen thousand living souls arises in each death Butrick documents as his own health fails: "My dear wife is now unwell, afflicted with ague. Her strength has been declining a number of days. I am also scarcely able to walk." The massive death count laid out flatly in a history book is captured on Butrick's pages in individual lives, with names and histories gone in an instant: "The poor little children are almost all dying off." It hardly seems real.

As I read, I find myself sinking most often into Butrick's frustration, into his screaming fruitlessly at the government carrying guns and pushing them onward. Maybe I connect with that impotence. I think of those children the government has caged, the immigrants living in fear near my house, the migrants dying of thirst in the desert, and I know I can change none of it. I want to write a diatribe, to scatter social media posts and letters to legislators, but those efforts seem as pitiful as Butrick pouring his anger into a diary.

But he didn't only scream into the void. He suffered; he marched. He did something. To what end? How did breaking down his body help the poor children dying off? What good did his watching mass death and suffering do?

What I come back to when I juggle *empathy* and *justice* is an argument from social ethicist and scholar of religion Jonathan Walton. Walton argues that an ethical lens, at least in a Christian tradition, requires looking for the most vulnerable in every situation and asking how a decision will affect them. This, to me, makes everything simple enough for action. The right thing to do isn't weighed down by pro/con lists or subcommittees. It's a simple calculus: How will this affect the most vulnerable?

Butrick couldn't stop what Jackson set in motion, what had been coming before the country had even given itself a name. But he could walk alongside it, put himself in it. Witness it.

....

In the end, Chief Little Will is a myth. It doesn't take too much reading before the white savior of William Thomas hits the ground, his horse trotting away into the sunset.

Much of it is true. He represented the Eastern Band, was adopted by Yonaguska. He fought off the American government with the weapon it respected most: bureaucracy. He played a central role in the perseverance of the North Carolina Cherokee people who remained. But he probably wasn't made the white chief of the remaining Cherokee people. Witness accounts of Yonaguska's death make no mention of him naming Will Thomas chief, and other accounts suggest Yonaguska tasked Thomas with protecting tribal interests in DC, not taking over as leader.

But I didn't need William Thomas to be a Cherokee chief to claim him. I just needed him to do the right thing. And he does.

Until he doesn't.

He's a walking contradiction: He personally bought food and clothing for suffering North Carolina Cherokee people in 1838, and yet he also helped the government track down Cherokee people escaping from other states. While fighting for the Eastern Band's right to remain in their homes, he also speculated in lands freed up by their removal. Perhaps this duplicitousness only added to his credibility among the white politicians of Washington, DC; perhaps that's why he was able to save the Eastern Band in the end. But it's hard, on this side of history, to align many of his actions into a seamless narrative.

What's more, his ahead-of-his-time belief that everyone—"white man or red man"—carries inalienable rights doesn't line up with his fervent support of the Confederacy a few decades later. When North Carolina seceded, he rode home and persuaded the Cherokee people to fight for the South, eventually leading a group into battle in east Tennessee to scalp wounded Union soldiers. He refused to lay down his weapons until May 1865—one of the last rebels in the country to surrender.

Two years later, he was declared insane and sent to an asylum. He lost his land, his money. His mind. He died in a mental hospital in 1893.

....

Behind my office on campus, they dug. A few hundred yards from where I parked my car every day, archaeologists and soon-to-be archaeologists came out of the ground with bits of life from millennia ago. Somewhere beneath what was soon to be an intramural field, stone ovens and corncribs revealed Tali Tsisgwayahi, Two Sparrows Town, one of the first Cherokee settlements in the mountains, now covered in pavement and buildings and me.

When I learned about those thousands-year-old artifacts just underfoot, that word *emplacement* arrived. The townhouse mound where the Cherokee residents of Two Sparrows Town built and replaced, built and replaced for generations—building up on the lives of ancestors—was pushed over by the university in the 1950s. To make way for the education and pyschology building.

Now the university digs before it builds, pulling up signs of life and documenting them in a collection named after Two Sparrows Town. They do this work in consultation with the tribal historic preservation office. They teach Cherokee language classes. They try to do better.

But really what I thought of most when I considered the stone oven that I might have walked over last week is the flash of a human life. My tininess was made only tinier when I considered the thousands of years indigenous people had lived on this land before Prestwoods and Joneses started hoeing corn and killing hogs. A short drive from campus waited Judaculla Rock, a hunk of carved-up soapstone. It's indecipherable, a petroglyph with no clear origin. The markings and drawings may have come from the hands of early Cherokee people or an even earlier prehistoric tribe chiseling into the flat rock at the end of the Ice Age. What was clear was life has long been here and, let's pray, will long hereafter be. What was clear was that William and I are the faintest of notches on a thousand-mile timeline.

The nationalist fervor of the day appeared clownish on that timeline. That clinging to a narrow American identity was so obviously desperate and doomed that it made me want to scream and laugh all at once. And yet we carried on, as we'd carried on since we declared our independence: sorting out who belongs and who doesn't.

All these ways and words for becoming something, living into one's citizenship: native-born, naturalized. Impressment, emplacement. Is it claimed or given, earned or lived into? Can it be taken away by a British sailor on a whim? By an army of volunteers marching you west? By a system declaring you property, inhuman and disposable?

What I most saw when I drove by the American flags recolored blue to support police (and simultaneously to disparage Black Lives Matter) was a reminder that any flag could turn against you, at any moment. The Confederate flag had been repurposed over and over, always finding new ways to attack and sort. No national identity was ever safe. Someone with power could decide one day you don't belong, and it wouldn't matter if your ancestor's stone oven was buried in the ground beneath you or if your family survived enslavement so you could walk these streets to sell cigarettes. You could never truly prove you belonged.

Not even spit in a beaker could make you American, no red, white, and blue encoded in your DNA. When the genetic decoding came back to me, there was no word of citizenship, but it ciphered me as, unsurprisingly, white as grits: my ancestry 100 percent European, mostly from the British Isles. And, also not surprisingly, to be very Neanderthal.

I realized quickly I would make a terrible 23andMe commercial, no surprise ancestor or geography in my results. *I always thought I was white, but then I got my reports and saw I'm . . . linen white.* No grand reveal in this advertisement.

But I dug and dug, and after a couple days of sorting through the material, I found what looked to be the far-off children of Binah scattered across the country, carrying in them the genetic ghost of William Thomas Prestwood.

Dear William:

I write to you from a machine forged of metals pulled from the ground by slaves. I never think of them. They're across the globe, down in the dark of the earth. Some of them are children, their fingers bloodied and backs warped as they mine what's needed for these words. Without any effort at all, I can blink them out of existence. I can eat sushi and type this letter, my ears plugged up with music made in an electronic room somewhere else.

Today, William, in our America, there is no more legal slavery. Today, Willis and Eliza and Harriet and Ira and John would be free. Free to attend school and marry and ignore you.

Today, William, there are more slaves than ever before. We have the good taste to keep them out of sight, to stash them in fields and factories far away. To move them in darkness from town to town, passports locked up out of reach. And they're cheap. You'd not believe how little it costs to enslave a human body, a human life, today.

I've never knowingly seen an enslaved person in the whole of my life. I sometimes imagine you walking past worn-down Black bodies on the way to mail a letter, seeing in the eyes of a man walking into the mine his very soul, knowing for a moment, before tamping it down, that the color in those eyes is as rich and complex as your own but walking on anyway. I can't understand that. How can you live in the midst of such torture, of such soulless evil?

Easier instead is to rearrange all the paths to mail a letter so that you never need to see those eyes. To form a world where the labor that holds you up is perched on the backs of people in countries poorer than yours, more desperate than yours, across ever-widening oceans and stashed behind shiny, respectable industries. This is how I move through my days—putting on shirts stitched together by enslaved people in Vietnam, driving to work in a car fueled by oil fought over forever, typing on this machine snapped together of materials dug out by tiny, enslaved bodies inside a Chinese mountain. All of these products come to me boxed-up, washed clean of any smell or sign of human work. Sanitized.

You see it, I'm sure? The sneaky hypocrisy that's crept from the shadows as I've been yelling while reading your life. I was ready to travel back in time to keep you from Binah. To demand you to see yourself in her children. And all the while, the people I enslave here have been feeding and dressing and entertaining me without making a sound. If I had a time machine to track you down, they would have built it.

I've been thinking of writing to my great-great-great-great-grandchildren lately. Wondering what I should say to them, how I'd present myself if they dug me up in two hundred years.

I'll be honest: I reckoned I'd come out pretty clean. A family man. Upstanding, salt of the earth. Gentle. I have no enslaved mistresses. I rounded up no Cherokee families. I bathe my children and read them books.

And yet, lately, I realize the only thing to write to these far-off sons and daughters is *I'm sorry.* To beg: *I'm not a monster.*

They will unearth me in 2220 and not understand how I could stomach stepping onto an airplane that burns up the atmosphere, slowly boiling the planet they'll inherit. How I drive sixty miles to work, dumping poison into the air they'll breathe. I will plead with my descendants about how I didn't know what to do, tell them about how it's all too big, too systematic, too woven into everything for me to make a change.

Everything you would say to me.

And what of these children in cages? they might ask. In the summer when our government began locking up children at the southern border, taking them from their parents and never returning them, I took my family on vacation. We sat our boys in front of dancing dolphins; we ate ice cream. Meanwhile, my country kidnapped children.

I could write to my great-great-great-great-grandchildren that I wanted to do something. That they must believe me. As we sat in a coffee shop and the news arrived on my phone (my slave-labor phone) I considered packing us all up to drive (in my war-fueled car) to the border. What might happen, I wondered then, if we marched to those cages. If we rattled those chains. If we screamed and cried and demanded freedom. If I showed my young boys other young boys who had been wrapped up by the insidious notion that their bodies mattered less than ours. I thought of leaving the theme park and going straight there.

But what good is it? This is what I'll need to convince my generations-later children: All has forever been lost. I'm but one man, dressed in the armor of slavery, surrounded in earth-killing machines that I need to live.

And yet. This damned optimism woven in me by my family or the theology they handed me—that there is forever healing, that justice is a single body in front of a tank. Our individual lives, which draw to a close with every breath, can bear witness, can try to unsettle the foundation of an out-of-plumb world.

I know you can't tell me how to live such a life. Just like I can't tell you how to live yours, with yet another war rolling across the sky and your mother growing frail and your children tall, but what we can hope and pray is that when we're laid into this North Carolina dirt, the lives we've passed on will understand, just a touch better, how to make peace out of thin air.

PART VI

Ə5ςς37ζ 27

Passing On

♐♒ *Advice for My Sons* ♌♒

March 20, 1823

My dear sons, learn eloquence; not barely what you say, but the proper manner of speaking.

42

Across the creek there were screams. My people were over there—Grandma had recently joined her husband and parents and aunts and uncles. My mom's family, too: Her grandparents and their kin all lay in the ground off Townsend Road. We heard the screams on this side, in the land of the living, just above the barn and Asbury and Clementine's house; the creek lifted the sounds cleanly from the cornfield and ushered them to us like lost children.

I knew no trumpets had sounded. There was no resurrection beside Lively's cow pasture in Fruitland, North Carolina—only high school kids dressed as the undead, slinking through the woods and outbuildings to make buses of church youth groups and entangled double dates shriek for their lives for ten dollars a pop. Still, I wanted to ask them to keep it down over there: My ancestors were sleeping.

I set out from the barn in the pitch black, avoiding the crunch of vans and buses as they barreled down the dirt road to experience the Haunted Farm. Without intending it, I was suddenly ten years old and disappearing into the woods to escape imagined enemies. I crossed the bridge, but when I heard a car approaching, I dropped off the road and dashed into trees. Wrapped up in darkness and the eternal games of my boyhood, I made it to the edge of the field, avoiding headlights and Soviet agents, and ran through the pasture until my muscles gave out. I crouched down in the cornfield as a tractor pulled a trailer full of thrilled and scared and bundled-up civilians back toward the zombies and chainsaws and the cemetery holding the people I'd come from. It was a full-body thrill to be invisible, to be a ghost amid the spectacle.

Once I eventually drifted my way into the makeshift parking lot in the pasture, I accidentally spooked the kid collecting parking money. He nearly fell backwards at the sight of me emerging from nowhere beside him, and I tried to muster something human and cordial—"Hey there"—as I stepped into the bright lights and paid my money to be haunted.

The whole operation I'd sneaked into was my mom's cousin's. As was the case across most of the county, that farm hadn't really been a farm for a couple decades; there was little money in it anymore. Horses ambled around during the other eleven months of the year, when the porta-potties and bright lights and rows of cars were gone. The silo was mostly empty, and the barn sheltered only a few run-down machines. This—the kids and screams and smoke machines and me in the month of October—*was* now the business.

After I'd swiped my card, I fell into line behind a young couple seemingly sharing a sweatshirt and considered striking up conversation about how those headstones just over there belonged to my family. *Isn't that weird?* I might say, gesturing at the graves as they squint into the darkness. *I mean, if anyone is haunting this farm, it's them.* Then I was imagining the ghost of Grandma floating into this crowd while everyone shivered and death metal blared from a hidden speaker. She was yelling, *Boys!* and giving that penetrating stare I ran from decades before. Then came Nanny wagging a crooked finger from an easy chair. Great-Grandma Maxwell and her amputated leg wheeled through overhead. I was smiling to myself at the gathering of frightening dead women when I realized that no one should ever come to a haunted farm on Halloween by himself. Especially when that person was thirty-six years old and couldn't control the urge to talk about genealogy and nostalgia with kissing teenagers in the woods.

The line crept. Above the hundred or so people waiting their turn and the loud music, a giant screen played a compilation of scenes from horror movies. Something in the field down by the creek rose in ten-foot flames every ten minutes or so. A bird-looking creeper walked through the crowd staring at us, until he was eventually subbed out by a lumberjack zombie who took over this freak-out-the-queue shift. The groups huddled to contend with the thirty-degree night, alternating between screaming and laughing at loud noises and dead-eyed teenagers. I stood among them alone, pulling my hat down and thinking about ghosts.

The Christian tradition I come from and carry on in tells that we'll be called up from the ground to live on a new, perfected earth. A world without pain, without intolerance and arthritis and hatred. The prophetic images given in Isaiah I carry with me the most: swords bent into plowshares, the lion lying down with the lamb.

I get that vision, but then I do sometimes wonder about the particulars of resurrected bodies. Are we flesh and blood on this new earth, smooth skin and perfect cholesterol? Do we come back as we died—Grandma forever eighty-seven; William seventy-one? Or are we revived in our best bodies—my seventeen-year-old, competitive-sport-every-season flesh; William riding into this new world on horseback, calling out for Mary Norwood with a full head of hair?

I don't worry with these thoughts much. It's either true or it's not. It'll either happen or it won't. There's no preparing for it, no changing it. We're called, I believe, to work toward that perfected earth now (the bent swords not the headful of hair), not to sit around waiting for the horn to blare. We're called to avoid the cult of the afterlife future.

And, yet, there I stood in the subfreezing night imagining the ancestors I knew and the ones I'd never met reaching up out of the ground in taut, shiny bodies to smile across the field at me and say, *Hey there.*

....

William's mother dies on a rainy day in 1841, the day after my birthday. On the day I'll be born 140 years later, he writes that she's sick. By the next day, she's gone. He draws and fills in a heart in the margins of his notebook; then he builds a coffin.

November 21: Buried

Evander, William's eldest, is twenty. He buys up much of Nancy Prestwood's estate when William administers the sale of her property: three cows, a yearling, two pigs, a chest, a pot, an oven, two chains, pothooks, a bell. Evander's preparing for a life on his own, taking up his grandmother's goods to make it so, and it must feel like yesterday that William lifted the tiny boy and the whiskey dram on that spring afternoon.

Alas, William is fifty-three, and nothing stands still. Evander is now the age William was when he started scratching on these pages, when he first recognized he needed to make some life choices: "either marry MN, or keep Bachelor's Hall, or travel." Not on the list was move to the mountains with Mother and dig for gold, but of course Evander doesn't listen to him when he offers advice about the future, about how unpredictable the world will forever be. How there's no planning for what's coming. He's a good boy, says *yes sir*, but William can see the disengagement swirling in those eyes when he starts up about becoming a grown man with purpose. *The desire of my soul is that my son should be a man and not a child all his life.*

William writes a letter to his father. Is something shifting in him amid all of this—the death of his mother, the adulthood of his son? Perhaps he can't avoid the truth of it: He misses his father. But this longing is a wave of warped nostalgia, a desire for a memory too far off to hold in hand, for a past that never really existed. He wants what could have been, not what was. He writes with the news. Maybe he mentions the gold. Maybe he mentions his discovery of reciprocals. Maybe he mentions the never-ending surveying work for the Harshaws, slowly chipping away at that black hole of debt.

He could mention about the sale of Mother's belongings. About how it should have been him, TP, fending off a drunk Nathan Clark at the estate sale, about how it should have been TP handling all of this, in fact: the cataloging of a life, the placing of value on her coffee mill and coffee pot as if they're only things and not extensions of her. TP should be the one deciding to collect $1.25 for what was always offered after the back door creaked closed, its handle worn to grooves where her hand held it tight but never will again.

Better, maybe, to share the news of Nancy's passing in a flat report. *She went peacefully*. But now he'd better be getting on to plant the potatoes. *Your son*, he'll sign off, and he'll mean it in more ways than the pen can convey.

....

When my 23andMe results arrived, I scrolled through the pages absentmindedly, not sure what much of it meant or what I was looking for. I doubted anything revelatory would appear to me, especially after seeing the single-color pie chart up front, tracing all my ancestry to the British Isles. But within a few clicks I sat up a little straighter, leaned in a little closer. There, sitting above me on the colorful, prebuilt family tree ending in me, was my uncle. Beneath him, in surefooted print, read "Father."

I thought immediately of the electrician who'd come to our house a few weeks before. After working for an hour or so, he connected the dots of my family. "I played basketball for your daddy," he said with some clipped wires in his hand. "Knew your grandparents—they were great people. Yep, now I see it," he nodded to himself as he looked into me.

"Yeah, guess I'm looking more and more like him these days." It's a line I've repeated often after moving home and having these dot-connecting exchanges all the time.

"No—more like your uncle, I'm sorry to say."

"Oh," I managed with a polite smile before leaving him to his work.

Sitting with my DNA parsed out in charts and lists on my phone and hearing that electrician's words echo in my head, I needed a few brain-spinning beats before I understood. My uncle is my father. My father is my uncle. Genetically.

My dad was born in the bathroom where I washed my hands before every meal at Grandma's. He came too quick to drive into town one early May morning, so the doctor drove a hearse, which doubled as an ambulance, into Fruitland to bring the baby into the world. It went smoothly enough—bottom smacked and cord cut—until the doctor realized another baby waited in Dad's wake. In a rush, they swaddled my father, rested him on the basin of the toilet, and readied Grandma to load into the hearse so she could deliver her next baby in the hospital. They were halfway down the driveway when someone realized they'd left my infant father on the toilet.

Dad's twin brother came along an hour or so later, a matching baby to lay in my grandmother's arms. Two bundles of identical DNA. Two times the diapers and mayonnaise sandwiches.

My dad had never sent his saliva away to understand who he is, but his twin brother had, so in the black and white of the human genome, Uncle Danny was my father—half of my DNA. His son Ryan, my cousin, was my half brother.

I understood all of this, but also I didn't. How could I look more like my uncle than my dad? How could my dad and his brother look different at all? Aren't they packaged the same, the same men in their skin? How could those basic building blocks change?

A geneticist friend explained it to me—a guy still saying "basic building blocks"—like this: Genes are like burners on a stove; they can be turned up or turned down by the world around us.

There was at once something obvious and miraculous in this. Of course we can change, but also, how astounding that we can change. Our very foundations can be altered, are being altered in this moment. I found impenetrable hope in this knowledge. We're raised up from nothing by the people who come before us. They copy themselves, give themselves away to makes us. But the people here now—the people who surround us, who touch our lives might genetically alter us with that touch, might adjust everything we're made of so that we're different in our very core, changed at a cellular level by the company we keep.

Cutting that hope, of course, is the possibility of what lies lurking inside us, what might be brought out without our knowing, what dead ancestor might emerge some unexpected night to take control of our living lives.

. . . .

They staggered us into the woods, sending each group down a dark trail when the coast was clear. The rest of us watched them disappear and waited for the screams.

"You're here by yourself?" the worker asked suspiciously when it was my turn to wait at the head of the trail and stare into nothingness. A sheriff's deputy stood by her, overseeing as people set off into this horror movie trope, and he too looked over in amusement at her question.

"Just me," I smiled, but she only gave me a look I deserved and then released me into the forest to be haunted.

It took longer than I expected for them to come for me. After a couple minutes of me crunching along down the trail, something leapt from behind a tree, a gruff voice swirling as the creature landed inches from me.

It did nothing for me. My heart rate was steady, I looked into the made-up kid's eyes. Maybe I smiled.

I didn't know if it was being alone out there or if it was childhood knowledge of those woods or if it was the detachment I'd fashioned by calling the trip *research*, but I watched the jump scares like one might a science fair. I observed curiously.

Some of the zombies were visibly annoyed to put in the effort and get no return on this investment. I tried to encourage them—"Whoa, that was a good one, man," I said to a dejected one. "Oh! Smart hiding spot, didn't see you coming," I offered to another, but I didn't know if my praise would ring true without shrieks. *It's not you, it's me,* I wanted to say to each emerging figure, but instead I kept winding through the woods toward the barn.

The Haunted Farm was the busiest Halloween spectacle on this side of the state, voted the Best Haunted House in the whole of North Carolina. All month, church vans and buses and pickup trucks had crunched down Townsend Road past the Prestwood land. Even though it was out there in my familial nowhere, it was easy to see why. It was an impressive outfit—hordes of teenagers in complicated garb and careful makeup, barns and outbuildings full of lights and smoke and electronic scares. Plus, the whole of the experience was wound into a story, a mythical center to all the fear: an Appalachian feud carrying on even after everyone is buried.

The Lively and Tate families, the story went, had been and would continue to be spilling blood over that plot of land, over access to Clear Creek, over the

Romeo-and-Juliet tale of Missy Lively and Billy Joe Tate. On the night the couple had planned to escape and elope, his body was found in these woods and Missy was left standing, screaming by Clear Creek in her white dress. She lost her mind and vanished.

That was the story crafted to make sense of the crazed butcher who had just rushed me from the corner of the shed. I was into it. I love a little history with my zombie apocalypse, which was why I was wondering if there could be any truth to the blood feud as the man with a chainsaw stepped from the cornfield and chased us down. The tractor pulling us to the creek couldn't outrun him, so he climbed onto the trail, laughing maniacally as the chainsaw roared above us and people screamed for their lives. I gave him a thumbs-up as he stepped back off.

By all accounts—which is to say my cousins'—Asbury and Clementine's house across that creek is haunted. As a child I heard the stories and the evidence: A man had murdered his wife, chopped her head clean off. Her spirit still haunted that old house, and we could hear—and often heard—her ghostly head rolling down the stairs. Thump, thump, thump.

Some years ago, I did the research. On paper, I found Asbury buying the house and 124 acres from a Freeman family in 1906. But no Freemans had been murdered in the process, no severed heads conveyed in the sale, so I wrote the thumping off as an empty ghost story aimed at impressionable children.

But then a tape emerged. A distant Prestwood cousin shared a newly digitized audio recording of Azalee Prestwood, Nanny, telling stories about life long ago. On the recording, these cousins who'd grown up in Georgia prompt her with questions on a visit to the mountains, probably sometime in the 1970s or early '80s, and she fires back in her natural prickliness. A cousin asks if horses drove the wagon. "Well, what else, Marjolie, did you think pulled it?!"

"They tell this about this place . . ." the recording opens. Then she recounts the story about the same as I'd heard it from older cousins as a boy—severed head, spirit haunting the stairs. Only, she provides a clear ending: "That old man got ashamed of hisself, and he went out here and hanged hisself on an apple tree between here and the highway."

The biggest difference in her story, recorded before I was born, was the name. She connects the grisly details to the family who'd owned this land before the Freemans, farther back than I'd researched. "It was old man Pinner who owned it, and he was real mean. And he was abusive to his wife."

Clementine Prestwood, granddaughter-in-law
of William Thomas Prestwood, in her handmade
wedding dress, 1881

The rest of the recording is full of details of the Prestwoods moving here from Lenoir, where William lived, of loading the boxcars with steamer trunks and driving the livestock with a schooner wagon. She tells of typical Sunday dinners and the work to keep a house and a farm. She returns over and over to Clementine, her mother-in-law. "She was the smartest woman I've ever known."

Mostly, she tells of Clementine's work, of everything it took to keep the place running, of how she rose before anyone else to dress the chickens and milk the cows and fetch the water. From the wings, a nephew chimes in to say Asbury worked hard, too, but Azalee is having none of it: "She would be a-sitting in that room of a night, making the girls a dress by lamplight, and he would've already gone to bed and be a-snoring."

But then the head would come rolling down the stairs, and Clementine'd run and jump into bed with Asbury—"clothes and all."

In everything Azalee tells, there seemed little exaggeration, so I wondered if I'd missed the murder after all, if I'd stopped my earlier research too soon. Maybe I'd doubted the story like I'd doubted Grandma when she introduced me to William and his ciphered life.

As the tractor aimed us back toward the haunted farm, I was thinking of the stories left behind by generations long gone and the murdered Pinner wife. A pale woman in a tattered wedding dress rocked in a chair out front of the barn, her dead eye tracking us. I wondered if that Pinner ghost was confined to the Prestwood house, forever thumping the stairs, or if she might slip out of a night to sit here with Missy Lively? Maybe they'd stroll down to the creek together in the dark, recalling old, alive times? What might they conspire to do together on this land now with all the time in the world?

Really, what I knew when I'd finished at the Haunted Farm and slipped off into the darkness above Clear Creek was that I had more digging to do. That there was always more to uncover, more to come to life. That the past rarely stayed put.

"There, that's the end of my tale," Azalee says as the tape clicks off.

43

To find any trace of Binah's children, I followed William's brother-in-law Hiram Clark across archives. But his life left hardly any paper trail. In the 1830 census Hiram was listed as the father of five children and the slaver of one woman. But in 1840, the number of enslaved had risen to four.

When I found that record, I presumed to know each of their names: John, Ira, Eliza, and Harriet. The suspicion I had formed from the scant entries across William's pages took shape in that census data: William sold Binah's children to Hiram sometime after the dispute with Martha. There they all were, save Willis and Sylvia, still in Burke County and in the hands of Celia's brother.

But the math quickly caught up with me: What of the previously enslaved woman? In 1840, there ought to be five lives counted.

The solution, I feared, came in an entry in 1839: "Store & H Cl sold Harriet." The missing number was Harriet, sold away without another word before the census work arrived. The journal of 1840 has vanished, so if William ever mentioned her again, I couldn't find the symbols to reveal it. I had only that entry on March 18, the day my mother would be born and the day Harriet's mother was laid to rest.

But I shuffled more pages and zoomed into more grainy copies anyway, just in case there was some chance that I could put down on this page more than a name for a whole lived life. So that I could see what life might have followed hers.

At the end of 1842, Hiram Clark is in jail. The news comes by letter, but William makes no mention of the why or where. No mention of his level of surprise by this development. He carries on in the mines, playing the lottery with a pickaxe. The world is strange this winter. In mid-January a snowstorm appears with thunder and lightning. The next night William hears a meteor noise from the northwest. He turns fifty-five the next week and is glad to be marveled still by the world, even as Helen's young child dies and he's tasked with chiseling a headstone. He tinkers with equations, discovers latitude. There is so much still to find, so many mysteries within reach. He spends many days measuring the surface of the earth before dropping down inside it to find something that might yet change his life.

By the end of January, Hiram is free again; his symbol—[ϟ|—shows up alongside a note that Sal Clonse is mad. William writes nothing of Ira, John, or Eliza. He writes nothing more of Hiram. February brings lots of snow:

Feb. 4, 1843: Snow deep.

Feb. 5: Melt smartly.

And more astrological disruptions follow not far behind: "Hear meteor burst." The days are "high windy."

Soon, Evander will marry. William won't record this fact, but in September, Evander and Harriet Clontz will come together. Evander will gather up the belongings of Nancy Prestwood that he bought and set out to make a home, the first of William's children out on his own.

Of course that's not right. Willis is gone. Harriet is gone. But they've never been on their own and they've always been on their own. They've never really had a home to leave.

Something is changing in William's life. His children are not children. Cicero will soon marry. Then Robert will marry his cousin Catherine. Before long, J. W. McLeard will come asking for Polly's hand, and that'll drive William to sketch that upside down heart again on his pages, his only little girl soon to marry and leave Burke County.

And in the midst of all of it, William Thomas Prestwood of the Chesterfield Prestwoods will become a grandfather. Evander and Harriet will welcome into the world a little girl, but William's record of this life change, of this little girl named Gooly Ann brought into his and Celia's arms, has been lost. It doesn't make it any less true, this empty record, those lost pages. In 1845, William is someone's grandfather and his mother is dead and his children are leaving and his back aches and the world is full of marvel. He hunts and hunts for veins to open. He notices he can still catch a lady's eye.

....

My dad and my uncle dad are not only—or not exactly—identical twins. They're mirror twins. To see high school photos of them is to see the same image flipped, my dad using his left hand to part his hair on one side, my uncle his right on the other. They confused defenders on basketball courts across the region at that age, looking the same until they pulled up to shoot or drove into the lane.

No one knows exactly what causes this mirroring in some identical twins, but the going theory is that the fertilized egg waits longer to split than in other sets of identical twins. By the time the egg splits, some characteristics are already taking shape so that each new egg takes with it an opposing map. In some sets, this mirroring can even appear in internal organs, one twin's very heart flipped.

It's also possible that these changes are the result of environmental changes within the womb, genes already being turned up or turned down because of what my grandma ate or which side she slept on. From the moment we're conceived, our DNA is already shuffling. I imagine the maps of our bodies with tectonic plates just beneath them—everything laid out but unsettled.

My uncle and I both share a knee condition—a disease in medical terms but nothing life altering. Osgood-Schlatter disease results in a hard bump below the kneecap, inflammation of the patellar ligament. An Adam's apple for my knee. Mine appeared when I was ten or eleven; it's brought on from sports—jumping and running so much that the growth plate is beat up from repeated use. But it was also always there, lying in wait from the moment of fertilization. I inherited it, and there may have been no escaping it, save for sitting still during my preteen years. Growing up on basketball courts while my dad was coaching and jumping from trees in our woods shifted my tectonic plates enough that they raised up a painful little mound I'll carry with me forever.

And yet my dad never pushed his plates in the right directions to collide. Maybe his left-handedness saved him. Both my uncle and I sport these bulges on our left legs, the legs we planted and leapt with most often. No matter the case, Dad's genetic capacity for the disease waits inside him, yet he never brought it to life; his knees are smooth. *No—more like your uncle, I'm sorry to say.*

Really, this plate tectonic image I've fashioned is wrong, upside down. The word *epigenetics* describing this natural process of genetic shifting suggests something *upon* our genetic code, a magician's cape tossed over us so that we might appear changed in any moment.

Even more magical than this ever-shifting genome is that many of these changes can be turned back. Unlike our locked-in genetic code, epigenetics can be reversed—the stove turned back up or down. *Abracadabra*, torso and legs reattached. A whole man again.

Learning about this—our codes and tectonic plates and magician capes—often has me pondering what's happening in my skin in any given moment. It's a fruitless effort but overwhelming nonetheless. *Will this second bowl of ice cream unlock something genetic?* is not a thought a healthy person has. Every action can't be a potential origin story for a genetic trait. And yet learning that inside us all wait new versions of ourselves is unsettling—and thrilling. As is the realization that inside of us may also wait older versions of ourselves waiting to be brought back to life.

....

ϟL is how she appears in 1849, CR. It is November when William first writes of her, and beyond the enciphered initials, her identity is a mystery: "Fuck'd CR. Made bad out."

Since Binah's death nearly twenty years ago, William has recorded no infidelity. He's tended the fields and his children, disappearing into the mines and far-flung surveying jobs to escape. He's hell fussed with Celia and occasionally gone to her, but these visits have become less frequent. He hasn't recorded sex with his wife since last October, since he stayed home and fiddled on a rainy day, since the snowbirds appeared and he went without dinner. This year he's sixty-one and his children are gone, and he ought to feel old, but suddenly he feels brand new. He feels like a William he hardly remembers: a William on a horse in the flatlands of South Carolina.

As 1849 draws to a close, hardly a week goes by without CR appearing on his pages:

November 23: School. Met and fuck'd CR.

November 25: School. CR. Fuck'd her.

December 7: School. Fuck'd CR.

December 12: School. Tried fuck CR. Couldn't. Nt. Home.

Sure, he feels his age from time to time, but he can't deny the spring in his step even if it fails to appear everywhere in his body all the time. He mines gold and teaches school and ends the year—and most nights—thinking of CR. "Sweet CR."

As a new year begins and William turns sixty-two, he and CR find more places to disappear. Closets, hills, lofts. A fence post. Eventually there's enough routine to meet at "old place." The meetings grow more and more frequent, but they're not all rainbows:

January 4, 1850: Disappointed by CR.

January 18: Tried fuck CR. Could not.

January 21: Rain. CR. Could not.

January 26: School. Fucked CR.

January 27: School. Fuss Celia.

William begins to qualify these rendezvous, assigning to many a rating:

March 2: Met CR. Good.

March 19: School, Lenoir. Met CR. Midling like.

March 26: Met CR. Nothing done.

April 15: School. Met CR. Very good.

May 7: School. Met CR in field. She hug good.

May 18: CR good in closet.

May 20: Met CR. She out of fix.

September 21: School. Muster. CR loft. Best.

October 30: Miller's salt. CR closet. Sweet.

November 3: CR closet. 12 months since begun.

Meanwhile, Fabius marries Delilah Setzer. William doesn't record it. He does record fixing a clock and splitting boards and getting honey, but this marriage receives no mention on his pages. No matter: On my family tree, lines are connected anyway, though it'll be some years after this wedding that Delilah delivers a boy named Asbury who'll bring his family to Fruitland to move into a house that may be haunted in 1906.

In 1850, Fabius is a newlywed and William feels like one.

December 6: Great, fresh.

December 12: Dreampt I was president.

December 17: CR barn. Good.

44

Hiram Clark died in 1846 with no will. There's no record of the date that I could find, hardly anything at all recorded about his life or death. With some searching, I turned up a legal dispute over a piece of his land some years after he passed: his wife and daughter pressing the court to return them their father's property. This daughter, Catherine, was married to Robert Prestwood, William's son and her first cousin. That document noted Hiram passed away "sometime in 1846" but offered no other details.

Half of 1846 is missing from William's record, so if he noted Hiram's passing anytime between January and June, it is out of sight. I suspect, however, the day is December 21, when William visits Nancy Clark's house and sketches a filled-in heart in the margins of his tiny notebook, his usual mark for a death. Even if that guess is right, I don't know how Hiram went. Suddenly, it seems.

A few months prior, William writes that Eliza has died. I don't know if this Eliza is his Eliza, Binah's daughter sold to Hiram, but I do know that sometime between Hiram's death in 1846 and 1850, those enslaved children who are no longer children are gone again.

When Hiram's widow, Polly, appears in the 1850 census, it's only her and her biological children living near Lower Creek. There's no mention of Ira or John or Eliza or any other enslaved lives. Maybe she sold them to pay debts. Maybe they'd been sold before Hiram died. Maybe they managed to escape. Maybe one of them died on August 8, 1846, likely in her early twenties—the second of Binah's daughters to die young.

All I knew for sure as I lost Hiram Clark in the records was that the last, barely cracked-open door that might have revealed something about the lives of Binah's children closed with his death in 1846. No paper trails remained. Hiram Clark in the ground, the children scattered or laid to rest, I was left with nothing more to search save first names—and the code of my body.

....

23andMe's website makes the world clean and ordered. The tangled-up strands of DNA inside me appear there as straightened, organized dashes. These dashes of varying lengths are my chromosomes; the 23 are no longer paired, snipped strands of thread but are now straightened out and color coded before me. Nothing blurs or bends—everything takes its place easily, as if there could have been no other way. The exactness of the segments listed on the page reminds me a little of William's precise pages, but here I'm seeing only one symbol listed over and over: ———.

This is also a code to crack, of course. Every day when I roll out of bed, I'm decoding those dashes a touch, figuring out just who I am. Or, if I'm being honest, some days I may bury everything deeper into symbols, not sure of who I am or not willing to hold the magnifying glass close enough to see.

When my results arrived, I examined the neatly arranged segments of my body, and then I searched for others. The browser spun, and DNA matches snapped together, producing names, sometimes faces, of family. I found the childhood friend whose house held a lawn jockey statue out front listed as a fourth cousin. I found the face of a girl I crushed on in middle school as my second cousin. I found the name of a real estate agent whose signs popped up across the county. I saw lots more names I'd never seen, people I've never known and probably never would, people who were all connected to me somewhere in the past, somewhere inside me.

I followed those strands as they thinned and fell away until I arrived to names with whom I shared hardly anything—0.41 percent, 0.39 percent of DNA. We were probably fourth cousins, 23andMe told me. Then again, we might share a single ancestor only, not a set—making us half cousins. There's not much there, the subtext suggested, and yet those removed half cousins displayed pie charts far more colorful than mine in their profiles, each one filled mostly with the purples of sub-Saharan Africa and varying blue slices of Europe. I counted the generations that might bring our distant lives together and landed smack in the middle of William's.

What seemed true on the screen, with a handful of Black lives connected to mine somewhere in the 1800s, was what I'd long suspected was true: William was the father of Binah's children. The descendants waited on my computer screen, our connection written into the clean code of dashes on the screen—the overlap in our bodies is a single, colored line.

I hovered over the *Message* button and thought back to the message in a bottle I tossed into the ocean of Ancestry.com a couple years before, hoping to reach Virginia Presswood two decades too late with news of William and Binah: "I'm sorry I don't know more." Like then, I wondered what exactly I was after. Was I the messenger? The seeker? For whose sake would I clack the keys and press *Send*?

It was mostly mine. There was no need to kid myself about that. I wanted to know what life followed William and what it meant for me—and the life that would follow me. But stepping into his pages had revealed to me the many layers of privilege wrapping me up, and an unexpected one was genealogy.

Years ago I'd have seen the puzzling over family trees as a hobby of the retired, the detective-y cousin of bridge or pickleball, but by now I knew the very opportunity of sleuthing in a quiet room in the library was a possibility afforded to only some Americans. Enslavement still robs people even today of this possible knowledge, this forged connection. I heard the words again from that twenty-year-old Ancestry post: *Unfortunately since we as slaves were never allowed to be family orientated we may never know. Love from your possible family in Chicago. A black man born in Mississippi.* It was the *we* in that post that caught me every time, the blurring of timelines, the overlapping of the past and the present, the perpetual robbery.

The opened-up life of William Thomas Prestwood was more than a quiet genealogy room: It was an entire house, furnished with secrets in drawers and feather beds made to lie down on. If, from this abundance I'd been given, I could share the smallest portion—a name, a possible lineage—it was something. It was a tiny debt William could afford. So I clicked and wrote of what I knew. William and Binah. Willis and Eliza and Sheriff Boone and Hiram Clark. Me.

45

In July 1851, my great-great-great-grandfather nearly catches my great-great-great-great-grandfather with his mistress: "CR did not meet me. Fabius saw me." But CR stays away, and William is left with only the memory of the previous weekend, when he met her in the cotton patch, to satisfy him. Or the many rendezvous of June, coupling in the closet and the barn, "in loft, first bin."

This affair, now in its second year, is growing more dangerous. A mere two weeks after Fabius nearly spots the pair, Jess Craig sees William ducking off to get ahold of CR after school. How long, William must wonder, will it be before word is back to Celia? Does he care? Would she?

The once-weekly secret meetings have grown more frequent. He and CR might be in "old place" or "usual place" or "near Corpeny mine" or, occasionally, in a real bed three times a week. William carries on teaching and searching for treasure. He pans for gold, and then he and Fabius find a new vein to split open. He "hunt[s] a blue stone near well place." He sees the northern lights. And he can't quit CR, even if these meetups are drawing attention. Just a month after Fabius nearly sees them, he meets her near his house again anyway: "good."

Meanwhile, his clan grows. Fabius and Delilah have a boy, David. A few weeks later Cicero and his wife have a boy, John. Evander and Harriet have their first boy; they name him William Thomas. William and Celia have taken in his niece Caroline. When someone named Franky dies suddenly in October, William and Celia also take in her child. The house is active again, and at the end of the month, all his grandchildren crowd into his house for the first time: "Had 5 grandchildren together."

Only, it may be six grandchildren. Earlier this year Rebecca Crump, sixteen years old and growing with child, swore to a judge the baby was Sydney Prestwood's. Nineteen and William's second youngest, Sydney denied he'd fathered any baby. *Above all things, my sons, do not SEDUCE innocent girls.*

Rebecca's father had died when she was a little girl, so she entered 1851 pregnant, with only her widowed mother to rely on. They brought a bastardy suit against Sydney, and he promptly bolted to Mitchell County to start a new life. Once or twice a week William visits Mrs. Crump's, perhaps checking in on Rebecca as the baby grows. He puts away her cabbage and mends her fence. Somewhere near the county line, he delivers Sydney some of his clothes, and Celia isn't pleased: "gave me hell."

Rebecca delivered her baby, also a boy, in August, just after Fabius nearly caught William fooling around. The court settlement awarded her forty dollars for Sydney's bastardy. So in October 1851, four of William's grandchildren are baby boys, born within a few months of one another. Despite—or maybe because of—Sydney's skipping town and leaving Rebecca alone with a child, she names the baby Joseph Sydney.

At that, I can only think of Binah naming her baby Willis, a not-so-veiled acknowledgment of that young white teacher who brought her here from the South Carolina lowlands as property and took from her the word *no.* But Willis is long gone now, perhaps with children of his own, children who'll never crowd into William and Celia's house for Sunday dinner.

....

In his sixties, free, and far from Burke County, Willis marries a woman twenty years his junior named Eve. They buy a house in Cape Fear, and he gives her his new last name, Jordan. He lives into old age, farming until he passes from this earth.

Or Willis lands not far from the place he'd been born, from where his mother had been taken in 1813 and buried two decades later. Once free from the Goodrums, his enslavers after William and Nancy Prestwood, he marries a woman named Jane and they raise many children in Marion—children that are theirs, children they've taken in. He teaches all of them to read. One of them he names Thomas.

Or Willis becomes Willis Blackman of Cumberland, North Carolina. He works as a turpentine hand and marries a woman named Nancy. They fill a house with children, and he sometimes tells them of his time mining gold, of his time on the run from the great-nephew of Daniel Boone. But about so much more, he remains quiet, preferring instead to sing bouncy songs after supper, making room for Mack, the two-year-old, to crawl into his lap even though he ought to be in bed. Despite her best efforts, Nancy often succumbs to Willis's silly optimism, tapping her toe to the songs, believing against all evidence to the contrary that tomorrow will always be better than yesterday. He's trained the children in the ways of practical jokes, and Nancy can never trust that a small child won't pop from a cabinet or around the corner, always with that same twinkle Willis has willed into his eyes. She loves Willis so much that she never speaks of the sounds he makes when he dreams. She wakes and heats the kettle, waiting a beat before turning, his face by then set into sunshine. "Oh, hello there." He winks, and life could never be better.

Or Willis dies before turning twenty. Only another uncounted life eaten up by the enslaved South.

Or Willis lives alone, taken to Alamance County after 1833 by Hiram Clark, his body beaten into a machine to work that land day in and day out. He jumped the broom with a woman whose name it's now too painful to remember. They had a daughter, whose name he's forced himself to forget. She was taken not long after her second birthday. He looked—for years after the war ended and his wife died, he looked. But what could he do? All he could do, it seemed, was just what he'd been doing before the war ended: work that farm and sleep on that same sack of feathers and hay he'd been given. And so each day he wakes and works and finds himself sometimes staring into the distance, sometimes considering the movement of the stars, but mostly dreaming of those deep, dark mines, praying one might one day open up and take him home.

Or he's Willis Cramartie of Whites Creek.

Or Willis Barco of Shiloh.

Willis Baker of Sanford. Willis Shaw of Lake Lanning. Willis Morrisey of Turkey. Willis Hamlin of Leaksville.

A couple dozen men named Willis and born in 1817 show up in the 1870 census, spread across North Carolina, free Black men and finally counted as such. Any one of them could be Binah's son. Or none of them.

Most likely, perhaps, of all the Willises who survived slavery and war and were counted in the 1870s census as free men, is Willis Jeffers. He's in a community called Bruce, situated in Guilford County—a place William mentions in 1833 when Willis is on the run and Hiram Clark is whisking him away. In 1870,

Willis is fifty-three, has been hired on a farm, can read and write. Six children and his mother-in-law live with him and his wife. And beside "race" on those scanned, blurry pages, the U.S. government names him as "mulatto."

....

One of my distant cousins wrote back. Of the eight people who seemed likely descendants of Binah and William, one wrote back, and his last name was familiar: Corpening, or as William wrote it after heading to the mines or sneaking to meet CR day after day, Corpeny. He'd grown up in Burke County, not far from where William and Binah lived and died. And, because the world sometimes works like this, that far-off cousin who was likely one of Binah's sons and I went to the same small college, missing each other by only a year.

His family tree, as far back as was traceable, held many names that were scattered across William's pages: Suddereth and Dula, Kincaid and McKesson. In the 23andMe chatboxes, we compared notes. He'd heard stories of ancestors coming off Harshaw's plantation, of others winding up with a Clarke family. His grandmother remembered tell of enslaved children and Hiram Clark, but as we shared and searched, we found nothing verifiable, really—only outlines of stories and the shared segment in our bodies.

Still, I was spinning scenarios: What if the Harshaws bought the children when Hiram died in 1846? What if Harriet is sold to the Harshaws in 1839 and later sold to Squire Dula? What if she is *the* Harriet Harshaw Dula that Leslie McKesson writes about in her book?

I lost hours tugging at those tattered and disconnected threads before finally settling into the knowledge that there was no knowing. Not really. There would never be answers to hold carefully in my hand and examine from every angle. My Corpening relative and I talked about college and a little of our lives now, but the past was only smoke.

A better question I might have been asking, a question more revealing than how I was connected to far-off kin online, was why I need the surety, the tied-up bow, the carefully plotted narrative. Maybe I wanted to find something undeniable amid all the gray of William's life, a straight line away from the racial disfunction of America, toward his guilty part within it (and away from me). It would be true if it was on the screen, solid and in color. He fathered those children. The computer caught him. The ancestor I'd come to know so intimately had not only passively benefited from a country built on slavery but had also stepped boldly into it to take what he wanted. Then he sold away the remains.

Or perhaps I was simply looking for another living, breathing soul with whom to process this attachment to the long-gone William Thomas Prestwood. *What does all of this mean?* I muttered to myself as I went back into the diaries week after week, like a certain sixty-year-old man disappearing into the mines, sure there was something to find to change his life.

Of course it was selfish to seek out another person tangled up by William so that I could ask, *What does it mean? Why does it matter?* Especially when that entanglement reached back to Binah, to a relationship that was born in bondage and resulted in children who died young or were shrugged off like used parts. What hubris to ask the descendants of Binah to make sense of this for me.

Before long, I heard back from another half cousin online. He was in DC, and we tossed around more theories. He suggested I search for Willis in the 1870s census, and I found Willis Jeffers and all of the other possible lives of Willis there. I sent him the court document detailing the fight over Binah's children. He consulted his grandparents. He told me of some possible connections in Virginia, leading me to wonder about who of Binah and William's children moved north.

As I should have expected, we found nothing conclusive. We may be connected on his grandmother's side, but from genetic testing she'd learned her grandfather hadn't been her biological grandfather at all. More smoke.

After we exhausted the little we could find, I asked. I was parked outside of a feed store to get cell reception, and I asked because I not only wanted to know for me, but I also wanted to know for him. *What does it mean?* What did it mean to find yourself descended from a man like William Prestwood, to know his DNA was there whether you wanted it or not?

"This is just," Winston said into a phone hundreds of miles away so that satellites caught his words and immediately sent them down on me, "an American story."

46

In William's world in 1852, there's a content, sometimes secretive, rhythm to his days. He goes to the gold mine. Or he says he's going to mine and meets CR instead—in a closet or loft or stand of pines. Sometimes he goes to the mine *and* meets CR just after, suddenly not minding his empty-handedness. As always, he teaches. Perhaps as he's aging, he cares less about how comprehensive the classes are for the young scholars. They daydream more. He does, too.

Fabius, now a young father, is working his land, so William "holps." Together they plant *oker* and build fences and roll logs. Sometimes William sets out to Fabius's house but meets CR in the shadows instead. *Good.*

Sydney returns briefly. He meets Rebecca at Fabius's: semineutral territory. Surely she brings little Joseph Sydney, now a year old. Surely Sydney wants to see him. Then again, maybe he's sticking to his story even now, even after his parents and siblings have taken up the slack. He is no father. He's only come to see his family, to drop in on his older brother, and is surprised to find Rebecca there, a squirmy child in her lap who looks at him too closely.

All around William there is the endless mess of life. Someone named William Avery kills S. Fleming. Jonathan Suddereth marries the Wakefield girl. It rains. It snows. He fusses with Celia. Luther is bit by a snake. A flood comes on in May.

Andrew Baird sends a letter from Alabama in late September. After so many tiny headstones, he and Nancy finally had those children—children who have now grown. Little Marcus is twenty-one. Margaret is twenty-two. William takes a few days, but he writes back. There's so much to report and yet so little. The grandchildren abound—some claimed and some unclaimed. Some so far gone they'll never be found. He's found and lost love. The mines call to him still. He dreams in such unexpected times of Mary Norwood, which frightens him. He's a sixty-four-year-old man, and yet this long-dead woman still haunts his sleep, beckoning him into lives unlived.

Neither his sister nor his brother-in-law needs to know any of this—they only need to know the leaves are turning and the summer birds are vanishing and life carries on. People here have been talking of temperance. Is that in the air there? No, he hasn't heard from their father, but oh how he misses Mother some days. How she would love on all these tiny baby boys at William's feet. How she would want to know about the heat down there in Alabama.

It was another lifetime when William would have whispered to a sister about a mistress. And that was Martha, anyway, not little Nancy—Martha who will likely never speak to him again after the fight for the lives of Binah's, of his, children. But he might at least tell Nancy that he's feeling like he's not felt for years. It's more than lust, he would plead. CR has colored the world in new ways. His spine is straighter, his fire hotter.

As 1853 begins, William turns sixty-five and builds a fire and stretches out a blanket. He's no longer surprised by how easily he can stretch out on the ground like a younger man, how spry he's become.

> **January 17, 1853:** 65 years old. CR on blanket by fire. Good.
> Home.

....

I dove into deed books and newspapers with Nanny's ghost story and came up where I started: murderless. Sure enough, I found Burrell Pinner, but I found no suicide, no decapitation. His wife, Ellen, outlived him by nearly a decade. No matter how long I searched or how many local historians I pestered, I uncovered no grain of truth in this story we'd passed down for generations. So why its persistence? Why the unexplained white shape in the window of that old house from a photograph years ago? Why the noises that sent my great-grandmother—*when I was a new bride*—jumping out of bed for fright? That sent me running into the field as a boy?

Or better yet, why all these stories of killed and abandoned women—the Pinner ghost drifting out to Missy Lively along the creek, Frankie Silver reciting her poetry at the gallows, Binah telling William MN would only scold him? "We tell ourselves stories in order to live," Joan Didion famously wrote, but what about these stories of life floating on after death? Do we tell ourselves these stories to keep the past alive, to keep our ancestors here with us? To make sense of what lingers? Or are they mere correctives: Don't murder your wife or you'll hang yourself in shame. Don't break up young love or they'll haunt your farm forever.

"We look for the sermon in the suicide, for the social or moral lesson in the murder of five," Didion continues. "We live entirely . . . by the imposition of a narrative line upon disparate images." Meangingfully whole.

I wonder what disparate images hang around my family's land to have created the story encircling the old house above the barn. That lonely farmhouse on a hill? A gnarled old apple tree apart from the others? A whistling breeze loosing the last leaves from the trees?

A student wondered aloud in class recently if a family ghost story might be a kind of inherited trauma taking shape. Whether the floating figure in an old house is real or not, the living, breathing people here have been hardwired to feel and sense the pain—to see the ghost. And, perhaps, to give it meaning.

So far there are no clear answers from researchers about transgenerational trauma. Many scientists in the growing field of epigenetic research believe enough studies have shown trauma can indeed be inherited, that trauma leaves a kind of chemical impression on someone's genes. And this impression can be passed down. This epigenetic change—the turned-up or turned-down burner eye—doesn't alter the gene itself but changes how it's processed. And the new instructions show up in the next generation's skin.

The biology to fully understand this idea, however, isn't clear, and critics believe too much causality is being assumed without enough evidence: *We tell ourselves stories . . .*

I like the stories, though, and am of a mind to believe our bodies can do miraculous if not terrible things, even when we can't parse out the *how*. If trauma can be laced into our inheritance, I wonder how the DNA from Binah and William took form in the children and children's children down the line. How might the segment I share with Winston on my eighth chromosome behave differently for him than it does in me? What other messages might it carry?

Even if there was no murdered Pinner woman thumping down the steps above Clear Creek, I had my Prestwood ghost story in William. He was haunting my head; I was writing him letters; he was coming to life. I was finding the disparate images to make a whole man, to impose the narrative. But I wondered what story Winston would tell about Binah had her pages been discovered in an abandoned house in Wadesboro, North Carolina, instead. What form would she take if conjured by someone carrying the story of her body in theirs?

What of Celia? Or any of the women before her? What of CR? I thought of Azalee setting the story straight about Clementine Prestwood, about who really did the necessary and unseen work on that land. The women on William's pages were mere footnotes. Of them, I could write next to nothing, could impose no narrative. William used them. William loved them. William sold them. William William William.

All I had was his code on the page and a code in my skin, and so I kept conjuring him even as I knew that he haunted the lives of so many around him—and may still do so today—whether we feel it or not.

....

When you send your spit to 23andMe, machines pull it from the tube. In assembly-line fashion, this sample of DNA is sucked up, labeled, and readied. Waiting are tiny chips, built to catch some of your genes like tiny nets. The spit and the genotyping chips are heated in ovens so that the DNA bakes in, adhering itself there for decoding.

Once free from the heat, the chips are stained, washed, and lit up. The unpacking of our bodies is essentially a sterile light show—an array of flares that reveals the curved and clipped threads that are our chromosomes. The lights beaming from the tiny cooked chip are our letters, the As, Cs, Ts, and Gs that make us *us*.

When I learned about just what this deciphering looks like in a lab, it felt too . . . magical. Tiny chips produce lights and then red and green constellations expose who we are? But what do the fairies do? The crystals?

I assumed there would be more whirring computers and fewer ovens and tiny bathtubs. Surely no beaming lights. It's as if they take our saliva and produce a hologram from it, projecting a translucent version of us on the wall.

But that's not me floating there in green and red. Not fully. The results splashed on the screen are limited, only the portion of my genome that 23andMe has handpicked to align with what they know about certain genetic variants and percentages. Despite the clean ordering of the results on my account, the process is a fragmented, crowdsourced guessing game. Compared against everyone else's colorful ghosts, I know I have only a typical likelihood of developing asthma; I won't likely develop Celiac disease or gallstones. Chances are good I won't flush red when drinking alcohol. I have a genetic variant for muscle composition found in many professional athletes, which I wasted, but also explains why I must stretch seventeen thousand times each day so that I can touch my toes and not wake up permanently bent over.

I won't likely have a bald spot. (I do.) My big toe is likely longer than my second. (It's not.) I likely weight less then two hundred pounds. (I don't.)

Despite the straight lines and pretty colors displaying my genetic code across a computer screen, nothing was as clear as I'd hoped. I couldn't be sure that the half cousins I'd messaged are indeed the descendants of Binah and William. The generations matched and some locations matched, but some other results didn't line up—some expected descendants don't share DNA with each other, And then other results lined up but in unexpected ways.

No family trees helped this far back, especially when the lives of enslaved people were torn limb from limb and left scattered, so I tiptoed on bits of guesswork. I tried to pull in more genetic matches—more crowds with which to source—and those connections only seemed to make everything more complex. The pretty colors of the 23andMe site began to feel gray.

All that was certain at the end was that I had relatives whose ancestors hailed from sub-Saharan Africa. But not all of those relatives traced to Binah. Not all of them traced back to Prestwoods. The more I searched and the more I compared, I found Black men and women on both sides of my tree, all of us connecting a few generations back.

In the poor mountain lines of my family's past, I'd found hardly any evidence of slavery. Until William, it seemed the rest of my tree had come out of the antebellum South pretty clean, many of them fighting for the Union. But then what about these cousins? What about this 0.5 percent of shared DNA, the three segments I shared with a Black woman in Texas, segments we received from some other shared ancestor four generations back? Owning a human life, I was learning, wasn't a requirement for using it.

Quickly the little knowledge I thought I had to share with my genetic matches—Binah and her children scattered in the mid-nineteenth century—was simply a story, a story built of smoke and lights. A ghost story.

47

William is elected county surveyor just a week after his birthday and romantic fireside celebration with CR. He's sworn in on January 25.

Daily, this means more surveying. More correspondence. More travel. Less mining. Even his rendezvous with CR grow less frequent, but he makes a way to see her most weeks:

> **February 15, 1853:** Smith. Mrs. Crump. Jo. Corpeny. Puett. CR loft.
>
> **February 17:** Wrote Harsaw's. Took handkerchief by mistake.
>
> **February 25:** CR closet, bed. Jo Corpeny.
>
> **March 8:** Holp Cicero. AE bought hog.
>
> **March 17:** CR loft. Caroline [the cow] come in.

He's doing work across the county, his diary quickly becoming only a list of names of men for whom he's doing work—Fleming, Corpeny, Kent—and locations of his affair:

> **August 3:** Jo. Corpeny. P Fleming. CR closet.
>
> **August 4:** Election. CR flat. Saw her cunt. Rain. Voted for S Dula, R Wakefield, clerks.
>
> **August 10:** CR old place. Good. Survey'd JW Shell.
>
> **August 11:** Met CR, old place. Survey M. M'Call.
>
> **August 29:** Mule kick me. Nt. W Shell
>
> **August 31:** Survey H. Porch. Sundries. Nt. Home.
>
> **September 7:** M. Crump. CR in field near old place.

William's father dies the next day. I don't know when word arrives to Burke County—William writes only "home" for September 8, 1853—but 150 miles away in Chesterfield, South Carolina, the ninety-one-year-old TP lets go. A week later, an obituary runs in *The Charleston Mercury*:

> Thomas Prestwood. Cheraw, Sept. 14, 1853 — ANOTHER REVOLUTIONARY SOLDIER GONE. — Died, on the 8th inst. at the residence of his daughter, after three days illness, Mr. Thomas Prestwood, in the ninety-second year of his age [*sic*]. He was a soldier of the Revolution, and the last survivor of that glorious struggle in this section of the country. He served under Col. Kalb [*sic*: Kolb] until the death of that brave officer, and then under Gen. Marion until the end of the war. He was born, raised, lived and died in Chesterfield District.

Had word made it to TP before he died that William had been made county surveyor? William didn't write to him to say, but perhaps someone did. It shouldn't matter. Shouldn't mean a thing what TP thought. William hasn't been to South Carolina for five years and might consider for a flash making the trek back to the Cheraw District as his father is laid to rest. But he can't. He won't. He's busy with never-ending jobs. His scholars. CR.

He leaves not a mark on his pages for TP's crossing over, not emptied nor filled-in hearts. Instead, he sets out for CR. They meet in the hollow above the spring. Good.

William checks in on Mrs. Crump weekly, sometimes more. Little Jonathan Sydney is on his feet now, wobbly but persistent.

William is doing more and more work for Mr. Kent, too. How old is Archilus now? Seventy-five? Seventy-six? He's got a decade on William, and yet he's set up house with Ann, who can't be but forty-three. A fine woman. Surely a woman like that, a woman so full of life, must bore of creaky old Archilus Kent. William must bore of him, too, as they stare gravely at the land and envision lines laid out there.

William's at the Kents' more than he needs to be. He might not admit that to himself, but he surely knows. And yet he goes back. Week after week he takes Ann's hand when she offers it as he steps inside. Stands on the porch longer than he should once Archilus has hobbled off to something else.

Fabius and Delilah have a little girl, Mary. They baptize her, and William sees his family grow before his eyes. He plows the potatoes and meets CR at the lumber house. His life is good. He's happy. Content. But he may as well stop by Kent's tomorrow just to see what's about, to reach out for her hand.

....

As I watched William sneaking off with CR week after week, I caught myself thinking back on his courting days, the heat amid the snow in 1819 (*Felt Celia's cunt. She touched my prick. Snow)*. What would that thirty-one-year-old have said to the old man fooling around behind Celia's back? In those days of only ב ב ב, would he have ever imagined a time when he'd want to climb into barn lofts with other women? I wish I knew anything about Celia to know what brought them together other than heat and snow.

After Sarah and I had been dating for a couple years, I found a picture of her as a child, four or five years old. I saw in that girl's expression the ghost of a face she made still, and for some reason, seeing her in that old photograph, locked in time there with the woman she was to become lying in wait in her skin, I experienced a stretching wide of everything I'd already felt. I loved that little girl, which made no sense because I didn't know that little girl. But I also knew that little girl. That little girl sat beside me even now.

I recognized then that what I felt I felt in ways far beyond the moment I felt them. I knew that whatever was happening was about more than the pleasing shape of her body. Or the cute wrinkle of her nose or thrill of her laugh. I recognized then that I loved her in a way so deep and wide that I would love her in any age. That smirk appearing on her baby face would appear on her seventy-year-old face. And I loved that already. I loved it in a way that I couldn't understand or articulate then, but I recognized there was a timelessness at work that I hadn't yet considered. And that was suddenly serious.

Of course we'd changed since then. We weren't those twentysomethings on a beach in Belize. We were on opposite ends of the couch, worn out and talking about taxes and packed lunches. *Write to me about this deep and wide love when you're sixty-five*, William might say.

But I imagined that face—at four and twenty-two and seventy-five—and it always set everything right. Even when the pretty woman across the coffee shop said hello and held my eye for a beat too long and a kid was home sick and another had soccer practice and I had a deadline and Sarah had a hearing and we'd been running ragged and hardly had a chance to say more than *hello* for days on end, she was still a smirking little girl but was also a new woman I was getting to know after twenty years together. There was something to that, something deep-set and immovable, and reading William's life in closets and writing letters to William continued to remind me of that, even if it was because I couldn't see Celia's face and I couldn't know why he was in the loft with sweet CR week after week. I was grateful all the same.

....

When William finally kisses Mrs. Kent, the weather has turned cold and Archimus has gone off somewhere. She's *Mrs. Kent* on his pages, and he makes no effort to figure a symbol for her now—she remains ϬLς ξ478.

> **November 3, 1855:** Come by Kent. Kiss Mrs. Kent
>
> **November 14:** Bradford execute E. Prestwood's horse. Mrs. Crumps.
>
> **November 17:** Kiss'd Kent. Lenoir.
>
> **November 18:** Fuck'd Mrs. Kent.

The next day William is back in the loft with CR.

William has taken to numbering his sexual encounters. A kiss is merely a kiss, but a roll in the hay or, as is the case the next time he and Mrs. Kent strip down, a roll in the hog pen, warrants a number. So far this year, he and CR have had sex twenty-nine times. As 1855 ends, he and Mrs. Kent are up to two.

But as William enters his sixty-ninth year, Mrs. Kent doesn't reappear. He is sued by Bagle. Luther, who is eighteen, has run away and come back and is now fighting with his brother. But CR is still in the loft and is still good (2).

Of late, numbers have appeared sometimes beside his recorded stops at the widow Crump's house too. He checks in on Mrs. Crump, on Rebecca, on his grandson often. He brings her corn and sorts her papers. But lately he does more. By June, she's up to number three.

These new numbers—Mrs. Kent, Mrs. Crump—may be why CR threatens to end it all in August. She and William have sex for the twenty-third time in 1856, but she's done. William sketches a heart on his pages:

> **August 12:** CR fence (23). She will quit me.

He goes by Mrs. Crump's the next day, but no number appears. Of the visit, he only reports that he "got alchemy mill."

Though William doesn't record it on his pages, Cicero's wife has died. Their son, John, is five, the same age as the fatherless Joseph Sydney. Rebecca Crump is twenty-one years old now and, like Cicero, raising a boy alone. As often as William stops by the Crumps' these days, he visits Cicero. He helps hoe and plant the garden. Does what he can.

Before long, all of this—Rebecca Crump left pregnant by Sydney, Mrs. Crump widowed a decade ago, Cicero standing here alone after his wife's passing, little John and Joseph Sydney climbing trees out back—comes together. Cicero marries Rebecca; she and Little Sydney, as William calls him, move in. William continues stopping by Mrs. Crump's anyway, but not only to offer help. After all, Mrs. Crump was once Betsy Setzer—a young woman who young William hugged and gave ginger and lay with. This fire has long ago been lit.

Then Rebecca is pregnant again, this time by a different Prestwood man. One she has married. They have a daughter, Margaret, five days before William turns sixty-nine. He sends Sydney a letter to let him know about this half-brother-cousin and then stops by to check in on Mrs. Crump.

Amid all of this, CR doesn't keep her word about ending it. They're in the old place and the loft, William scratching in numbers each night. Neither William nor she can quit this. And while he may want to stay faithful to his mistress, before long he's also penning a number beside Mrs. Cragg, too. Inside, William can feel another William emerging—a version of himself sliding back into place, his genes shuffling to reconstitute a former self.

Sydney comes the next month, letter in hand. There's a "great fuss" at Cicero's. William tries to keep the peace, but what does Sydney believe he's owed after running off to leave a sixteen-year-old girl alone with a baby? Does he think he has some say? William writes to Sydney to reconcile a few days later, but the damage is done.

He sees Mrs. Kent the next day. Is there still fire there? He thinks there might be, with a little kindling, but he heads off to see Mrs. Crump instead, with the stated reason, perhaps, of talking about this domestic mess of their children, but afterward he goes back home to write down the number two beside her name, ϭLς ϟL|ϭə. Then he climbs back into the loft with CR—*sweet loft*.

Dear William:

I'm up to 1857. You've been reelected county surveyor. Your kids are having kids.

Here, my kids are damming up creeks and playing soccer as the leaves turn. We're in our first cold snap, and my body is remembering how to close in on itself. I feel those muscles relearning what it means to grab a doorknob and prepare for frigidity lying on the other side. Do you know this feeling? Shoulders hunching, everything tightened and braced.

That boy that Delilah and Fabius had in July, Asbury—he'll lead to me. He'll move away in fifty years, buying some land and an old haunted house deeper in the mountains, and I'll come later, after Albert and Betty and David. I hope you'll hold him for me.

Next month there's an election here. That's true for you, too. You're planning to vote in favor of free suffrage, I know. You won't be alone. I'll tell you now, it'll pass by wide margin. It took only seventy years, but this requirement of owning land to earn the right to vote will fade away in North Carolina before you know it.

You're smart enough to see the danger, though. More freedoms are being afforded to white men while freedoms are stricken from Black lives. This can't last. These rulings and elections and Dred Scott and Frederick Douglass and John Brown and Nat Turner and Willis and Harriet and the ghosts of Sylvia and Binah and Cato. Free states and slave states. Our country is a tinderbox.

Before it lights up, I wanted to write to tell you everything gets better and everything gets worse. I wanted to tell you about Asbury. I wanted to tell you to brace for the cold. I wanted to tell you you're wrong. I wanted to tell you thank you. I wanted to tell you sorry.

48

"How many other children did he father?" someone asked me once after I told them about William and all of his symbols. I explained about Binah, about the guesswork and her children.

"But what about all these other women?"

Somehow, I'd never considered that, never considered that in all of his running around—in his twenties and his sixties—he might have fathered children from Darlington to Burke counties. But of course, he may well have left a trail of bastardy suits across two states. And those descendants may be waiting on my computer screen, too. All of us with Osgood-Schlatter but not knowing why.

None of them would know of William, just like many of Binah's descendants will never know of William. And does any of it matter? I felt guilty when it became clear that tracing our connected lives back to Binah wasn't as clear of a shot as it seemed. I wondered if I should have kept William and Binah to myself instead of throwing my guesswork at strangers on the internet. I had only possible ancestors, only never-ending maybes. But no one I talked to through 23andMe was surprised to learn of a white slaver in the family tree. One of them wrote to me, "My cousins and I have grown up knowing 'who old folks said' their grand/great grandparents were." It was an open secret that somewhere in the family tree waited a William Thomas Prestwood.

What my results had revealed to me was simply that William Thomas Prestwood wasn't the only William in my family tree. Despite only faint traces on paper of slaveholding in my family history, I came from a forest of Williams. An everyman's story. From the cradle and beyond the grave. An American story.

. . . .

He can't deny it. Before long, William will be a seventy-year-old man. His mother is dead. His father is dead. Sure, he's a man about town—and pig pens and barn lofts—but the people around him are smaller, more fragile. Take Elizabeth Crump. She may've never been the most enthusiastic of women, but she stayed on her feet with the nonstop work. He's known her to come alive not on her feet, too. But of late, she hardly seems herself.

Mrs. Cragg has taken ill, Sanders died last month, and now Celia is wheezy at night. More than ever the human body seems so particular, so finnicky. William is fine; he carries on. He rides to Lenoir to buy some shoes. He digs a new vein and boils sugarcane, but he must admit he feels uneasy about all of this. The cold and age and eternal darkness.

Maybe CR senses this, or maybe she's back to her usual misgivings. "She will forsake me," William writes as fall approaches. Last week Mrs. Crump, too, was "in a fret." William tries to make everything better, back to normal. "Made friends her," he writes of his next visit to Mrs. Crump, but CR appears to be gone for good. The affair over. *Forsaken.*

It's cold, and Celia has gotten worse as fall has set in. "Bad off," he writes in October. It's not only the weather that's chilly when he sees CR in December: "CR, cold reception." He writes no numbers. They climb into no closets or lofts. Nothing is good. Nothing is sweet. Everything is ending. William sticks close to home with Celia being so poorly. He hauls manure and plants onions and writes letters to his sons, but most days only "home" appears on his pages as his wife grows sicker.

Celia survives the winter. The birds return, and so William heads back out into the world, surveying across the county. CR is no longer a usual stop on his outings, gone entirely from his pages and life. Nor are there numbers for Mrs. Crump. Or Mrs. Kent. Or Mrs. Cragg. William T. Prestwood, upstanding county surveyor, is all anyone sees along Lower Creek.

Cicero and Rebecca have another child, a boy they name James. Sydney comes to visit, but this time does so in peace, perhaps having accepted the state of the world. Polly and her husband come to visit from Wilkes County. William is glad for his children to be back in one place—glad for the sound of their voices and predictable bickers, but glad mostly because he fears Celia may not make it another winter. Fears no one will.

In August, he's right. She takes a turn:

August 18, 1858: Home. Celia bad off.

August 19: Home.

August 20: CR. One kiss.

They must all know now, William and his children—and CR. Celia is fading. CR must've heard the news in town and thought of William alone in that house, his wife dying, and she returns a year after quitting him. One kiss.

In the months to come, William will be home. He and CR will kiss when she lingers outside to check on him, but nothing more. He won't quantify or qualify her visits. He'll be by his wife's bedside until November 3, when she finally lets go:

> **November 3, 1858:** Celia died ♡♥
>
> **November 4:** Buried. Dined Cicero.

....

In the car-rider line to pick up my children, I called another newly discovered and distant kin on the phone. As the line inched forward, I told her of the little I knew of Binah and her children. We talked about family trees and looked for shared branches in the South. As always, we found only possibilities. Only edges of stories.

That week I had spent time talking to genecists, hoping to clear the fog of the 23andMe connections, but through those conversations, I had only learned that everything gets hazier the farther back we go. On a screen, I could see clear as day the segment I shared with Cheryl in Chicago—it was purple and undeniable—but I couldn't find anything to connect us directly to a man who laid his wife to rest in November 1858. We could be connected by some other branch in some other story. If not Binah and William, then some other lives we'd never know. As we spoke, we landed upon the only thing that was sure: We were connected by enslavement somehow. It was coded into us.

We promised to stay in touch with updates, and I hung up just as I saw the wild, red hair of my boy bounce from the school, the dark hair of his brother in tow. Because I'd spent the afternoon in enciphered pages, I thought of Celia when I saw them. What I had learned by then was that just as she was laid into the ground, she was also laid into my skin—into my boys' skin. In all my Prestwood people. In us, she haunts that house on the hill, haunts the Haunted Farm, haunts the woods surrounding Grandma's, haunted that car-rider line on a breezy spring day.

The boys climbed in, backpacks stuffed beneath feet and perfunctory *fines* tossed back to me when I asked questions. What a world this is. I thought I ought to write to William to tell him about schools these days, about the surveyors we saw along the road on the drive home, about his wife's continued life in the back seat of my Subaru.

I ought to tell him that despite everything that's gone unsaid and unnoted across his pages, his symbols have revealed to me that we're inhabited by unknowable lives, lives as rich and messy as our own. I have half a mind to pull out the Ouija board to meet them all, but all I have to piece them together are stories and court records and decoded DNA. And, of course, in the case of one man mining gold at Corpening's in 1858, I have decoded symbols stretching across a life's worth of worn pages.

But I didn't write to William. He was busy dying. I made my kids a snack and tried as hard as I could to forget the past and ignore the future and be only amid the goldfish and sliced apples and iPad games before this one life made of many was gone.

....

In the weeks after Celia's passing, William and CR sit for a meal for the first time in their recorded lives. His house is still Celia's house, filled with her clothes and smells, but what's missing—her just around the corner, the light snore in the afternoon chair—fills more space than seems imaginable. Walking CR through the front door and guiding her to the table cuts this cumbersome absence. He expects it to feel like a betrayal, but it only feels like a meal. It is Christmas, and she stays the night.

December 25, 1858: CR Breakfast and dinner by ourselves

And then it is 1859 and William is seventy-one years old, a widowed grandfather mining gold. Out of habit or embarrassment, he and CR still climb into the loft to draw close after he completes a surveying job. It is still good. "CR. Kiss and fuck sweet CR. (1). Loft."

Wild geese pass and he drinks brandy. He votes for that little Vance boy he met years ago on the way back from Mother Town, now a young man running for Congress and soon to be a governor amid war. William takes a surveying job in Shake Rag. He dyes wool. He has a "lovin discourse" with CR. His grandchildren run through. His children check in. He is an old man, but life abounds.

September 1, 1859: Home and Cicero. Splendor this night.

September 2: A. Borealis appeared with night. Mrs. Crump, she at E Cragg wife frolic.

He doesn't know it, but his corporeal life is nearly over. He may feel it in his lungs as a rain comes on ("upset chest"; "home, stupid"), but CR comes inside again ("bed") and he surveys in the cold. He digs new veins and continues to not find gold. He writes and appears in court, but as the fall of 1859 drags on, William's days run out of ink. He stops by Mrs. Crump's one day ("not home") and surveys Kincaid's another. Then, just after he visits J. Corpeny on a Friday in November, William Thomas Prestwood of the Cheraw District of South Carolina, a forgettable man, has only enough life for a final entry, a final earthly act: Sweet CR.

And then he's gone.

....

But, of course, he's not. *Gone* is not the nature of this life. It is wispy and persistent, seeping into cracks in our skin, not something easily undone. It is dust and will be dust, forever in our hair and under our feet, and so William is not gone. I am William. William clings to us, just as TP and Adam clung to him. Just as his pages opened with resurrection, so do they close in 1859. These lives trail us so that we're turned around, never sure who's following who. And yet somehow, of all the letters in my skin and all the lives haunting mine, this one down the mountain in Burke County I can see, if only as a sketch. A filled-in heart. It is a miracle: I ought never have known of the secret affairs of William Prestwood. But he's before me now, and I'm behind him, and to know him is to better know me. Lo, I am one of his sons. He is one of mine.

4215

On a day when the world is on fire, I drive without thinking to Prestwood land. I leave my car at Grandma's empty house and walk into the woods, imagining that everything happening elsewhere—war and protest and death and floods—sloughs off, unable to find its way along the paths only we know.

I end up where I often end up when I set out into this land without direction: on Asbury and Clementine's porch, overlooking the barn and cemetery. Asbury's grapes still grow, though he's been dead nearly a century. I eat one at a time before the birds and bees set in on them.

Down the hill, someone has laid a big rig trailer across the creek. The shell of it serves as a makeshift bridge, and from here it looks like a narrow house, mid-construction, hovering dangerously over Clear Creek. I consider descending the hill to try it out, but the irrigation ditch is wide and wet, and the field is smothered in mud, and I'm growing older every day. Better, I think, to sit here and imagine it. Better, I think, to watch the hawk being chased off by sparrows.

William made a mess of his life, and I'm glad to know it. It's better, I think, to know of Betsy Gandy and Mrs. Kent and E. Raby and CR. Of enslaved children sold somewhere. Of their descendants taking my calls to make sense of the world with me more than 150 years later. I'm better off than before, when I had only the clarity and righteousness of mountain poverty in my family tree, only flat names in a family Bible, only this breezy land spreading out before me. Here on these pages is the monied, slaveholding ancestor of the plantation South—and he's all mine.

I'm glad, too, that William died before his boys set off to war. When he was laid into Cajah's Mountain, he didn't know that they'd nearly all die, pulled under by disease and minié balls and Gettysburg, Pennsylvania. My great-great-granddaddy Asbury was four when his daddy took up arms, never to return. He was two when William passed. Before his tenth birthday, Asbury had lost his uncles, his father, and his grandfather, and yet years later he'd marry Clemen-

Asbury Prestwood's house today

tine and grow a family in this very house where I eat his grapes. He'd raise up teachers and preachers and farmers and mailmen who would tell me stories and release me into these woods. He'd make it.

This, I've come to know, is what I want for my boys: a solid place to stand. When the world is shaky, they can set their feet on this land. If I die or we're at war, they'll have this: a bare hill surrounded in rabbits and brambles, a haunted house growing century-old grapes, a family of headstones waiting just across the water. It's not much, but it's a place to stand still and know that all that's come before us grounds us, grows in us even now.

On this porch on a bright day, I understand nothing about time, and that settles me. In this moment, William has died and William is courting MN and William has sold Willis and William is reading my letters. We are fighting for independence and greed and fear, and we are standing in front of tanks and hiding Cato. We are having babies and laying babies to rest. We are chasing hawks and planting seeds. We are still here even when we're not. And that's something.

On any given day, an echo of William's life might resound in my body, might turn up a gene, and I'll find myself somehow changed by a confounding, maddening nineteenth-century man I'll never know and I'll always know. I won't resist it. I welcome these hauntings, these passed-on lives coursing through me long enough to animate me and give me a shot to fade into the background while I'm alive—to love the lives around me before I'm scattered, too, into a hundred other bodies. Letter by letter, the lives passed onto mine spell me out, another short line in a story started long ago. As I sit on this creaky old porch and breathe in this perfectly empty day of far-off fires and big rigs across creeks, I want only to get a few words right while I can. Learn eloquence, William says to me, and I won't, but somebody someday will. Maybe one of my boys.

Years ago, when I found William's headstone and considered lying down there in the empty cemetery to whisper through the dirt to him, I might have told him I'd learned his code. I might have left him a note in a hand only he could decipher. Maybe just before the storm sets in, I'd write to him, 3 XL384 8[4ς4 X2Lſςς2 8[58 8[4] б5] 2|8|5ς8 б4, Λ4ϟ2б4 б4. *I write these words so that they may outlast me, become me.* And then I'm gone.

Acknowledgments

If you've read this book, I'm grateful to you. If you've purchased this book but skipped straight to the acknowledgments, I'm grateful to you, too. If you've just found this book discarded in a trash can, lying open to this very page, what are you doing with your one wild and precious life? Still, gratitude.

Writing a book is an odd mix of the solitary and communal. For long stretches this book was only scattered notes and stacks of books and white pages stuck to walls and me sitting amid it all, trying to find my way. But even in those hours of holed-off lonely work, I relied on so many others.

For giving me spaces to write—and affix nonsensical notes to walls—I'm grateful to Brenda Coates, Sally Massagee, and the crew at Robinson Design Engineers, especially Philip Ellis and Joshua Robinson. And to so many coffee shops. And so much coffee (sponsor me, Independent Bean Roasters).

But it wasn't only sitting in rooms alone. It takes a village, etcetera.

Thanks to Elena Passarello, Jessie van Eerden, Meredith McCarroll, and Sarah Viren for reading this manuscript in its various iterations and offering up smart questions and advice. Thanks to Will Duffy and John Penniman for letting me talk through the many roadblocks in the project while driving the winding roads to campus.

I sought out smarter people than I to figure out what questions to ask and then where to find some answers, among them Todd Lyda, Heather Coan, Bret Riggs, Elizabeth McCrae, Scott Philyaw, Rob Ferguson, the volunteers at the Henderson County Genealogical and Historical Society, and so many librarians, but especially the folks caring for these bizarre diaries in the special collections at the North Carolina State University libraries. Thanks to Jessica Swaringen for helping to scan and sort so many diary pages. Thanks, too, to Douglas Marks for writing the program to allow me to do this: [3, 626.

I owe the students in Evan Gurney's Literary Asheville class at the University of North Carolina-Asheville for letting me take over their class for an afternoon and think through some thorny issues in the book. Shining stars, all of you.

To aid in the research and writing of this book, I received support from Western Carolina University's College of Arts and Sciences faculty research grant and the Office of the Provost's scholarly development assignment. Shout out to my colleagues in English Studies, the most supportive academic department on earth.

Thanks to the *Oxford American*, especially former editor Maxwell George, for seeing something worthwhile in the early stages of this project. Other early bits of this book appeared, in different forms, in *Cutleaf* and the book *Letter to a Stranger: Essays to the Ones Who Haunt Us* (Algonquin, 2022). These publications were shots in the arm. Likewise, Cassie Mannes Murray and Zoe-Aline Howard believed in the book when it wasn't yet a book and then helped to give it shape and momentum.

Big thanks to my agent, Justin Brouckaert, for being such a savvy editor and unrelenting champion. 9,485 drafts later, we made it!

I owe so much to the late Nathaniel Browder, an ever-curious code breaker, and his daughter, Betsy Browder Wilson. Without the Browders, I'd never have known William Thomas Prestwood. My world would be smaller.

Huge thanks to the team at Blair, especially publisher Lynn York and my editor, Robin Miura, for seeing and believing in this strange project. The act of handing off a book like this is wildly personal, so I'm so very grateful for the care and concern it received in the hands of everyone along the way, from messy draft to real-life, glowing book: Arielle Hebert, Michael Levatino, Jessica Griffin, fact-checker Laura Traister, cover designer Laura Williams. And then thanks to Pine Street Publicity for sending the shiny thing out into the world.

Lastly—and obviously—none of this would be conceivable without my family. Thanks to my parents, David and Joy, for helping with anything and everything without question. Thanks to my sister, Kristie, for always having room for my kids to crash through the front door. Thanks to Sarah for going to that Charlie Brown musical with me when we were eighteen and then marrying me and then letting me make space to write my little words. Thanks to Abraham and Ezra for being the best Abraham and Ezra and thus helping me become a better me. And thanks to William Thomas Prestwood, a man long dead but alive nonetheless.

5/3 May 1813

T 11 ∠408 ς∠12ɩ. ∠264 ∧ς ∠.∠. ς8227 8

W 12 7.² / ς4∠∠389 82 3. 622 ∠4

F 13 X478 ∠8.12144 61884 .X^m 1595 8 7

S 14 X^m 159.7 ς28 5X59. X478 61584∠. ∠

S 15 X478 ∧∠ɩ.ɩ. ς3ʋ4 g∠4gg 64728.∠12
ς478 Mss ∂.∠ 148842. σ131637ς 14∠

S 16 ∠537. 0374 6. ∂2X411 65 77. ς1438..

M 17 X478 ∠14484∠Γ8417.. 82. -5.. ∠24∠4∠

T 18 X478 82 ∠1. ∠8 12154

W 19 X478 82 ⌐ς47425ɩ 61584∠. ς8595ɩ X26∧

T 20 X478 7.∠22∠. &c. ∠21. ∠224ς ∠264 82 7

F 21 ∠264 82 -2758157 ∠22∠ς

S 22 ∠264 1264. 4.ς5779 157 ς478 64 148

S 23 X478 6408376

M 24 ∠408 ς∠122ɩ. X478 1.5.

T 25 7.² {6²1217 ∠264

W 26 7.² {74657747 X^m 6²14271.5 81378

T 27 7.² M.ᵗ (∧)

F 28 7.² ς13ʋ.7.ς.Γ.

S 29 X478 2ʋ4∠ ∧1.∠∠44∠. ∧∠38.g5779 8
..1595 157. Γ3ς18. X478.. 41355 75ʋ

S 30 ∠274 13 -2745'. ∠264 ∧9 ∠313g2

M 31 ∠408 ς∠1221. X478 1.58